Lessons in Progress

Lessons in Progress

State Universities and Progressivism in the New South, 1880–1920

Michael Dennis

University of Illinois Press
Urbana and Chicago

Manufactured in the United States of America
♾ This book is printed on acid-free paper.

Library of Congress Cataloging-in-Publication Data
Dennis, Michael, 1967–
Lessons in progress : state universities and Progressivism
in the new South, 1880–1920 / Michael Dennis.
p. cm.
Includes bibliographical references (p.) and index.
ISBN 0-252-02617-9
1. State universities and colleges—Southern States—History.
2. Education, Higher—Social aspects—Southern States—History.
3. Progressivism (United States politics)—History.
I. Title.
LB2329.5.D36 2001
378.75—dc21 00-009308

C 5 4 3 2 1

To W. Fitzhugh Brundage and Frank V. Dennis, mentors

Contents

Acknowledgments

Students often use the term "mentor" to describe anyone in a supervisory capacity, but Professor Fitzhugh Brundage demonstrated that mentoring means more than revising chapter drafts. His erudition and careful, thorough scholarship established the standard that I am still trying to meet. Through agonizingly demanding questions, Fitz forced me to dismiss facile graduate student assumptions about the South and about American history. He taught me to go beyond surface impressions, to pose questions about the past and make connections to the present that have molded my thinking since. At academic conferences, during the publication process, and throughout the uncertainties of a tight job market, he provided unflagging support and honest advice. Most important, he offered the example of what a professional historian should be. That is, I imagine, what a mentor is supposed to do, and for all of this I am very grateful.

No less an intellectual influence, Professor William Link read the manuscript and challenged me to expand my historical perspective. By pointing out factual infelicities and oversights, particularly on the critical role of the University of North Carolina during this period, he improved this book immensely, and I am very grateful for his comments. Of course, he is also absolved of any remaining transgressions.

I would also like to express my sincere gratitude to Professor Thomas G. Dyer, whose insights, research leads, and comments on an earlier version of this work were indispensable. I am grateful as well to Mary Hoffschwelle, who offered a fresh perspective on Charles Dabney through comments on a paper that I presented at the Tennessee Conference of Historians. In addition, Roger Geiger provided useful and constructive criticism of an earlier draft of the chapter on Walter Hill and the University of Georgia. I would like to thank Professors Klaus Hansen, Robert Malcolmson, Richard Fuke, William Cormack, Geoff Smith, and the late George Rawlyk, whose memory follows me at Acadia, a place very dear to him, for their teaching excellence and indefatigable support. I owe a special debt of gratitude to Professor Barry Moody and the history department at Acadia University for their professional support and uncommon decency.

I would also like to thank John Heiting, archivist at the University of South Carolina; Richard Shrader, archivist at the Southern Historical Collection; and Joe Rader, archivist at the University of Tennessee. In addition, I am tremendously grateful for the assistance rendered by the staffs of the Hargrett Rare Book and Manuscript Library, University of Georgia Libraries; the Alderman Library, University of Virginia; and the Manuscript Division of the Library of Congress. Pam Conley at Trent University Library provided lifesaving assistance in the final stages of revision. When this book was light years away from publication, Richard Wentworth at the University of Illinois Press graciously read it and offered valuable advice. I am grateful also to Carol Anne Peschke for expertly editing the manuscript and for breaking me of an obsession with hyphens and commas. Theresa Sears of the University of Illinois Press also provided invaluable guidance throughout the process.

For cheerfully enduring the vicissitudes of an academic career, I am forever grateful to my wife, Melanie. Finally, I want to thank my mother, Catherine Dennis, and my father, Frank Dennis. My father's example has guided me from the beginning, and a line in a book is a paltry way to say thank you for that.

* * *

An earlier version of chapter 3 appeared as "Schooling along the Color Line: Progressives and the Education of Blacks in the New South," *Journal of Negro Education* 67 (Spring 1998): 142–56.

An earlier version of chapter 8 appeared as "Reforming the Academical Village: Edwin A. Alderman and the University of Virginia, 1904–1915," *Virginia Magazine of History and Biography* 105 (Winter 1997): 53–86.

I am grateful to the Hargrett Rare Book and Manuscript Library at the University of Georgia Libraries and the University Archives and Special Collections at the University of Tennessee for permission to use their materials.

Lessons in Progress

1

Progressive Educators and the State Universities of the New South

At the turn of the century, southern middle-class professionals joined the national crusade to impose order on a society in flux. In the American South, universities provided leadership and intellectual guidance for this movement. Although devastated by the Civil War, southern universities recovered to assume an unprecedented role in southern life. Revitalized by the progressive creed of bureaucratic efficiency, southern leaders of higher education set out to rationalize not only the university but all of society. Colleges that were marginal during the antebellum period became powerful agents of social change in the New South. At the core of this transformation in southern higher education was the commitment to social service.

The administrations of four university presidents exemplify educational progressivism in the New South. The central reformers in the movement and the figures in this study are Edwin Alderman, president of the University of Virginia (UVA); Samuel C. Mitchell, professor at Richmond College and president of the University of South Carolina (USC); Walter Barnard Hill, chancellor of the University of Georgia; and Charles Dabney, president of the University of Tennessee. They were representative of the progressive educators who became increasingly conspicuous in the executive offices of southern state universities. Infused with the progressive ethos, they joined a growing number of faculty and trustees who shared in the creed of southern progress.

Their administrations reveal the ideological convictions that underlay educational modernization. An examination of the work of these reformers illustrates the impact of progressive universities on the New South. It also illuminates the way in which progressivism transformed higher education in the region. More than architects of university modernization, progressives such as Mitchell and Dabney became figures of regional prominence. Forging links with southern reformers and northern educational philanthropists, progressive educators extended their influence beyond the limits of the campus.

Readers familiar with the history of southern education will note the absence of an extended analysis of the University of North Carolina. Certainly, UNC shared in the progressive impulse to remodel the southern college. Parallels have been drawn between initiatives for university extension, departmental reorganization, and professionalization at the UNC and the institutions featured here. But UNC was not a focal point of the analysis for a number of reasons.

Unlike those at the Universities of Virginia, Tennessee, and South Carolina, UNC administrators did not play a significant role in the regional reform movement during the period considered. Charles D. McIver, a UNC graduate and a leading member of the reform movement, had his greatest impact as president of the North Carolina Normal and Industrial School for Women. North Carolinians who loomed large in the progressive movement, such as Edwin Alderman and Charles Dabney, did so in other states. Although Francis P. Venable, president of the UNC between 1900 and 1914, supervised reforms that in some cases outdistanced his contemporaries' efforts at modernization, he declined the role of university booster and activist. His successor, Edward Kidder Graham, was more attuned to the currents of university extension and social service. His administration is discussed in chapter 4 and the epilogue.

The UNC did eventually become a paragon of university progressivism, but it did so in the period after this study. The groundbreaking sociological studies of Howard Odum and Arthur Raper, the scholarly excellence of the university press under William Couch, and the social criticism stimulated by the Institute for Research in Social Science awaited the university expansion of the 1920s and 1930s. Ultimately, the UNC evolved into the representative modern university that none of the others could match, at least before 1920. In the 1930s Chapel Hill brimmed with the progressive energies unleashed throughout the South; its place in state higher education is discussed in the epilogue.[1]

Although the history of common school education in the South has attracted the attention of scholars, higher education after Reconstruction remains largely unexamined. Countless leaders in the southern progressive movement had affiliations with regional universities. Yet surprisingly little research has been done on the link between these institutions and the movement for greater efficiency, economic progress, and some measure of social justice. Furthermore, the literature on the impact of progressivism and the New South "creed" on the southern university is negligible. In a 1981 historiographical essay in a book titled *Education and the Rise of the New South,* the authors tersely point out, "The role of higher education in the emergence of the New South deserves more attention."[2] Education historian Jennings L. Wagoner asked that "closer study" be given to "the degree to which Southern colleges and university leaders of the New South looked outward as well as inward . . . as they wrestled with the demands of the New South creed."[3] This study attempts to address both of these concerns.

Southern universities were at the forefront of the southern progressive movement. Propelling reform was the vision of a New South revitalized by practical education. By providing leadership in regional reform efforts and scholarly analysis of social problems, southern colleges furnished the laboratory for progressive educational reform. Through educational revivals, state-level campaigns, university extension, local tax initiatives, and a steady stream of propaganda, southern progressives sought to improve the quality of education, at least for whites. Northern philanthropists and white, middle-class educators worked to establish a network that linked high schools to universities. By 1915 southern universities and common schools had begun to reflect the image of bureaucratic administration envisioned by progressive educators.

Destitute after the Civil War, universities were compelled to seek assistance from Redeemer governments that were indifferent to the needs of higher education. Financially strapped state colleges ravenously accepted federal grants to support technical education. Under the control of administrators who believed that education should uplift the prostrate South, universities adapted themselves to the task of economic and social progress. Although many private universities embraced the creed of southern progress, their denominational affiliations and financial security led them down different paths. Leading educational progressives such as James Kirkland of Vanderbilt and Warren Candler of Emory emerged from private southern universities. Historians have been more interested in examining these educators than the progressives who administered the often destitute state universities. This study makes some effort to redress this imbalance.

New South educators believed that economic regeneration required professional education and training in the practical sciences. Advocates of practical training, they subjected the classical tradition of the antebellum southern colleges to withering criticism. The school and the university were not repositories of rarefied knowledge but agents of social advancement. To educational progressives, the university was the capstone of a social system that replaced rural isolation and individualism with progressive democracy. Central to this new democracy was the university-trained technical expert. The ideological landmarks of the South's educational revolution were indistinguishable from those that dotted the landscape of southern progressivism.[4]

Social service became the rallying cry of progressives in higher education. Infused with New South optimism, reformers championed educational improvement as the linchpin of regional economic rejuvenation. They promoted social reform and expanded the influence of the university through extension lectures, farmers' institutes, and faculty service to governments and private enterprise. College presidents encouraged the fusion of government agencies with academic posts as well as the connection of faculty members to southern reform organizations. New South educators also championed agricultural extension programs. In their struggle to wrench financial support from miserly governments, they claimed that a modernized university would stimulate social change. In so doing, they transformed universities from obscure and often elitist colleges into instruments of the modern state.

Modernizing universities sought to become institutions of social leadership in the decentralized South. Confronting a political culture premised on the values of individualism and local autonomy, progressive universities promoted social coordination and expert leadership. Social stability, racial stratification, and regional cohesiveness were the central tenets of southern progressivism. University leaders portrayed themselves as the voices of rational and controlled social development. Rather than an isolated observer of southern change, the state university of the New South was a catalyst in the movement for southern progress.

Progressivism recast the internal structure of the university. Like the corporate monoliths of the early twentieth century, modernizing southern institutions of higher education increasingly adopted the language and methods of progressive administration. Making university administration more efficient was a central concern of the leaders of progressive-era higher education. The efficiency imperative spilled out over the walls of academe and into the channels and tributaries of educational reform throughout the region.

The effort to constrain women and blacks within socially sanctioned spheres of "appropriate" education was another function of the effort to rationalize southern universities. Progressives were convinced that education had a role to play in preserving black economic and racial subordination. University administrators elaborated an intellectual defense for industrial education, a type of technical training designed to transform blacks into a highly exploitable source of agricultural labor. Similarly, progressives endorsed women's education, but they carefully prescribed courses of study that would not threaten conventional notions of gender and domesticity. Despite these restrictions, women exploited educational opportunities to carve out for themselves a larger sphere of independence. And despite their own caution, progressives who welcomed women into the crusade for public education unwittingly opened seams of political and professional autonomy that women widened aggressively.

Progressives sought to professionalize university teaching and to expand the opportunities for university-based professional instruction. Their efforts reinforced occupational exclusivity and the social prestige attached to their work. Participating in the nationwide movement for professionalization, southern universities produced trained technicians for the South's expanding urban industrial complex. University-trained lawyers, dentists, doctors, civil servants, teachers, business administrators, and entrepreneurs entered the ranks of an expanding middle class. Through professional and technical instruction, state universities accelerated the process of class formation in the New South.

At the same time that the state university encouraged the coalescence of a new middle class, it contributed to a complex process of state construction. Pursuing a broad program of modernization, progressive educators sought to link the university to the state, to fuse university departments to state agencies, and to assimilate the university's objectives into those of an embryonic, regulatory polis. Administrators such as Hill and Dabney espoused a reform agenda that for the most part protected fundamental cultural and social values. Even while they sought to control change, others extended the implications of social reform to express aspirations that southern progressives did not sanction. The modernizing southern university was both an agent of social reorientation and a bulwark of southern tradition.

While progressives wrestled with the relationship between higher education and society, they also grappled with pedagogical theory. In a suggestive article on post-Reconstruction universities, historian Joseph Stetar analyzes the southern version of the late-nineteenth-century debate at northern universities over the ideals of higher education. Using historian Laurence Veysey's pedagogical categories, Stetar suggests that southern colleges maintained a stronger adherence to the values of liberal culture and mental discipline than their northern counterparts. In the North, utility and research became the dominant pedagogical values after the Civil War. Although he admits that utility—the philosophy of practical education for social service—made inroads at southern universities, he argues that it failed to replace the ideals of Christian education and liberal culture.[5]

Certainly, southern universities in the early twentieth century weathered a torrent of conflicting arguments about the function of university training. Despite the tempest over higher education, though, many southern administrators adopted practical education as their guiding principle. And although the research ideal was by no means axiomatic by 1915, progressive educators at state universities encouraged research as a professional obligation for university faculty. Research for purely esoteric purposes was anathema to most university progressives. The trend toward a practical pedagogy did not preclude classical training; instead, it achieved an uneasy equilibrium with the traditional curriculum. But the university presidents examined in this study subordinated liberal culture and Christian education to practical education.[6] In this way they fostered universities that reflected the values and myths of the New South.

This study draws upon the contributions of several historians of southern progressivism and southern education. Dewey Grantham, in his book *Southern Progressivism: The Reconciliation of Progress and Tradition,* has convincingly demonstrated that southern progressives shared the objectives of the national reform movements but defined the southern movement according to regional traditions. In the name of regional stability and social justice, southern progressives made a virtue out of racial oppression. Thomas Dyer's *The University of Georgia: A Bicentennial History* reveals how progressive educators such as Walter Barnard Hill and David Barrow eagerly pursued university modernization. His book is perhaps the best example of an institutional study that explores the relationship between higher education, culture, and society. William Link's *The Paradox of Southern Progressivism* and his earlier book, *A Hard Country and a Lonely Place,* illuminate the tension inherent in the progressive effort to "democratize" society while administering programs based on bureaucratic centralization. As Link demonstrates, conflict arose between progressive reform and southern traditions of local autonomy and community control. Progressives in higher education also spoke the idiom of democracy while endorsing reforms that, at times, seemed antithetical to popular participation.[7]

Although this study relies on a corpus of existing literature, it contributes to an understanding of issues that many historians have yet to address. No study examines several state universities against the backdrop of an emerging New South. Nor is there any sustained discussion on the relationship between progressivism and the state universities of the New South. Mitchell, Alderman, Hill, and Dabney have received some attention in intellectual histories of the post-Reconstruction South. Yet the examination of these reformers against the landscape of southern progressivism remains incomplete. Historians have also overlooked the impact of progressivism on southern higher education. Additionally, this study illuminates the structural changes generated by university involvement in state construction and class formation. Rather than peripheral cul de sacs of speculative reform, state universities were the laboratories of southern progressivism.[8]

* * *

University modernization grew out of the movement for educational reform that spread throughout the South at the beginning of the twentieth century. By national standards, education in the South was abysmal. According to one historian, the region's public schools at the beginning of the century were "miserably supported, poorly attended, wretchedly taught, and wholly inadequate for the education of the people." More than any public institution, the South's schools compared unfavorably with those of the rest of the nation.[9]

Southern state universities were not far behind. Endowments for southern colleges were meager at best; many schools were entirely dependent on federal grants for survival. Income derived from state expenditures was pathetically small. The average salary for college professors in 1901 was approximately $840, whereas in 1893 the average salary at 100 northern schools was $1,470. The value of buildings at southern universities was a meager $19,000,000 of the national total of $146,000,000. Financial stringency was exacerbated by the profusion of schools competing for tuitions. Many had only a tenuous claim to college status, operating largely on the strength of their preparatory departments. The leading competition for many was not another college but the region's equally dismal high schools. Institutional overlap diluted college admission and graduation standards. Often, the curriculum of southern universities differed little from that of many private academies and high schools. Robert E. Blackwell, president of Randolph-Macon College, surveyed the bleak landscape of southern higher education in 1911: "No university well enough equipped to do genuine research work, and twice as many professional and polytechnic schools as are needed, and none of them able to give our people the advantages that northern and western institutions offer." If southern revitalization depended on educational progress, then its universities as much as its common schools needed attention.[10]

The education movement was built on the efforts of Reconstruction-era "intersectionalists" to promote industrial education for African Americans.[11] The Peabody Education Fund, created by northern philanthropist George Peabody in 1867, and the Slater Fund, established by Connecticut entrepreneur John Fox Slater, provided most of the money and the leadership for early efforts at school improvement. Organizing the activities of the Peabody and Slater funds was Jabez Lamar Monroe Curry. Astutely, Curry mediated between northern paternalism and southern white suspicion. He pioneered the evangelical-style appeals to educational reform that distinguished the school campaigns of Edwin Alderman and North Carolina reformer Charles D. McIver. Although Curry died before the crusade reached its crescendo, he became the model of educational activism for southern progressives.[12]

Expanding the sphere of educational reform was the objective of progressive journalist Walter Hines Page. Working as an editor for the North Carolina *State Chronicle* in the early 1880s, Page championed industrialization, agricultural improvement, and education as the means to southern progress. When Edward P. Moses, superintendent for public instruction in Goldsboro, implemented graded schools, Page gave him unqualified approval. In addition to supporting grade school improvement, he advocated instruction in engineering, a State College of Agriculture, and technical education for blacks. Page distilled much of his educational program into the "Forgotten Man," an address he gave at the North Carolina Normal and Industrial School for Women in June 1897. He advocated a public school system supported by local and state taxation. Linking productivity to knowledge, Page solidified the New South connection between education and social progress. Although he was not an active reformer, Page's criticism of southern illiteracy and cultural torpor brought the issue of education to the attention of a wide spectrum of southerners. Other progressives, such as Josephus Daniels of the Raleigh *News and Observer,* joined him in propagating the message of educational uplift. It was only in 1898, though, at a meeting of southern reformers and northern philanthropists that the ideology of southern educational reform crystallized. Here, the reform movement took institutional form.[13]

That year, Edward Abbot, pastor of St. James Church in Cambridge, Massachusetts, and Hollis Burke Frissell, president of the Hampton Institute in Virginia, a northern-financed technical college for blacks, convened the Conference for Christian Education at Capon Springs, West Virginia. Attended by a small number of undistinguished educators from both sections, the conference reaffirmed the Reconstruction-era missionary program of instruction for blacks and Christian education. But in adopting a regional focus for education reform, as well as by redirecting resources from the development of sectarian to public education, the conference departed from the missionary credo. The next year, the conference distinguished itself even more clearly as a vehicle of public education by abandoning its religious association and its alliance with missionary education.[14]

The 1899 meeting was also a turning point for the educational movement in the South. There, a coalition of northern philanthropists and white middle-class educators solidified behind a program of education for social progress. The dominant northern members included Robert C. Ogden, department store entrepreneur and long-time educational activist; George Foster Peabody, native of Georgia who made his millions as an investment banker in New York; and William H. Baldwin Jr., vice-president of J. P. Morgan's Southern Railway Company and trustee of the Tuskegee Institute since 1894. The rest of the northern wing consisted of J. L. M. Curry and Walter Hines Page, both transplanted from the South, and Wallace Buttrick, a Rockefeller representative.

The southern group was dominated by a cadre of North Carolina educators that included Charles Dabney, state chemist at the UNC and future president of the University of Tennessee; Edwin Alderman, president of the UNC and future president of UVA; and Charles D. McIver, president of the North Carolina Normal and Industrial College for Women. Joining them were Hollis Frissell; Philander P. Claxton, who would later work in the Dabney administration at Tennessee and as federal commissioner of education; and Edgar Gardner Murphy of Alabama, leading southern opponent of child labor, advocate of black education, and organizer of the Montgomery Conference on the Race Question.

Meeting at the Capon Springs Conference, northern philanthropists and southern educators found common ideological ground on the principles of universal education, white supremacy, and industrial education for blacks. This consensus required northern reformers such as Ogden to subordinate black education to the southern demand for white schools. Southerners such as J. L. M. Curry argued that regional advancement for both races depended on the education of the region's whites. They, in turn, would supervise the education of blacks. Ideological convergence also required northerners to accept the southern insistence on freedom from interference in race relations. Again, southerners insisted, regional progress required racial harmony, which could only mean white political dominance. Cooperation between northern activists and southern reformers was easy, though, considering that philanthropists had no quarrel with southern convictions about black inferiority and labor control. They also agreed on the benefits of industrialization, the use of practical education in socializing laborers, liberal capitalism, and social efficiency. After the ideological gestation provided by three annual meetings at Capon Springs, the Conference for Education in the South was prepared to disseminate its message throughout the South.[15]

The Fourth Conference for Education in the South was held in Winston-Salem and was marked by the attendance of several prominent northern philanthropists, who arrived at the meeting on a train provided by Robert Ogden. Addresses by Charles Dabney and Charles D. McIver featured endorsements of technical education for both races as well as public support for education.

Most importantly, the conference resolved to support a regional movement to raise public consciousness about education. The participants endorsed a proposal from Charles Dabney to create an executive board that would coordinate the reform movement. In addition to approving what would be known as the Southern Education Board (SEB), the meeting also authorized a propaganda bureau to be headed by Dabney.[16]

Although the SEB would evolve into a bureaucratic organization, it was intended to operate as an instrument for educational evangelization. Organizers were careful not to give the impression that the board controlled the campaigns. Cooperating with local leaders and educators, usually the state superintendent of education, the board launched education campaigns that took on the character of evangelical revivals. Complementing the revivals was the deluge of propaganda unleashed on the South by Dabney's Bureau of Investigation and Information. Yearly meetings of the Conference for Education in the South held throughout the region popularized the state campaigns and gave organizers a chance to plan strategies. Throughout, university presidents took an active role in the board's programs. Their institutions not only lent assistance to the school campaigns but also benefited from the changes stimulated by SEB activism.[17]

Southern college presidents were conspicuous on the SEB. Alderman, then president at Chapel Hill, was an original member, as were Charles Dabney, Charles McIver, and Hollis B. Frissell. Walter Hill became a member in 1904. Samuel Mitchell became a member in 1906 and collaborated with the board both as an educational reformer in Virginia and as president of USC. Rather than marginal supporters, the figures in this study assumed leading roles in the southern educational movement. Part of this program included improving state institutions of higher education, but much of it concerned coordinating state education agencies and standardizing public schools. Equally important, Alderman, Dabney, and Hill spoke as representatives of the conference and the SEB. Organizing the board's reform initiatives, they also formulated the ideological justifications that accompanied its policies.

The Winston-Salem conference gave rise to another organization of paramount importance to the southern education movement. Attending the conference as a guest of Robert Ogden, John D. Rockefeller Jr. became convinced that the cause of southern education deserved generous financial support. Persuaded by his son, the elder Rockefeller created the General Education Board (GEB) in 1902 with an endowment of $1 million. The board's activity was not restricted to the South. Considering the condition of southern education, however, the board's influence in school development was greater there than in the rest of the country. As well as conducting systematic surveys of education in each southern state, the board cooperated with the SEB to advance rural elementary education in the South, establish a framework of high school education, promote educational efficiency, and finance farm demonstration work. In 1907, Edwin Alderman had the distinction of being the first southerner appointed to the board.[18]

As is often noted by historians of education, the trustees of the SEB and the GEB formed an interlocking directorate. Ogden, Peabody, Curry, Baldwin, and Buttrick were all founding members of both organizations. In addition, representatives of both boards supervised the activities of other philanthropic organizations, including the Peabody and Slater funds, the Anna T. Jeanes Foundation, created in 1907, and the Phelps-Stokes Fund, established in 1910.[19]

Although they never held the pursestrings of philanthropy, Alderman, Dabney, and the others were intimately connected to this powerful network of northern benefactors and southern elites. Ogden, Baldwin, and Peabody collaborated with state university presidents in countless campaigns for local taxation, secondary school improvement, and university extension. University progressives became experts on southern educational reform. As much as the region's common schools, southern state universities came within the philanthropists' sphere of influence.[20]

The southern education movement did not slip silently by isolated enclaves of higher learning. Instead, it incorporated state universities in a concerted effort to uplift the South through educational reform. Not all southerners rejoiced in the education crusade. Progressives in higher education met resistance to reforms aimed at centralizing authority in bureaucratic structures and professionalizing public instruction. More than some of their adversaries would admit, state universities were transformed by the progressive ethos of efficiency and educational service.

There was nothing inexorable about educational modernization; it stemmed from the agency of individuals committed to a particular conception of education in the South. This conception bore the distinctive marks of the New South creed and pedagogical utilitarianism. After 1920 southern state universities were still poorly financed, small, and academically undistinguished institutions. However, they were no longer colleges of the antebellum period or even of the Reconstruction era. How they became institutions closely connected to an emergent bureaucratic state and deeply involved in the social life of the South is the story that follows.

Notes

1. In addition to these qualifications, the objective of the study was to illuminate the struggle of progressivism at universities not typically regarded as institutions of social leadership. University modernization in South Carolina and Tennessee highlighted the cultural obstacles that confronted progressive reform. By comparison, the UNC enjoyed an atmosphere favorable to educational reform. The heartland of educational reform, North Carolina, also supported its state university more generously than did the state governments of Georgia or Tennessee.

2. Neufeldt and Allison, "Education and the Rise of the New South, 276. The role of higher education in the nation at large has drawn more attention recently. See Geiger, *To Advance Knowledge,* and Leslie, *Gentlemen and Scholars.*

3. Wagoner, "Higher Education and Transitions in Southern Culture," 108. For another lamentation on the inadequacy of research on higher education in the South, see Dyer, "Higher Education in the South since the Civil War," 127–45. See also Urban, "History of Education."

4. Despite the fact that education was a lesser tenet of the New South creed, Thomas Dyer argues that southern colleges and universities absorbed the values of the New South ideology as "they scrambled to adopt technological, scientific, and agricultural emphases that would keep them in step with the emergent mania for industrialization," in "Higher Education in the South since the Civil War," 131.

5. Stetar, "In Search of Direction," 341–67.

6. Veysey's analytical categories are useful for understanding the development of higher education in the late nineteenth century. Mental discipline and piety, dominant in the antebellum period, held that academic instruction should train the mind to think logically and the soul to contemplate moral truth. Proponents of mental discipline believed that instruction in Latin and Greek best provided the former and moral philosophy the latter. Advocates of liberal culture believed that education should cultivate aesthetic and moral sensibilities. This could best be accomplished through an appreciation of Europe's great literature and the achievements of Anglo-American culture. More secular and liberal than mental discipline, liberal culture was antithetical to the narrow specialization encouraged by the ideal of research.

The research ideal was largely an import from German universities pioneering in classical philology, linguistics, and the social sciences. This pedagogical philosophy valued pure research for no other purpose than the expansion of knowledge. Academics should conduct rigorous scientific investigation in pursuit of empirical truth. The generalities of liberal culture were anathema to the research enthusiasts. Exponents of utility accepted specialization and the value of professionalization but subordinated it to the service of practical social needs. The value of education was measured by its application to tangible social problems. See Veysey, *The Emergence of the American University,* especially chapters 1–4.

7. Grantham, *Southern Progressivism;* Dyer, *The University of Georgia;* Link, *The Paradox of Southern Progressivism* and *A Hard Country and a Lonely Place.*

8. Clayton, *The Savage Ideal.* For a study that adopts the ideological bias of the progressives themselves, see Bailey, *Liberalism in the New South.*

9. Woodward, *Origins of the New South,* 398.

10. Ibid., 436–38, including quote; information on salaries at northern schools is found in Veysey, *The Emergence of the American University,* 390.

11. Link, *The Paradox of Southern Progressivism,* 128.

12. Ibid., 128–29. For a discussion of the paternalistic ideology espoused by the trustees of the Slater Fund and by most middle-class southerners who supported black education, see Finkenbine, "'Our Little Circle,'" 6–22.

13. Bailey, *Liberalism in the New South,* 132–37.

14. Link, *A Hard Country and a Lonely Place,* 102–8.

15. Anderson, *The Education of Blacks in the South,* 84.

16. Link, *A Hard Country and a Lonely Place,* 102–8; Anderson, *The Education of Blacks in the South,* 83–85.

17. Grantham, *Southern Progressivism,* 248–49.

18. Anderson, *The Education of Blacks in the South,* 85–87; Grantham, *Southern Progressivism,* 248. Whereas the SEB depended largely on the benevolence of Peabody and Ogden to pay its field agents, the GEB had few financial concerns.

19. Anderson, *The Education of Blacks in the South,* 85–87; Grantham, *Southern Progressivism,* 248; Harlan, *Separate and Unequal,* 85–90. An example of the educational hegemony exercised by this tightly knit group of reformers is the activity of Robert Ogden in 1906. In that year the northern philanthropist was simultaneously president of the Conference for Education in the South, the SEB, the GEB, and the board of trustees for the Hampton and Tuskegee institutes. The officers of the GEB had abundant resources to fund their activity. By 1909 the GEB had received $53 million from Rockefeller; by 1921, the total contributions amounted to more than $129 million.

20. Anderson, *The Education of Blacks in the South,* 87; Harlan, *Separate and Unequal,* 85–87. Another telling example of the philanthropic oligarchy was Wickliffe Rose, who served as a member of both the SEB and the GEB, agent of the Peabody Fund, trustee of the Slater Fund, and secretary of the Rockefeller Sanitary Commission.

2

Thinking about the New South: Educational Modernizers and Progressivism

Although progressive educators saw themselves as people of action, they devoted considerable time and energy to thought. Their ideas about progress, history, and social change established the ideological parameters of the southern education movement. They shared common convictions about the function of the university in the advancing South. Social progress meant material abundance through universal education and technological advancement. At the center of their plans for regional advancement was the modernized university.

Progressive educators shared a milieu infused with the cultural and social values of the white, middle-class South. They spoke the same language, filled with symbols familiar to the unreconstructed Confederate and the self-consciously new southerner. Their ideas or discourse were sewn together with the thread of sectional consciousness that permeated both the liberalism of George Washington Cable and the racial extremism of James K. Vardaman.

Southern progressive educators belonged to the same reform organizations. Many corresponded and met with each other, and each turned to the experience of others for guidance. For example, Edwin Alderman addressed Charles Dabney's Summer School of the South at the University of Tennessee and Samuel Mitchell's University of South Carolina (USC); Dabney and Walter Hill collaborated in the movement for national aid to education, and the latter cooperated with Alderman on the Southern Education Board (SEB); Alderman and Mitchell worked together on the Virginia Education Commission, a state-sponsored reform organization; both Hill and Mitchell addressed the 1904 meeting of the Conference for Education in Birmingham and, as members of the SEB, they cooperated in planning and executing educational reform.[1]

Southern university presidents formed a close-knit intellectual community. Their speeches and writings reinforced deeply held convictions about social change at a time when reform of any kind was met with suspicion. By no means were they theoreticians of striking originality. Even so, they were bold reformers who premised their movement on the belief that ideas have the power to change social conditions.

Principal among these ideas were the tenets of the New South creed.[2] The creed maintained that sectional reconciliation, regional industrialization, and racial adjustment would pave the way for southern rehabilitation. Although rarely articulated as a coherent ideology, the creed of southern progress permeated the thought of progressive educators. Rejoicing in the South's liberation from the incubus of slavery, exponents of the New South ideology articulated a form of nationalism that would unite southerners in a program of sectional rehabilitation. By linking the promise of nationalism to an imagined tradition of southern unity, New South spokespeople hoped to deflect the accusation of sectional disloyalty.

Yet the appeal to nationalism included more mundane considerations. In the effort to reclaim southern control over racial policy, Henry Grady tried to calm residual northern fears about the plight of blacks in the South. Northern meddling, Grady argued, led to racial instability and an unfavorable climate for northern investment. Under the management of the "better" class of whites, race relations would be harmonized and capital investment protected from social upheaval.[3]

Chancellor Walter Hill saw no contradiction between nationalism and southern control of race relations. Nationalism and sectionalism were perfectly reconcilable, he argued, because the latter was premised on the "reasonable claim of universal validity that those who are in closest touch with any problem know most about it and are most deeply concerned in its judicious handling." Champions of the New South ideology used nationalism as a rhetorical lever to secure northern investment. Declaring virulent sectionalism dead, New South ideologues assured northern investors that the region welcomed the infusion of "foreign" capital.[4]

Echoing the exponents of the New South creed, Samuel Mitchell, president of USC from 1908 to 1913, celebrated the virtues of nationalism for the South. Far from capitulation to northern hegemony, southern nationalism represented a "return to an original course, from which it was temporarily diverted in the fog of the controversy over slavery."[5] Northern acknowledgement of the proud nationalist tradition forged by Washington, Jefferson, and Madison was binding the sections together. The charm of nationalism was rooted in more than tradition, though. "The frank acceptance by the South of the issue of the War as regards slavery," wrote Mitchell in 1908, "and the frank acknowledgement upon the part of the North of the blunder-crime of Reconstruction, have cleared the path of conciliation."[6] For progressive educators, northern acquiescence to a version of Reconstruction sympathetic to the South made northern involvement in regional development possible. Under the guidance of Columbia's William A. Dunning, Progressive Era historians created an interpretation of slavery, secession, and the "tragedy" of Reconstruction palatable to both northerners and southerners.[7] John Burgess, one of the leading northern architects of the myth of the Tragic Reconstruction, won Mitchell's approval for his severe "condemnation" of Republican radicalism.[8]

Shared racial prejudice facilitated a consensus on the meaning of the war and Reconstruction. Imperial expansionism in the Philippines and Latin America, accompanied by the vexing problems of colonial management, reinforced northern racial prejudice kindled by disillusionment with Reconstruction. Northern racism was bolstered by the popular Anglo-American ideology of social Darwinism.[9]

The imposition of "the sovereignty of the United States upon eight million Asiatics," Mitchell proclaimed, "has changed its view in regard to the political relation of the races, and has at last virtually accepted the ideas of the South upon that subject." He assured his readers that the South had no reason to fear a return of Republican fanaticism, considering that the party's leaders had dismissed racial equality as "vain imagination." In fact, intelligent northerners agreed that slavery was but one stage in the evolutionary adjustment between advanced and inferior races. Simply by misfortune, the South had found itself at the "bloody angle" in a worldwide process of racial development. The growth of urban centers teeming with strange and uncontrollable immigrants also helped crystallize northern racial consciousness. "This changing view-point is due, in part, to its [the North's] own frictional experience with negroes, Japanese, Chinese, and backward immigrants from Hungary and Poland."[10]

The education crusade itself harmonized northern and southern sensibilities. Although the Conference for Education in the South helped convince northerners of the wisdom of southern racial management by offering a "saner acquaintance with Southern conditions," it also "took the sting out of northern suspicion as to the fair treatment of the freedmen" by demonstrating the commitment of the region's better people to public support for black education. Coupled with northern assent to black disfranchisement, industrialization was helping to dissolve regional barriers. "The cotton mill owner in South Carolina and the iron master in Alabama," Mitchell exclaimed, "are, perforce, responsive to the laws of trade as they operate throughout the whole republic. To industrialize is, therefore, to nationalize the South."[11] Combining nationalism with the axioms of liberal capitalism, exponents of the New South creed offered up a vision of regional regeneration that preserved the essential features of a distinctive South.

Nationalism offered progressives a convenient rationalization for northern involvement in the education movement. Paralleling the revisionism of post-Reconstruction southern historians, chancellor Walter Hill argued that the South did not bear sole responsibility for the "peculiar institution." The North had collaborated in the slave trade. It was also responsible for the loss of the South's principal capital investment. Because emancipation was the source of southern poverty, Hill argued, the nation shared responsibility for "the peculiar Southern problem and . . . the inability of the South to meet these conditions." Hill justified northern support for southern education by linking illiteracy to the stultifying effects of slavery. Yet illiteracy for Hill was a blanket term for the South's many social ills, "the disabilities, the limitations, the shiftlessness, the degradation, the vice, the crime, that are generally associated with it." Northern funding of the Tuskegee and Hampton institutes warranted no censure from southerners, Hill reasoned, because it represented their acceptance of responsibility for a problem that was national in scope.[12]

Boldly, Walter Hill suggested that the legacy of slavery justified a resuscitation of the moribund Blair bill, which had been defeated in 1890. National aid for education would be less controversial than it was when southern members of congress defeated the Blair measure out of fear that it would finance black education at the expense of white political control. The Blair bill allowed segregation but prohibited racial discrimination in the distribution of funds. The bill's defeat was unfortunate for the South because money for education was to be distributed according to the percentage of illiteracy in each state. Considering the South's high rate of illiteracy, it would have received the largest share of the federal money. But Hill was confident that new legislation would avoid that most noxious of provisions found in the Blair bill: the allocation of funds for black liberal arts education. This would be accomplished by acknowledging that black instruction should be "largely manual, industrial and agricultural, so as to be adapted to the real needs of the masses."[13]

New South nationalism was inextricably bound up with its vision of industrialization and economic progress. Arguing that the defeat of the Confederacy liberated the South from the social stagnation bred by slavery, proponents of the New South articulated a program of economic expansion modeled on the northern experience of urbanization, industrialization, and scientific agriculture.[14] The South's "mastery of modern industrial forces," announced

University of Virginia (UVA) president Edwin Alderman in 1906, "gives to its rebuilding period the same aspects of steadiness and of grandeur that surrounded the period of its suffering and its losses."[15]

For Charles Dabney, president of the University of Tennessee, the South's demand for industrial productivity lay behind the crusade for educational improvement. He saw a direct correlation between education and the production of wealth. Echoing the jeremiads of leading New South boosters, he warned that the reliance on agriculture and the importation of finished goods "means continued financial and commercial dependency, continued slavery to every other class and interest—continued poverty."[16] Samuel Mitchell asserted in 1910 that economic adjustment was one of the crucial challenges confronting the South's educational system. Proponents of the New South creed also included agricultural development in their program for southern economic progress. Mitchell and others applauded the growth of mechanical and agricultural instruction at the South's state universities.[17]

Proponents of educational modernization were not caricatures of the voluble New South boosters. For one thing, the educational crusade belongs to a later period of southern history than the New South movement, which reached its apex in the 1880s. Although Atticus G. Haygood and J. L. M. Curry successfully attached public education to the New South program, educational advancement was subordinate to industrialization and agricultural diversification, at least until 1903.[18] University modernizers, on the other hand, emphasized educational reform ahead of industrialization and scientific agriculture.

The university presidents belonged to a generation of reformers that superimposed the ideology of southern progressivism on the framework of the New South creed. The crucial assumption underlying the New South movement was the belief that material growth represented social progress. Historian Dewey Grantham points out, "Although southern progressives typically went beyond the prescriptions of the New South creed in their advocacy of legislative action and social reform, they were convinced that social progress could not take place without economic development."[19] Combining this conviction with the antimonopoly tradition, a commitment to social efficiency, and the humanitarian impulse generated by the Social Gospel, reformers forged the ideological matrix that guided southern progressivism.

Rather than entrust social reconstruction to the unpredictable forces of industrial capitalism, as the exponents of the New South creed had done, progressives hoped that it would be administered by social efficiency experts. In the place of unfettered industrialization, they celebrated the school as the vital catalyst of social uplift. Walter Hines Page, southern critic and expatriate, made this point in his landmark 1897 address "Forgotten Man," which spelled out the intellectual justification for the education crusade.[20]

According to Samuel Mitchell, the crux of the problem of southern progress was school development. "Education represents a structural process in society. . . . The South has found in the school the latent potency that will create industries, uplift the masses, adjust racial differences, and regain political prestige." Mitchell endorsed the New South's reconciliation of industry and agriculture and claimed that education would assist in the development of southern resources. Resonating with pedagogical utilitarianism, he asserted, "Education here is addressing itself to the recovery of exhausted soils and to the diffusion of sound economic ideas."[21]

For Edwin Alderman, the social benefits of educational improvement were equally evident. "It has been settled," he wrote in 1906, "that it is a moral and economic error of the first magnitude to neglect the education of any of the people, and an economic necessity of the first magnitude to develop the productive power of trained intelligence." Alderman spoke for each state university president when he identified the university as the harbinger of a new, service-oriented education. "A State university must become the place that . . . relates closely the surest ethical and economic insights to practical problems of co-operation and relief." The university that failed to address current social and economic problems had missed its function.[22]

In the connection they made between educational development and economic growth, educators followed the lead of Edgar Gardner Murphy, one of the region's most illustrious progressives. Writing in 1910, Murphy argued that educational improvement would benefit the rising industrial order and the South's struggling agricultural sector: "We must put ideas into the ground if we are to get more money out of it. . . . If the South is to advance the wealth of the land, we must advance the practical intelligence of the labor which works it."[23]

Educational progressives did not relinquish liberal education in favor of technical instruction. Instead, they tended either to emphasize the practical benefits of liberal instruction or to synthesize practical and liberal instruction in such a way that the latter was made subordinate. In an article exploring the changes in university pedagogy, Mitchell criticized mental discipline as a philosophical justification for classical training. He disparaged the way in which the cumulative philosophy of learning had squelched "Spontaneity of thought, the will, the emotions, conscience." Language had its place in education, to be sure, but the study of modern languages should be preeminent. Mitchell argued that studying modern languages would benefit the enterprising businessperson.

Unlike the traditional method of teaching languages, which relied on textbook recitation, the practical, conversational techniques of modern language pedagogy would promote mental proficiency. Curiously, though, the progressive enthusiasm for a quantifiable, practical education reinforced the "cumulative" approach to learning that Mitchell objected to in the classical tradition.[24]

Mitchell was equally utilitarian in rationalizing the study of history and civics. Both subjects, he argued, instructed students in the duties of citizenship. History gave students an appreciation of continuity and change, linear progress, and the understanding of history as "past politics." The study of history also was valuable for moral instruction. History was nothing short of the "conscience of the human race," and its examination produced moral enlightenment. Reflecting the empiricism transforming the historical profession of the early twentieth century into a social "science," Mitchell applauded the strengthening of "moral purposes" that the study of history afforded, as students examined "this laboratory of motives, testing character and weighing acts." History should be studied as a highly specialized discipline with an emphasis on research and practical application.[25]

Dabney also castigated pedantic education. The image of the educated man in the antebellum South was a "cyclopedia of information from which anyone could borrow a fact . . . a vast storehouse of supplies." Rather than "a receptacle for knowledge," Dabney argued, the true scholar was a "gleaner in the field of science" and the university a laboratory for research. But he differed from Mitchell in his apologia for the classics. A harmonious balance, he insisted, should exist between the sciences and the humanities. "Let no one understand me . . . as depreciating the value in education of languages and literature. . . . Properly used these studies exercise many faculties." Unlike Mitchell, Dabney's synthesis assumed that the classics and the humanities should cultivate mental faculties not stimulated by the study of science.[26]

Dabney also conceded the humanities a broadening and civilizing influence. The liberal arts, however, were simply a "preparatory" education for professional studies. Liberal education would prevent the practical-minded specialist from degenerating into a narrow-minded philistine. Although he was no adversary of the humanities, much of his rhetoric was meant to ease the anxieties of traditionalists about the subversion of the classical curriculum by creeping utilitarianism.[27]

His administrative record at Tennessee illustrated his preference for technical instruction. He believed that the humanities should be protected, if only to disseminate genteel culture among an urban middle class often accused of boorish materialism. Yet the patina of liberal culture meant little in the scheme of progress: "Science, in the high sense, is the only true foundation upon which the superstructure of modern material civilization is built." The classics had their pedagogical place, but economic imperatives placed a premium on technical instruction. The South "awoke" in 1865 out of a "medieval night"—hardly a metaphor to curry favor with proponents of a traditional education—into a new day of science and material development. No doubt, liberal education would guarantee an ample supply of preachers and men of affairs. But because the progressives considered the technical expert the real power broker in the New South, the products of a classical education could expect a subordinate place in the new order.[28]

The "spirit" underlying the education crusade united school reform to the broader movement for social revitalization. Mitchell believed that the education movement was breaking down southern isolation by corroding the region's regressive "idiosyncrasies." Education was the mysterious solvent of social barriers, eroding the class structure in the South and assimilating the region to the "habits" and "sentiments" of the nation. Fostering literacy, disseminating knowledge, and encouraging the analysis of current economic and social questions, education had become "the platform of the party of progress." Education, he argued, was a vital component of the progressive movement's assault on southern provincialism and localism: "The school, the public library, the rural mail delivery, the daily paper, telephone, and better roads are common agencies in making them restive under the servile control too often exercised by professional politicians."[29] According to reformers, the school was the most important agent in the progressive campaign to uproot the pervasive ignorance demagogues preyed on.

The progressive vision of a South emancipated from rural isolation permeated Edwin Alderman's writings. Like Mitchell, Alderman believed that modern technology would solidify the bonds between the urban and rural South. At the same time, it would bind the region more closely to the rest of the nation. "The education of the country child and the general enrichment of rural life—and by enrichment I mean making the country a sweeter and happier place to live in, to remove its isolation and loneliness by libraries, by good roads, by telephones, by touch with the great throbbing world—are now accepted without dispute as fundamental tenets of public education."[30] Educational progressives fused school development to reforms that promoted social cohesion. Much like public health reformers, they believed that it was the task of the modern school to inculcate rural children in the values of middle-class culture. Juxtaposing rural backwardness to the wonders of a progressive social order, reformers such as Alderman never questioned whether rural southerners welcomed the attention of many well-meaning efficiency experts. "The social reformers of the post 1900 South shared this combination of the impulse to uplift and a certainty of the inadequacy of the uplifted," writes historian William Link.[31]

For Robert Ogden, inveterate educational reformer, the Conference for Education in the South encapsulated the progressive vision of a rejuvenated South: "Some are profoundly ignorant of the technicalities of education. . . . But all are with one accord in one place . . . by reason of a common belief in the beneficent power of education, and because each distinct element is essential to the spirit that must vitalize the Conference."[32] Progressives saw in the modern school the means of disseminating knowledge and encouraging behavior crucial for economic development.

Intrinsic to the progressive ideology was the idea of community. If individualism and local autonomy were the causes of the South's torpor, then the cultivation of an enlightened community spirit was crucial to the educational awakening. "It has been settled," claimed Alderman, "that the South is hereafter to place its chief emphasis upon community effort, rather than upon individualism." It was an "achievement of character," he asserted, that southern intellectual discourse had turned to the discussion of "communities and their aspirations and their developing genius for concerted action."[33]

Implicit in the community ideal was the principle of cooperation exemplified by the education crusade. "Co-operation is the lesson that we Southern people are learning rapidly," Mitchell announced. "This educational movement in the South is building up community life by making effective the cooperative principle in all forms of progressive action." When southern progressives spoke of cooperation, they often meant the organizational efficiency that accompanied the expansion of progressive institutions into rural life. "It finds application first in the neighborhood school," Mitchell argued, "but it rapidly extends itself to the public library, the demonstration farm, the co-operative dairy, good roads, the local factory, and the general enrichment of rural life."[34] Libraries and demonstration farms, as the reasoning went, would break down rural prejudices and nurture rational behavior.

The development of a community ideal was made possible only by the structural changes reshaping the postwar South. Mitchell argued that the demise of the plantation system and the subsequent rise of multiple forms of land tenancy made social interaction possible. In addition, racial segregation was ushering in the white solidarity implicit in the community ideal. "A community has taken the place of the old plantation. This spells progress." For Mitchell and other university progressives, the cooperative ideal was realized with increasing legislative appropriations for schools and colleges, the coordination of university entrance requirements and high school curricula, and the development of university extension work. However, the best examples of community action were the numerous state campaigns for local taxation in support of common schools launched after 1903. Rejecting the dreary isolation of the antebellum plantation, southern progressives redefined the concept of community to include the state and the South itself.[35]

The progressive notion of community represented a challenge to rural traditions and values. Imbued with a libertarian strain of republicanism, rural southerners of the nineteenth century cherished decentralized political authority and local control. Many jealously guarded their understanding of liberty and shared the Populist resentment of centralized political power even while they resisted Alliance efforts to regulate the market economy. Instead, many rural southerners chose to define freedom as opposition to government interference. As historian James Leloudis concludes, the efforts of Alderman and his allies to transform the University of North Carolina into an instrument of social engineering alienated rural southerners: "Many North Carolinians, wary of the growing power of distant monopolies in other areas of their lives, feared the emergence of an 'educational ring' that would eventually deny them control over their own children." Opponents of state aid to education were not backward-looking Luddites. They valued improved school facilities, but they opposed the movement to replace local authority with bureaucratic control and technical expertise.[36]

In harmony with the Populist regulatory impulse, progressive reformers adopted a more collective conception of community. Communities were bound together by "likemindedness," social sympathies, and an appreciation of the values of social efficiency and order. Progressive collectivism was not egalitarianism, however. Reformers infused their conception of community with middle-class paternalism. Progressive collectivism had little in common with the cooperative producer commonwealth espoused by the Farmer's Alliance and the Knights of Labor. Progressives believed that reform should come from a professional class trained in the techniques of social management, not from the grass roots. Progressive notions of community also incorporated the spirit of social uplift inherited from late nineteenth-century Protestant humanitarianism. With these assumptions about community, reformers confronted a tradition of individualism deeply rooted in southern political culture.[37]

Although many southerners defended local autonomy, progressives championed government intervention in the form of the modernized school. Edwin Alderman captured the essence of the community paradigm: "The social centre of gravity of the South to-day is neither the courthouse nor the hustings, but the schoolhouse and the university, and its prevailing mood is social sympathy."[38] Progressive educators portrayed the graded school as the model of the rationalized South. But Alderman and Mitchell argued that common schools and universities were interdependent units in a smoothly functioning organization. "The University embraces within its purpose all the educational agencies of the state [and] feels a keen interest in the progress of every school," wrote Mitchell.[39] This bureaucratic notion of education reflected the organizational impulse central to the progressive idea of community. Just as reformers sought to upgrade common schools to improve the colleges, they considered the state university and the rural schools partners in a newly invigorated social center.

An agent of social cohesion, the modern university would privilege social service over competing models of university organization. Here, Alderman made a clear connection between political culture and education. As part of the framework of modern administration, the American university was forced to negotiate between the growing demand for government efficiency and the traditions of political democracy. Autocratic governments such as that of Wilhelmine Germany functioned with "superhuman efficiency." Centralized and structured, the German government was capable of promoting social welfare and economic productivity on a scale unimaginable in the United States. German efficiency, of course, came at the expense of participatory democracy. Yet Alderman clearly admired German efforts to link science to material advancement and to celebrate technical knowledge as a "final fruit of civilization." The unfortunate price of democratic government was "waste and unscientific arrangement." Whereas European statism made efficient government possible, American democratic republicanism required good citizenship. Cultivating an intelligent citizenry, he argued, was the responsibility of American education.[40]

American universities would distinguish themselves from their European counterparts not on the basis of academic abstraction but in response to the conditions of American political culture. Alderman believed that the American college should not replicate the British ideal of higher education for the transmission of noble virtues. At the same time, the American college would transcend the rationalism of French higher education, which stressed "clarity of expression" and aesthetic excellence. Similarly, the German ideals of investigation and "organization" would be "comprehended" but incorporated in a higher synthesis of social service. Democracy required the "truth finder" and the "man of cultivated manner." More importantly, it needed a college professor conscious of broad social and economic issues. Ultimately, the social service university would encourage the extension of community life.[41]

In promoting community life, the service-oriented university would validate its status as an extension of progressive government. The university's role in state formation, Alderman suggested, might well be recognized by the expansion of the traditional threefold division of government branches to include education. The university would then function as a "coordinate branch of democratic government" that would produce a cadre of experts and "social-minded men" who would cooperate with "the state in its making." University experts would organize industry, encourage rural economic development, reduce the backwardness of country life, improve agriculture, rationalize public expenditures, elevate the public mind, and apply "scientific knowledge and business sense to its affairs." Equally important, university faculty would instruct the young in the principles of democracy. As functional elements of a regulatory, service-oriented state, modern American universities would be the harbingers of a progressive new day: "No just man can deny to it leadership as the chief constructive agent in the building of a new social order."[42]

In their preoccupation with community cohesion and organic images of society, southern progressives spoke what historian Daniel Rodgers has described as the language of social bonds. Rodgers believes this idiom was one of the "language[s] of discontent" intrinsic to progressivism. Repudiating individualism, southern progressives joined their northern counterparts by extolling a "consciously contrived harmony" and demonstrating a "new interest in the social and physical environment, the discovery of . . . new measures of social control, and a vivid, nervous concern with social cohesion."[43] Not only the school, but social and political institutions would be transformed from instruments of sectarianism into vehicles of social progress. As Alderman put it, "Southern politics is permeated with this thought of social progress and community effort."[44] Reflecting Hegelian motifs of the harmony between the state and civil society, progressives assumed a unity of interest between the people and elite reformers. Southerners had espoused the virtues of community before, most notably as an expression of the paternalistic relationship embedded in slavery. The progressive notion of community was much more artificial than the one sustained by the slave regime, however. Community in itself was not an end but a process toward the vague goals of progress and growth. The ambiguities of southern republicanism were resolved in the cold light of progressive community.[45]

As pervasive as the concept of community was in progressive educational thought, the idea of democracy renewed seemed to accompany almost every educational address or article. But progressive democracy was fraught with contradictions of hierarchy and cooperation, local control and state regulation. Similarly, progressive democracy combined a veneration of the people with an acceptance of black disfranchisement and elite government. As historian Dewey Grantham points out, progressives believed segregation and disfranchisement "were the touchstones through which the distinctions separating white men could be softened, white unity maintained, and a broader white democracy achieved." Middle-class reformers showed little sympathy for the idea of broad-based, mass political participation. Educators routinely disparaged what they saw as the average southerner's provincialism, resentment of outside criticism, preoccupation with race, and propensity for "sentimentalism." These convictions led progressives to favor paternalistic methods of social reform that directly contradicted their paeans to democracy.[46]

Democracy was a corollary of the community ideal. Democratic rhetoric provided ideological ballast for the effort to enlist financial support for public education. By offering practical education accessible to reasonably qualified whites, universities would become avenues of social opportunity instead of havens of exclusivity. Charles Dabney suggested that the rise of the state university paralleled the transition of southern society from an aristocratic to a democratic form of organization.[47] But never far from the surface of progressive democracy was the aura of elitism and hierarchy. Democracy and community were binary terms that expressed the overriding progressive desire to create a cohesive social order.

The emancipation of the "common man" was the main task of the modernized southern school, Mitchell proclaimed. Echoing New South critics of the plantation order, he reproached the "social stratification" of the South before the war. Slavery elevated a minority of whites and provided "immeasurable improvement" for blacks, but it degraded the sturdy southern yeomanry. Mitchell explained defensively that the education crusade was not committed to securing "privileges for a class," meaning southern blacks. Rather, it was dedicated to developing society by uplifting the multitudes of poor whites who "were once ground between the upper millstone of aristocracy and the nether one of slavery." Elevating the common people was a necessary prelude to social regeneration.[48]

What precisely, then, did progressives mean by democracy? Mitchell cited the efforts of progressive educators to use "every agency of civilization and progress to raise the neglected white people of the South to industrial prosperity, social efficiency and independence in political action." Democracy was the political flip-side of the conviction that the civilized society was the efficient one. Progressives excoriated the demagoguery and hidebound partisanship of the democratic South. Social reform, they argued, could hardly be expected from conservatives wedded to limited government and racial extremism. Yet for progressives democracy was not simply political purification. It also meant renewed economic vigor, together with the development of public services, exemplified by the modernized school. It also anticipated mass mobilization in the effort to create a more efficient and productive society. Instead of provincialism and squalor the "democratic" South would be distinguished by voluntary cooperation in social reform and greater state responsibility for social needs. It would also replace race-baiting partisanship and machine politics with public administration by technical experts.[49]

Inseparable from the progressives' veneration of the common man as the repository of democracy was their euphoria for social sympathy. Although as vague as their notion of community, "sympathies" suggested the white South's recognition of the need for a minimum of state regulation, racial stratification, and school improvement. "Steadfastness of spirit and purity of thought about public service have been stamped into the life of the South by its strange, sad history," Alderman claimed. But the South's resolution to use the state to promote social change was boosted by "social sympathy and practical faith in the common man."[50] As Mitchell explained it, the "bond of union in democracy is likemindedness." This likemindedness presupposed common habits, modes of thought, and "sentiment," which together ensured social stability.[51] Progressives suggested that this new, organic community had replaced traditional class and racial divisions.

It was the acceptance of organized mechanisms of reform that was transforming indigent southern schools into institutions of democratic education. Alderman argued that the New South had developed "an overwhelming public sentiment, with the social and political agencies necessary to sustain that sentiment, in favor of the education of all the people at public expense, thus making of a social system, semi-feudal in nature, a democracy in *social usage*, as well as in political philosophy."[52] The implication was that progressivism represented no challenge to the social order. Instead, it reflected broadly held convictions evoked by the crucible of war and Reconstruction.

Alderman suggested that education was beginning to reflect the progressive vision of democracy and social organization. Instead of emphasizing political rights, southern schools were promoting duty and service in their curricula. "The whole educational curriculum reveals the mood of the Southern mind in the effort made in it to discipline the will, to understand social and economic causes, and to see the life about it, not as an atom, but as part of a related whole."[53] The turn to bureaucratic thought, the belief that, as historian Robert Wiebe puts it, social unity could be based on "a frictionless operation analogous to the factory under pre-scientific management," helps to explain the functional tone of progressive democracy.[54]

For progressive educators, democracy was a mechanism of economic progress and efficiency, not a political theory of representative government. Fears of infringement on personal freedom were little evident in the writings of educational progressives. Rather than government by the people, Samuel Mitchell suggested that democracy was best understood as "fraternalism." By contrast, "particularism" and "provincialism" were anathema. Most shared Charles Dabney's conviction that political decisions should not be determined by raw public opinion. Like many Gilded Age elites, he feared that large-scale immigration, urbanization, and labor conflict would lead to social upheaval. The university could help prevent social disintegration by educating people for enlightened democracy. American democracy could be "saved" not only by education but by training leaders to mold public opinion in favor of intelligent policies.[55]

Instead of defensive sectionalism, democracy would mean system and predictability. It also meant a central role for the educational institutions in which Mitchell, Alderman, Dabney, and Hill had a vested interest. Here is how Samuel Mitchell described the function of education in democracy: "Hence, solidarity is a motive force in democratic education. . . . The public school is the exponent of Americanism. Agencies to the same end are the colleges of which a prime function is to give right orientation to their students." One wonders what traditionalists would have made of Mitchell's suggestion that the university's primary function was to "give right orientation." In any case, Mitchell connected the college to other agencies of social reconstruction. Institutions giving "right orientation" included "the press, which by its very profession makes for the public point of view; and general conventions, religious, scientific, and social, in which persons . . . advance a common interest."[56] Their ideas about democracy and education were worlds away from those dominant before the New South. For these progressives, mental discipline and liberal culture were replaced by the ideal of education as process. The task of education was not to develop mental faculties but to enhance civic-mindedness. But the civic virtue that progressives had in mind included the acceptance of middle-class leadership in social management.

The political theory of southern progressives bore a striking resemblance to that of their northern counterparts. As Robert Wiebe explains, northern reformers believed that political leadership was the responsibility of the "educator-extraordinary." His or her task was to elevate public opinion from emotional partisanship to detached rationality. According to Franklin Giddings, public opinion "is rational like-mindedness. . . . We can derive . . . no assurance that a stable popular government can be maintained in a nation which ceases to be hourly creative of genuine public opinion—the fruit of rational discourse."[57] Giddings sounded remarkably like Mitchell. Both imagined themselves in the role of the expert adviser. Bureaucratic thought was clearly evident in Alderman's ode to the "growing" South. He praised the South's passage from the stage of educational rallies and revivals to the stage of "constructiveness and technique." According to him, educational reformers should be concerned primarily with administering the "machinery and methods" of an efficient public education system.[58]

Southern progressives mixed bureaucratic thought with a diluted version of positivism that supported their philosophy of education. Southern historians have yet to examine the influence of positivism on the southern mind of the early twentieth century, probably because its sources are so obscure. There is no material evidence linking southern educational progressives to August Comte's "positive philosophy." Yet an undercurrent of pseudoscience, historical teleology, and statism suggests the influence of positivism on the larger intellectual climate of late nineteenth-century America.

Positivism assumed a variety of forms. In the United States many exponents jettisoned the authoritarian and pseudoreligious elements of Comte's system. They agreed with the fundamental tenet of positivism: Knowledge was restricted to phenomena that could be observed and verified by empirical methods of scientific investigation. Speculation about essences and "things in themselves," though interesting to the metaphysician, was outside the domain of the hard-headed scientist. Through empirical investigation, Comte believed, the scientist could arrive at an understanding of the fundamental laws governing phenomena, even social interaction. Comtean positivists vigorously rejected the individualism and materialism of Baconian induction.

In place of an atomistic conception of society, Comte substituted the idea of society as an organic composite subject to historical change. His theory that society developed through three distinct intellectual stages—the theological, the metaphysical, and the positive—combined empiricism with historicist evolutionism.[59] Comte's three stages were fixed within an evolutionary framework; widespread enthusiasm about science signaled the arrival of the positive stage, which would foster a highly regulated society administered by technocrats. In company with Hegel and Marx, Comte posited a unified scheme of interpretation. For liberals no longer convinced that Christianity could provide a stable foundation for their worldview, the scientific aura of positivism seemed to guarantee intellectual certitude.[60]

According to historian Gillis Harp, positivism appealed to American liberals of the late nineteenth century for a variety of reasons. Courtesy of Darwin and Spencer, many intellectuals embraced positivism because of its emphasis on scientific predictability and hierarchical classification.[61] Positivism also suited the intellectual mood of the late nineteenth century, which exulted in "laws" of development and the inevitability of material and moral progress. More importantly, though, positivism offered a social theory that seemed to answer the complex questions of the Gilded Age. "Scientific sociology could deliver European civilization from this crisis by resolving the central tension of contemporary society, that is, the opposition of order and progress," Harp explains.[62] Could it not do the same for America? Evidently, reformers such as Lester Frank Ward and Herbert Croly believed it could.

Positivism was a philosophy of action and reform, not speculation. The science of society would help illuminate political discourse by delineating the things that were amenable to reform.[63] However, its most important contribution was to the transformation of American liberalism. Comtean positivism provided a scientific rationale for consistent government intervention in society. At the same time, it justified the technocratic managerialism that accompanied an increasingly bureaucratic, corporate order. Efficiency experts could legitimately intervene in society without disrupting social harmony. Decisions made previously by political partisans would be transferred to disinterested technical experts. Responsible for maintaining social order, efficiency experts would harmonize competing interests while maintaining industrial productivity. "It was mostly this elitist/organizational impulse that was taken up by Progressives at the turn of the century," argues Harp. Theorists such as Albion Small and E. A. Ross extracted from positivism its emphasis on social stability and expert administration. Yet American liberalism also absorbed corporatism from the positive philosophy. Comte's theory saw semiautonomous groups rather than individuals as the crucial agents in the new society. Premised on a hierarchical division of labor, positivism's organic conception of society accommodated modern corporations by portraying them as natural products of social evolution.[64]

According to Dewey Grantham, the positivist preoccupation with reconciling progress and order was the guiding principle of southern progressivism. This does not necessarily make educational progressives positivists, of course. But positivism was at least one powerful source of progressive thought about social change and the role of professionals in the modern order. In their explanation of democracy as a process fostering social sympathies, educational progressives echoed organic themes central to positivism.

Similarly, the corporatist conception of community that progressives espoused, which included a hierarchical division of labor and an interventionist state, resonated with positivism. In their criticism of "atomistic" individualism and their celebration of efficient cooperation, progressives spoke the language of positivist sociology. Lamenting the lack of educational coordination in the South (which Alderman was able to overlook in a haze of New South optimism two years later when he praised the region's "genius of school organization"), he claimed that "Each phase of the great process is thought of as an isolated unit, as a separate atom, rather than as a different state of an organic and related process."[65] Organic metaphors were by no means unique to positivism. They permeated Hegelian philosophy and Darwinian science. Yet, when seen in conjunction with the other elements of positivist sociology reflected in southern progressive thought, the lineage with an Americanized version of Comte's positive philosophy becomes clearer.

Positivism was above all progressive. By uncovering the laws of society, positivists believed that managerial experts could make discrete adjustments to the social order that would promote progress but preserve stability. To a considerable extent, this is how progressives viewed education. Educational institutions were meant to "give right orientation" to students, not instruction in republican virtue and liberal democracy. Education was crucial to southern material progress because it existed solely "in order to yield continual returns of efficiency and power," as Alderman put it. The South still lacked a clear understanding of the "relationship of school life to the other activities of social life, nor of education as a great social factor modifying and affecting civilization as a whole," he insisted.[66] Mitchell believed that the educator should not be a bookish pedant but a social technician who could discern the laws of progress: "They must be given the conspectus of the whole circle of society, with its limitless interplay of human forces." And what was the place of the southern college in this scheme, Mitchell asked? "To create and to energize the idea of social progress, of national integrity, of industrial justice, and of spiritual power." Applying science to industry and sociology to the region's "baffling racial conditions," the new class of professionals would guide southern development through the treacherous waters of modernization.[67]

To educational progressives, the advent of bureaucratic management represented the South's transition from the stage of revivalist social reform to the period of concrete achievement. But "construction" required the continuous formation of public opinion in favor of public education—the "educator extraordinary" that Robert Wiebe described. To meet this demand, Alderman explained that the Conference for Education in the South and state cooperative associations would evolve into the organizations envisioned by Comtean positivism: "They should become permanent bodies, efficient organizations, to watch with eternal vigilance the state of public opinion. The great demand for the future, however, is to be not so much with public agitation . . . as for sound basis of action, of intelligence in the scientific use of the moneys made possible by an aroused public opinion." The educational reformer that Alderman imagined sounded much like the technocratic experts celebrated in Comte's social theory. Scholarship was secondary to the teacher. Most important was "technical training in administration, in the history and principles of adjusting education to the needs of a free people." Technique rather than knowledge would be required of "a highly trained expert in educational work." His responsibility was to "build" the educational infrastructure rather than generate public enthusiasm. Instead of appealing to conscience, the educator of the future would "inform" the masses of the need for greater efficiency. Alderman's educational bureaucrat was a man "who can go into a community and teach that community how to build a good schoolhouse, and how to order its curriculum in the interest of the child, for the use that life will demand of him."[68]

It was in large part the college's ability to produce professional experts that justified its claim to practical social service. Positivism thus gave intellectual credibility to professionalization: "Is it not significant that the expert is finding a larger place in our democracy? What is the meaning of the present tendency to govern by commissions? Does it not all signify the increasing importance which the people attach to special knowledge, and their belief in the duty of trained men to labor for the common good?"[69]

Similarly, the positivist theme of expert leadership informed Charles Dabney's thoughts about civil service reform. Writing to Walter Hines Page in 1894, then assistant secretary of agriculture Dabney announced his plan to coordinate the government's various scientific agencies within the Department of Agriculture. Administration by scientific elites is what he had in mind: "A great national department of Economic Science is the dream of the scientific men of Washington. We have all the elements of it now. . . . Only one thing more is needed—a permanent scientific director, to form the keystone in a perfectly formed and united arch of scientific agencies supporting the industries of the people."[70] Much like Lester Frank Ward, Dabney espoused a philosophy that combined an uncritical faith in science with bureaucratic thought and positivist empiricism. By the 1880s, this philosophy had become dominant among Washington's growing civil service community.[71]

Southern progressives were neither models of Frederick W. Taylor's scientific managers nor dogmatic exponents of Comtean positivism. No doubt, corporatist and bureaucratic thought were fed by intellectual sources that went beyond positivism. The Social Gospel, the organizational impulse inherited from mobilization for the Civil War, the cooperative lexicon fostered by the Southern Alliance, the social and economic conditions in the South after Reconstruction, and the New South ideology shaped the thought of southern progressives. But positivism was an important intellectual thread in the fabric of progressive thought.

Ultimately, conformity characterized progressive educational thought more than bold intellectual dissent. For the most part, progressives did not openly defy southern social conventions. Their writings and speeches respected southern racial orthodoxies. However, many educational progressives did belong to the group of liberal intellectuals George Washington Cable described as the "Silent South." This may be why Samuel Mitchell's altercation with governor Coleman Blease, in which the governor accused the president of taking money away from the education of white girls for the education of black men, is so remarkable. Yet there were some who were not so silent. In 1905, Hill published an article that questioned the South's intellectual freedom and called for greater tolerance of dissent. Although it did not match the audacity of John Spencer Bassett and Andrew Sledd, two southern academics who brought opprobrium on themselves for questioning racial inequities, it represented a tone of criticism uncharacteristic of university administrators.

The occasion of Hill's article, titled "A Plea for Tolerance," was an address given by Edwin Alderman at the Southern Society in New York. Alderman made the controversial suggestion that the South's current political leadership fell below the standards of its antebellum predecessors, exemplified by Clay and Calhoun. The comments angered senator Joseph Bailey of Texas, who declined membership on a committee that was trying to establish an endowment fund for UVA. Dexterously, Hill suggested that Bailey's leadership disproved Alderman's theory. However, Hill's point was not the accuracy of Alderman's observations but the propriety of Bailey's. "Have we freedom of opinion in the south? Must every man who thinks above a whisper do so at the peril of his reputation of his influence . . . or . . . the institution or the cause that he represents?"[72]

Hill rattled the cages of southern conservatives by praising the Trinity faculty who protected Bassett's position when threatened by his claim that Booker T. Washington was, beside Lee, the greatest man the South had produced in a hundred years. In a backhanded compliment that illustrated his point, the chancellor lauded the vitality of southern political leadership, which the North could not match if similarly trapped in the "deadly paralysis of intellect caused by the enforced uniformity of thought within the lines of one party." The Solid South was necessary for social order, Hill argued, but its advantages were purchased at the "fearful cost" of intellectual sterility. Whereas Alderman and others had obliquely challenged single-party dominance in the pages of the *Atlantic Monthly* and the *South Atlantic Quarterly*, Hill castigated the "illiberality" of southern thought more vigorously in the *Atlanta Constitution*.

Slavery and its defense explained the South's "morbid self-consciousness," its extreme sensitivity to criticism, which the sectional conflict and the "unspeakable indignities" of Reconstruction only aggravated. Instead of relinquishing identity, though, the South needed to preserve what was good and abandon its "monstrosities." Inquisition-like torture was a thing of the past (Hill was silent about lynching), but every vicious attempt to silence dissenting opinion represented "an abridgement of that reasonable liberty of thought and speech which is the . . . heritage of freedom and the indispensable requisite for the ascertainment of truth."[73]

The chancellor's article met with a mixed response. Some of the local newspapers chastised him, and others such as the Athens *Banner* gave qualified support. One staunch defender of the Lost Cause leveled an acrimonious attack against Hill in the *Constitution* and through personal correspondence. "I would rather live in the undefiled atmosphere of Caucasian simplicity," wrote Benjamin Blackburn in a sixteen-page harangue, "and be known among my people as a sincere exponent of the Southern view, than to sit under the approving hand of some self-appointed custodian of tolerant thought, whose pen is directed against the foundations of Southern civilization." No doubt Blackburn's views were shared by many defenders of the Lost Cause. What his letters confirmed, of course, was the accuracy of Hill's argument.[74]

Blackburn's attack illustrates the political minefield that progressives had to negotiate. Like his contemporaries, Hill had to mediate between racial moderation and the Southern way of life. Southern reformers walked a tightrope between criticism of suffocating conformity and defense of southern tradition. Chancellor Hill's moderate critique is important for this reason alone. Faced with defensive hostility, even Hill's muted plea took a measure of courage many liberal southerners could not muster. Writing to N. E. Harris, former law associate of Hill's and legislative representative, the chancellor suggested that his unpleasant exchange with Blackburn brought into sharp relief the political polarization of the South: Vardamanism against the "spirit of Grady and Gordon."[75]

Against racial extremism and demagoguery, educational modernizers did articulate a vision of a South more humane than the one they inhabited. Much of this vision included assumptions of class stratification incongruous with their democratic profession of faith. Despite the distasteful elements of their ideology, they did espouse a program of regional rehabilitation that included many of the tenets of an emergent southern liberalism. Furthermore, they fashioned an intellectual rationale for the prominent role of education in the New South.

Yet if progressives found adversaries among Vardaman's followers, they also found them within the walls of academe. Academic critics often were less concerned about progressive social policies than about the reformers' pedagogical philosophy. Progressives liked to portray the movement for technical instruction as a groundswell of enlightened support. Yet some were skeptical of educational modernization. Utility, the ascending pedagogical philosophy at most state universities, had by no means triumphed over classicism and Christian piety as the reigning orthodoxy in higher education.[76]

H. E. Shepherd of the College of Charleston expressed early misgivings about the changing character of southern higher education. Writing in 1892, Shepherd decried the "insatiable lust of numerical strength" displayed by fledgling southern colleges. Beyond the crass materialism of the drive for increased attendance, the pursuit of numbers had a deleterious effect on university instruction. Shepherd lamented that high-quality education mattered little "when brought to bear against the charm and magic of numerical force." Compounding the deterioration of university instruction was the "tendency toward a speedy and immature specialization." Without a broad education in science and classical literature, specialization resulted in "empiricism" and "charlatanism." The criticism of classicists such as Shepherd forced progressives to modify their utilitarianism to accommodate a plurality of opinion about southern education.[77]

John Kilgo, president of Trinity University and virulent critic of public higher education, assailed the progressives' evangelical-style reform. Educational advancement took gradual effort, Kilgo insisted, not the "emotionalism" of reformers preoccupied with immediate results. Progressive educators were strong on rhetoric but weak on substance: "There are a sufficient number of Southern educators who can talk, and talk, and talk, and keep on talking. But of ideas that look to a definite end and to genuine growth of culture and of a faith that draws to it the money necessary to sincere work, there are few." The Trinity president lumped educators together with New South journalists and politicians as a group that espoused "public faiths" aimed only at "immediate achievement." Kilgo accused New South educators of excessive "flattery" and smug optimism; attempting to attract investment in their universities, they used "superlatives with reckless extravagance." Like exponents of the New South creed, progressive educators obscured the disparity between promise and reality, which only harmed the movement for reform: "Such expressions as 'Our great colleges and universities,' and many others of the same sort, have been over-worked by educators in the South. . . . But beyond this public flattery as to the relative position of higher education in the South, there have been set false standards for the general public as to educational success. . . . It is a matter of numbers; scarcely ever a matter of the quality of training."[78] Kilgo was equally distressed by the tendency of evangelical educators to substitute quantitative for qualitative standards of progress. However, Kilgo did praise James Kirkland of Vanderbilt, the leading crusader for improved standards in southern higher education.

If not explicitly critical of the educational boosters, some educators placed greater emphasis on the movement to improve standards than on the crusade for public support. Elizabeth Avery Colton, chair of the Committee on Standards for the Southern Association of College Women (SACW), conducted a study of 142 women's colleges that illustrated the deficiencies of southern higher education for women. In 1912, Colton reported that only four colleges had been certified by the Southern Association of Colleges and Preparatory Schools. Lacking any national or southern standards to evaluate the remaining institutions, Colton devised a classification scheme that distinguished between institutions offering legitimate college studies and those "which are merely inferior secondary schools." Like her male counterparts at state universities, Colton complained that insufficient funding hindered university progress. But rather than measure university improvement by the standard of social outreach, Colton emphasized scholarly excellence.[79]

Colton pointed to several problems afflicting women's higher education. Although some institutions announced the college standard of fourteen units for admission, they did not enforce it. In some cases, the school's curriculum bore little relationship to its admissions standards. A full one-third of the institutions she examined failed to distinguish between students enrolled in preparatory, "special-study," and college courses. Most disconcerting was the concentration of students in preparatory classes and special studies, such as art and music. Administrators justified the numbers in the less rigorous special studies by appealing to the ennobling effects of the "social and intellectual life of the college" on the students. For Colton, it was wishful thinking because "in reality, the overworked professor, the immature fine-arts 'specialist,' and even the 'inspired' *prep* are apt to make the clear, keen, scholarly atmosphere of college life somewhat hazy." In fact, it was the propensity of southern women for specialized studies that distinguished a school such as the North Carolina State Normal and Industrial College from the more rigorously academic Vassar College.[80]

The solution for Colton was not to eliminate classical requirements or add industrial education. If anything, she called on colleges to purge "specializers" as well as those who "drop studies simply because they are difficult." Instead, she encouraged institutions to submit to the standards of the Association of Colleges and Preparatory Schools of the Southern States. Although Colton embraced the progressive tenet of educational rationalization, she objected to the notion that more was equal to better education. For her, the crisis in higher education was not the gulf between universities and social issues but the absence of unified college standards in the region.[81]

Certainly, progressives such as Samuel Mitchell were also concerned with defining the function of various levels of southern education. And although Kilgo's and Shepherd's observations were astute, they did not provide an exhaustive critique of the progressive ideology. Together, though, their observations suggest that the field of ideas about southern education was a contested terrain. Though not the only voice for improved standards, Colton's analysis suggests that women educators established pedagogical objectives that did not always include a connection between schooling and social reform. At least in Colton's case, rigorous and traditional standards were the measure of university advancement. Similarly, Kilgo and Shepherd criticized the fragmentation caused by academic specialization, progressive propaganda, and the hyperbole of the New South. Both were unfair to the progressives; neither admitted the sectarian interests underlying their criticisms. Even so, their models of education competed with those of the progressives. Educational progressives were compelled to sell their education program to a South that included those skeptical of reform and suspicious of northern do-gooders. But they also had to contend with rational, alternative conceptions of education for the South.

Although the South was no intellectual monolith, it was a place where intellectuals were obligated to defer to social conventions or face stiff reprisals. Hill's and Mitchell's experience would confirm this. Like all progressives, educational modernizers cast their reform agenda in terms familiar to white southerners. Drawing their ideas from indigenous sources as well as from wider intellectual currents, progressives sought to modernize the South without relinquishing its most cherished features. The progressive versions of democracy and community should be seen in this light.

Progressive ideas about educational modernization reinforced the social structures of the New South. But if progressives did not revolutionize the South, they did leave their imprint on the region's corporate laws, railroad laws, child labor legislation, public health laws and, perhaps most importantly, education system. The universities of the New South were the testing ground for the progressives' philosophy of education and social change.

Notes

1. For evidence of correspondence between the state university presidents, see Alderman's affable letter to Hill, December 11, 1904, box 4; Hill's letter to Charles Dabney, relating to the movement for national aid to education, March 9, 1904, box 1; and Dabney's invitation to Hill to attend the University of Cincinnati's inaugural exercises, box 3, Hill Collection, UGA. There is nothing intrinsically interesting about these letters; they only suggest that the university presidents under examination often corresponded with each other.

2. See Gaston, *The New South Creed,* especially chapter 2.

3. Ibid., 92–98.

4. Hill, "Southern Education a National Responsibility." An interesting example of the progressives' synthesis of nationalism and sectionalism was Edwin Alderman's solicitation of comments from several American intellectuals about southern contributions to the nation. Prompted by a lecture he was to give at Johns Hopkins in 1903, Alderman's survey received fascinating responses from Woodrow Wilson, Henry Adams, Frederick Jackson Turner, Thomas Nelson Page, Ellen Glasgow, Albert Shaw, and William P. Trent, among others. The letters appear in the Alderman Collection at UVA, but they are published together in an article by Robert Bush, "Dr. Alderman's Symposium on the South," 3–19.

5. Mitchell, "The Nationalization of Southern Sentiment," 108–9.

6. Ibid.

7. Novick, *That Noble Dream,* 76–80; Stephenson, *Southern History in the Making,* 8, 64–65; Grob, "Reconstruction," 199.

8. Mitchell, "The Nationalization of Southern Sentiment," 108–9; Mitchell, "Education for Constructive National Leadership."

9. On the parallels between race consciousness in the Jim Crow South and in late nineteenth-century American colonialism, see Hunt, *Ideology and U.S. Foreign Policy,* 78–81; historian Alan Dawley writes that "This attitude [racism] fit in well with the mood of reconciliation between North and South. . . . As northern elites asserted the duty of Anglo-Saxons to govern the so-called darker races of the world, they came to be more sympathetic to white supremacy in the South," in *Struggles for Justice,* 54; on the role of northern racism in the abandonment of Reconstruction, see Gillette, *Retreat from Reconstruction,* 363–80; for an interpretation that stresses the link between the subversion of the free labor ideology and the rise of northern racism, see Foner, *A Short History of Reconstruction,* 222–24.

10. Mitchell, "The Nationalization of Southern Sentiment," 111, 112.

11. Ibid. For Hill, addresses given by Phillips Brooks and the Conference for Education's Robert Ogden served as heartwarming examples of the willingness of northerners to embrace the doctrine of sectional reconciliation that admitted southern honor and "patriotism" in the Civil War. See "Nationalism Not Opposed to Truest Sectionalism," *Atlanta Constitution*, April 9, 1905, in box 7, Hill Collection, UGA.

12. Hill, "Southern Education a National Responsibility."

13. Ibid.

14. Doyle, *New Men, New Cities, New South*, 315.

15. Alderman, "The Achievement of a Generation," 241.

16. Dabney, "As Is Education So Is Production," 3; "Report of the President," *Trustees' Report*, 1887–88, Dabney Papers, UTK.

17. Mitchell, "Jubilee Address," 112–13; see also his article titled "Education for Constructive National Leadership," in which he argued that the teacher "must share the spirit of the statesman and regulate his work accordingly, for the school stands for a program of progress, economic, social, and political," 5. The educational panacea was made explicit by Edwin Alderman: "Our institutions needed to be democratized; our thought to be nationalized; our life to be industrialized, and the whole process was one of education." See Alderman, "Charles D. McIver of North Carolina," 108.

18. Gaston, *The New South Creed*, 106.

19. Grantham, *Southern Progressivism*, 25; also see "The Contours of Southern Progressivism," 1037–42.

20. Bailey, *Liberalism in the New South*, 136–37.

21. Mitchell, "Phases in the Educational Movement of the Day," 18–20.

22. Alderman, "The Achievement of a Generation," 239, 251.

23. Murphy, *Problems of the Present South*, 77–78.

24. Mitchell, "Practical Tendencies in Education."

25. Ibid.

26. Dabney, "Technical Education in the South," unpublished, undated address, folder #322, box 26, Dabney Papers, UNC; see also Dabney's unpublished address titled "Wanted: Scholars," folder #317, box 25, Dabney Papers, UNC.

27. Dabney, "Technical Education in the South."

28. Ibid. Although the humanities might elevate the sensibilities, the "future prosperity of nations depended upon the culture of scientific intellect." Progressive theories of education clearly favored inductive science over the liberal arts. "Ignorance may follow afar off in the path lighted by advancing knowledge, but when science leaves her, she falls into darkness and is lost." For progressives, practical education was the springboard to social progress.

29. Mitchell, "Phases in the Educational Movement of the Day," 20–21.

30. Alderman, "The Achievement of a Generation," 240.

31. Link, *The Paradox of Southern Progressivism*, 91.

32. Ogden, "The Conference for Education in the South," 272.

33. Alderman, "The Achievement of a Generation," 241; also see Alderman, "The Growing South," 10380.

34. Mitchell, "The American Spirit in Education," 256.

35. Mitchell, "Do Our Colleges Pay?" 219–20.

36. Leloudis, *Schooling the New South,* 113–21; quote on p. 113.

37. Link, *The Paradox of Southern Progressivism,* xi–xii.

38. Alderman, "Education and Public Service," in folder titled "Address at Inauguration of Edward Kidder Graham, 1876–1918," President's Papers, UVA.

39. Mitchell, The Ideal of the State University," 7.

40. Alderman, "Education and Public Service," President's Papers, UVA; see also "Can Democracy Be Organized?" Address to the Literary and Historical Association of North Carolina, Raleigh, November 9, 1915, Rare Virginia Pamphlets, "Edwin Alderman," vol. 43, UVA.

41. "Education and Public Service," 371.

42. Ibid., 372.

43. Rodgers, "In Search of Progressivism," 125.

44. Alderman, "The Growing South," 10381; Alderman emphasized the organic motif in an address titled "The National Spirit": "Our new philosophy, then, treats society as an organism and studies it; secondly, it is informed by intense sympathy; third; it has a genius for organization and co-operation. This genius for organization manifests itself not only in individual organization for the public welfare, but in passion for legislation . . . for the public welfare." The progressives' corporatist vision anticipated social modifications through political and voluntary mechanisms. Rare Virginia Pamphlets, vol. 43, "Edwin Alderman," UVA.

45. M. E. Bradford, a conservative social commentator, wrote of the southern conservative tradition, "Community was their prior ideal—an informally hierarchical social organism in which all Southerners (including the Negro insofar as the survival of the community permitted) had a sense of investment and participation. In brief, a patriarchal world of families, pre- or non-capitalist *because* familial, located, pious, and "brotherly." Quoted in Genovese, *The Southern Tradition,* 17–18. In contrast to the slaveholders' conception of community as a natural association based on republican precepts, the progressives cast themselves as social engineers of a community organized by the principles of efficiency, productivity, and order.

46. Grantham, *Southern Progressivism,* xvii–xviii.

47. Dabney, "The State University: The Institution of Democracy," unpublished, undated address, folder #329, box 26, Dabney Papers, UNC.

48. Mitchell, "Phases in the Educational Movement of the Day," 18–19.

49. Ibid.

50. Alderman, "The Growing South," 10375, 10382.

51. Mitchell, "Phases in the Educational Movement of the Day," 19.

52. Alderman, "The Growing South," 10375.

53. Ibid., 10376.

54. Wiebe, *The Search for Order 1877–1920,* 156.

55. Dabney, "The State University: The Institution of Democracy," 14.

56. Mitchell, "The Nationalization of Southern Sentiment," 113.

57. Wiebe, *The Search for Order,* 160, including quote.

58. Alderman, "The Growing South," 10376.

59. It should be noted that positivism and historicism did not share a peaceful coexistence. Historicism provided the foundation for nineteenth-century social science, but positivism venerated inexorable laws independent of historical variables. As political scientist Dorothy Ross argues, "Positivist sociology tended to turn all of history into a closed system." Once positivism had identified the natural laws supposedly governing society, "history developed by an inner logic along a precharted course, substantially immune to the contingencies of historical change." Ross, *The Origins of American Social Science,* 18.

60. Harp, *Positivist Republic,* 2–21 and chapter 5, on Lester Frank Ward; Biddiss, "Progress, Prosperity, and Positivism," 200.

61. Empiricism was nothing new to American thought. It was the bedrock of the "common sense," Baconian philosophy of the Scottish Enlightenment, which Americans imbibed from Thomas Reid, among others. What was new was the fusion of empiricism to grand theories of social explanation. For common sense tradition in America, see Turner, *Without God, without Creed,* 56, 76.

62. Harp, *Positivist Republic,* 18.

63. Ibid., 16–19.

64. Ibid., 18–19, 212–13 (quote on 213).

65. Alderman, "The Achievement of a Generation," 244.

66. Ibid., 248.

67. Mitchell, "The Task of the College in the South," 261–62.

68. Alderman, "The Achievement of a Generation," 246; also see Alderman to A. C. Gordon, October 28, 1912, in folder titled "Annual Reports," box 4, President's Papers, UVA.

69. Mitchell, "The Task of the College in the South," 262. Alderman was equally enthusiastic about universities meeting the demand for technical elites: "Its duty is not alone to provide preachers and teachers . . . but to provide as well experts in every phase of expansion in a complex new line, in engineering, in commerce, agriculture, the domestic arts, in public health, in public transportation, and public welfare generally," in Alderman, "The Achievement of a Generation," 251. See also Alderman's address (undated) to the Washington Association titled "The National Spirit" in which he extols the virtue of sociology and the scientific spirit (Alderman Collection, UVA).

70. Dabney to Page, February 21, 1896, folder #81, box 5, Dabney Papers, UNC.

71. Harp, *Positivist Republic,* 121. Harp argues that science provided for this group of government-affiliated intellectuals a progressive and reformist worldview.

72. Hill, "A Plea for Tolerance," *Atlanta Constitution,* February 12, 1905, box 7, Hill Collection, UGA.

73. Ibid.

74. Blackburn to Hill, March 25, 1905, box 5, Hill Collection, UGA. See also Hill to Blackburn, March 15, 1905; and Hill to N. E. Harris, March 21, 1905, box 5, Hill Collection, UGA. Blackburn objected strenuously to Hill's suggestion that economic interests lay behind the Confederate defense of slavery. Blackburn informed Hill that his comments were given added legitimacy by an endorsement from the Confederate Veterans of Atlanta.

75. Hill to N. E. Harris, March 30, 1905, box 5, 1905, Hill Collection, UGA. On reaction to Hill's address, see Mathis, "Walter B. Hill and the Savage Ideal," 31–34. Edwin Mims, a proponent of university leadership in improving educational standards, echoed Hill's insistence on intellectual liberty in the South: "Scholars—an increasing number, let us hope—are bringing to bear upon Southern life the influence of modern ideas and insisting on open-mindedness and cosmopolitanism as the prime virtues of progressive people." Mims, "The University in the South," 19.

76. Ayers, *The Promise of the New South,* 421.

77. Shepherd, "Higher Education in the South," 283–89.

78. Kilgo, "Some Phases of Southern Education," 137–51.

79. Colton, "Standards of Southern Colleges for Women," 458–59.

80. Ibid., 462–64.

81. Ibid., 462–64, 474–75; for more on Colton and the SACW, see Amy Thompson McCandless's insightful article "Progressivism and the Higher Education of Southern Women," 302–25.

3

Architects of Control: Progressives and the Education of Blacks in the New South

State universities were at the forefront of social reform in the New South. A new generation of university administrators and faculty members promoted university modernization and social service. As intellectuals, they became the architects of the southern education movement. But it was in their capacity as authorities on racial issues that progressive educators left an indelible mark. Politely distinguishing themselves from the racial extremism that sent lynching rates skyrocketing in the 1890s, progressive educators espoused a form of racial discrimination palatable to middle-class southerners. As educational experts, university progressives imparted an aura of intellectual legitimacy to a system of instruction designed to maintain black subservience. A group of university presidents and faculty members, not northern industrialists, became the leading propagandists for black industrial education.

Paradoxically, while university progressives advocated education for social improvement, they also propagated a pedagogical scheme that fit conveniently into a scheme for racial submission. Improved standards and the advent of research schools went hand in hand with black proscription. The history of higher education in the South is inextricable from the crystallization of the "highest stage of white supremacy."[1]

Progressives welcomed the stabilization of race relations after the 1890s. Along with most white southerners, they were convinced that segregation and black proscription would guarantee social order, economic progress, and white supremacy. Progressives believed that, having solved the race "question," the South could turn its attention to other pressing social issues. Disfranchisement had removed the threat that political power might be wielded as an instrument of black advancement. Edwin Alderman, president of the University of Virginia (UVA) since 1903 and a leading figure in the educational reform movement in North Carolina, echoed these sentiments in a 1908 article titled "The Growing South." Removed from politics, blacks would focus more constructively on achieving economic self-reliance. Equally important was the effect of disfranchisement on whites. Suffrage restrictions had removed a "frightful temptation from the politics of the white people" and placed the exercise of the vote "on the highest plane possible in a republic."[2]

Samuel Mitchell heartily agreed. Mitchell, a professor of history at Richmond College from 1895 until his election to the presidency of the University of South Carolina in 1908, was deeply involved in the crusade for educational reform in Virginia. Throughout his career he maintained close ties to both the Southern Education Board (SEB) and the General Education Board (GEB), the leading vehicles of educational reform in the region. Writing the same year as Alderman, Mitchell claimed that the constitutional limitation of the suffrage since 1890 had "removed the fear of negro domination" and "opened the way for increasing independence in political thought and action."[3]

If anything, southern racial moderates portrayed disfranchisement as an accomplishment in social engineering. Instead of the barbarism of extralegal violence, intelligent southern opinion had "settled" on white political control and social separation. The South's policy toward blacks would now be generated from "a scientific habit of investigation as to the facts of his progress, coupled with an intelligent interest in his development." The comparatively sanitary policies of disfranchisement and segregation appealed to progressives who sponsored moderate change through discrete adjustments to the social order. Armed with "rational" techniques for maintaining white supremacy, progressives shielded themselves from the contradictions in their program for black uplift.[4]

In fact, as Mitchell asserted, racial conciliation was in perfect harmony with the principle underlying the progressive ethos: the "spirit of service." Racial moderates rejected the image of the black beast and replaced it with the paternalistic counterimage of blacks as dependent children. Discussing the alleged problem of black intemperance, Samuel Mitchell suggested, "Under the fairest conditions, this child-race, so clogged by appetite and passion, finds it difficult to get on well in the world." Morally and intellectually stunted by slavery, blacks were capable of racial improvement only under the guidance of liberal-minded southerners.[5]

Charles Dabney reinforced Mitchell's sentiments. A graduate of the doctoral program in chemistry at Göttingen University Germany, Dabney led the agricultural experiment station at the University of North Carolina before accepting the presidency of the University of Tennessee in 1887. From the inception of the southern education movement Dabney played a prominent part, assuming the leadership of the SEB's propaganda division, the Bureau of Information. In an address to the Conference for Education in the South in 1901,

Dabney implored southern reformers concerned about the education of blacks to recognize the "momentous fact that the negro is a child race, at least two thousand years behind the Anglo-Saxon in its development."[6] Harmless children, blacks nevertheless needed the supervision of their white superiors.

The moderates' views on racial control bore the imprint of the New South ideology. Espoused by journalists and entrepreneurs, the most notable of whom was Henry Grady of the *Atlanta Constitution,* it set out a program of economic progress through industrial development, peaceful coexistence with the North, and agricultural diversification. Above all, regional development required social stability, which in turn depended on racial harmony. Racial antagonism, New South boosters argued, would scare away northern investors. Equally important, economic advancement meant including blacks in the social order. As "racial accommodationists," the term historian George Fredrickson uses to describe moderate racists of the early twentieth century, progressives maintained the New South's commitment to biracialism but joined it to the conviction that black economic advancement and racial harmony were beneficial to the entire South.[7]

The key to the progressives' racial accommodation was education. The proper curriculum would equip blacks with the rudimentary skills needed by the new economic order. It would also inculcate them in the middle-class virtues needed for social stability. Thus educated, blacks would quietly assume their subservient but productive place in southern society. As Mitchell explained to P. P. Watson of the Colored Normal College in Orangeburg, South Carolina, the home, the church, and the school were crucial for encouraging in blacks the "habit of thrift, obedience to law, the love of home, kindliness toward one's neighbor, cleanliness of person" and a "hunger for practical righteousness."[8] Discussing the ever-thorny "race problem" in an article for the *Southern Workman,* Mitchell rejected the extreme solutions of deportation and repression. He argued that denying education to blacks would perpetuate ignorance and militate against progress. Alternatively, the slow and steady influences of education and religion would make blacks "more useful in industry and more moral in society."[9] Fitting comfortably into the New South vision of economic expansion, progressive theories on black development reinforced the idea that educational reform was no threat to southern orthodoxy.[10]

Progressive educators accepted unquestioningly the maintenance of racially segregated schools. Mitchell praised Mississippi "heroism" in bearing the burden of a dual system of public education. As a model for the South, Mississippi's system was providing the "capital, initiative [and] brains" for the education of the masses. Yet Mitchell feared that the Magnolia State's admirable "self-reliance" in funding segregated schools had its limits. National aid was needed to sustain the noble endeavor. Echoing Hill, Mitchell underlined the federal government's responsibility for educating those it had emancipated at great cost. Sparing no rhetorical expense, the president claimed that the future of southern society was at stake: "It if was right to use the national arm to free the slave and to clothe him with citizenship, surely it is right to use the same hand to fit him for civic efficiency. . . . Without this, freedom itself is a delusion to the negro and a menace to the white man." Segregated education stemmed not only from a concern for white racial sensibilities but also from the belief that the preservation of social order and white supremacy demanded it.[11]

According to Chancellor Hill, both blacks and whites agreed that segregated schooling was axiomatic for the South. Hill observed that many of "the intelligent negroes" accepted the wisdom of separate schooling on the premise that integrated education would threaten a "blending of the races . . . between the higher types of their people and the lower types of the white race." Such indiscriminate mixing, Hill argued, would prove deleterious to the "best interests of the negro race." Compulsory, universal, segregated education would become the standard in the South. Should white officials be less vigilant in the enforcement of compulsory education than expected, the determined efforts of southern blacks to improve the quality of education for their own children would compensate. The chancellor made no mention of how the South would guarantee an equitable distribution of educational revenues between black and white schools.[12]

President Alderman also accepted the a priori rationality of segregated education. In his 1906 assessment of the achievements of a generation of southern reformers, he concluded dogmatically that public schooling for all children regardless of race, class, or religion was a settled issue, "provided that the children of the white and black races shall be taught in separate schools."[13] Two years later Alderman reiterated his point, stressing the beneficent effects of "absolute social separateness"[14] for racial advancement. Educational segregation, progressives maintained, was but one component of the neopaternalist program for black uplift and white racial purity.

For progressives, according to historian James D. Anderson, African-American education was primarily a question of political economy. Southern white educational reformers and their philanthropic northern allies believed that "the right schooling could train laborers to be better citizens and more efficient workers." Progressives "viewed universal education as a sound investment in social stability and economic prosperity." No less committed to black subordination than their extremist adversaries, racial accommodationists considered education rather than repression a more effective method for accomplishing the same objective.[15]

Committed to maintaining a compliant, black agricultural labor force, educational reformers from both sections applauded the Hampton-Tuskegee model of industrial education. Northern architects of the southern education movement first came into contact with the region through their support for the Hampton Institute. Founded in 1868 by former military officer Samuel Chapman Armstrong, the Hampton Institute enshrined the theory of industrial education. Simply put, theorists of industrial education held that practical training in the skills needed by southern agriculture and industry was best suited to the educational needs of blacks. On the other hand, literature and philosophy was fancy book-learning unnecessary for agricultural and industrial menials. The school's practical curriculum reflected Armstrong's conviction that a "particular combination of hard work, political socialization, and social discipline would mold the appropriate kind of conservative black teachers."[16]

White educators and philanthropists were not the only proponents of industrial education for blacks. Booker T. Washington, an African American educated at Hampton, became one of the leading voices for the Hampton philosophy in the 1890s. In 1881 Washington became principal of the Tuskegee Institute in Alabama. Reflecting the influence of his years at Hampton, Washington espoused the virtues of practical learning for black economic advancement. Education should help blacks improve their homes, their livestock, the land they tilled—in short, to become more efficient agricultural laborers. But Washington held out the hope that economic self-reliance and the habit of thrift would open avenues of social mobility. Classical colleges failed southern blacks by producing teachers who neglected the concrete needs of the schools and communities they served. Schools should not simply produce "ladies and gentlemen." Instead, education should prepare people for service and practical work.[17]

Critical to Washington's program was the favor of white southerners. Black classical colleges inhibited the cause of black education by failing to appeal to the better element of white people. Southerners had to be convinced that an investment in black education would produce the same results as public support for white education. Educated blacks would be more productive and more dependable citizens. Intelligent white southerners already believed; the rest now had to be convinced with evidence that "education has actually benefited and helped in some practical way the masses of the Negro people." Whites would certainly not disparage an education that reduced black crime and disease while encouraging "better service" to whites "on the farm or in the shop." Until black colleges seized the opportunity to persuade whites that money spent on education was not "a mere sop to the Negro race, or perhaps as money entirely thrown away," black education would languish. In the meantime, liberal arts colleges did a disservice to black education by creating a climate in which students "yielded to the temptation to become mere agitators, unwilling and unfit to do any kind of useful or constructive work."[18]

Certainly, Washington did not dismiss higher education altogether. However, like W. E. B. Du Bois, he believed that it should be reserved for the training of a "talented tenth." Unlike his formidable adversary, he considered Tuskegee the archetype of black higher education, training future leaders and educators as proponents of the industrial pedagogy. In his famous address to the Atlanta Exposition of 1895 he included industrial education in his program for black advancement. Casting down their buckets where they were, accepting political disfranchisement, adjusting to social inequality, blacks would find practical education a springboard to economic progress. In the Atlanta address Washington acknowledged industrial education as a "platform of compromise" between blacks and the white South. But the genius of industrial education was not confined to the American experience. Like Samuel Mitchell, Washington believed that the South was part of a world historic moment of racial adjustment. Industrial education was also applicable therefore to Europe, Africa, and Asia, places where "great masses are coming for the first time in contact with and under the influence of a higher civilization." Black schools of the Tuskegee persuasion were conduits of this racial solution.[19]

Robert Moton, principal of the Tuskegee Institute after Washington's death, celebrated the Hampton model for its contributions to black life in the South. According to Moton, the Hampton tradition had fostered among blacks a greater respect for "country life" and a recognition of the "dignity of labor—work of the hand." Confirming the function of industrial education as a mechanism of class control, Moton observed that "No single institution . . . has done more than Hampton to teach my race to believe in and respect work of the hands." Moton also reinforced Washington's conviction that technical instruction along the lines of the Hampton Institute created a point of consensus for northern and southern whites as well as southern blacks. At the same time, Moton attributed to the institute the flourishing of race pride and "race consciousness." The Hampton Institute had enabled the black person "to believe in and respect himself," an objective that united black intellectuals across the ideological spectrum.[20]

The Hampton model became many things for many people. Most importantly, it facilitated ideological convergence between northern philanthropists and southern educators. White advocates of industrial training from both sections celebrated the Hampton philosophy as a lever for black economic and social progress. It encouraged economic thrift, self-reliance, and moral improvement; it also placated southerners worried by the prospect of northern interference in southern management of race relations. At the same time it guaranteed the development of a class of exploitable laborers and a social climate favorable to northern investment.[21]

For blacks, at least according to Washington and his supporters, industrial education seemed to offer an opportunity for economic amelioration. It provided a means of achieving racial solidarity against political and social repression. Industrial education held out hope for a cessation of racial antagonism, even while it afforded blacks a measure of control over their destiny. Considering the antagonism of most whites to any form of black instruction, industrial education seemed a pragmatic compromise that would keep the channels of public support open for black schools. Many of the supposed benefits of industrial education proved illusory for both blacks and whites. Yet progressive educators embraced the Hampton-Tuskegee model as the only acceptable hope for black advancement in the South.[22]

For white educators, Charles Dabney clearly articulated the trajectory of progressive thought about black education in his address to the Fourth Conference for Education in the South in 1901. Dabney vigorously endorsed universal education and compulsory attendance laws for both races. Yet rather than nourish intellectual development, education should equip blacks with manual skills. It should also socialize them to a subordinate class position. "The negro is in the South to stay—he is a necessity for southern industries—and the southern people must educate and elevate him or he will drag them down." As a racial accommodationist, Dabney argued that the neglect of black education would lead to the debasement of whites. Neither Dabney nor his progressive counterparts seemed to recognize how this assertion contradicted the premise of their racial paternalism: the conviction that blacks were not degenerating ineluctably, as racial extremists would have it. Instead, they were innocuous but dependent children capable of moral and mental progress.[23]

Intellectually ambivalent, the element of self-interest in the case for black education was abundantly clear: Educate blacks to meet current economic demands or be prepared to accept the social consequences. On the basis of these assumptions, it was a predictable leap for Dabney to the doctrine of industrial education. Armstrong and Washington had "worked out a sensible plan for the education of the negro boys who come to their schools." Their practical curricula should be the archetype for public schools in the South. Celebrating industrial education, Dabney excoriated the idea that blacks should be educated in the liberal arts. "Nothing is more ridiculous than the programme of the good religious people from the North who insist upon teaching Latin, Greek, and philosophy to the negro boys who come to their schools." By dismissing the classical curriculum, Dabney signaled how far the southern education movement had departed from the ideals of the northern educational missionaries.[24]

Chancellor Hill made a more explicit connection between Reconstruction, federal intervention in southern affairs, and liberal education. While defending the idea of government support for education, black and white, Hill castigated the Blair bill of 1890 as an example of misplaced northern idealism. The problem with the bill, which would have given federal aid to states based on the proportion of illiteracy in each, was that it was "essentially academic." The bill made no racial distinctions and would have provided generous support for instruction in writing, reading, history, geography, and arithmetic. To Hill, the provision for liberal education was based upon the "erroneous idea" espoused by northern missionaries that "the children of the Negro race were ready and ripe for the culture for which the children of the Anglo-Saxon race had been fitted by long centuries." Although the bill would have benefited the South, with its high rate of illiteracy, Hill applauded its defeat. Furthermore, he criticized the unwillingness of its supporters to accept the "liberal and just view" that the distribution of federal funds should be controlled by white southerners.[25]

Fortunately, Hill reported, the management of race relations would be easier now that "there is almost a consensus of opinion, North and South, in favor of elementary education and in favor of industrial education." The chancellor attributed this state of affairs to the SEB and the Conference for Education in the South. These organizations channeled enlightened opinion toward the development of biracial education while bringing the issue to the nation's attention in a "rational form." The "wisdom" of the southern education movement lay in the recognition of its members that the "national" problem of black education could be solved only by white southerners. "If those of other sections wonder that we in the South hesitate to apply educational principles that seem truisms elsewhere," Hill theorized, "they may profitably remember that we are in immediate contact with the painful and depressing elements of the problem . . . vast shiftlessness, vice and crime."[26]

Under the aegis of industrial education, northern and southern whites decided to continue the education blacks had received under slavery. Like all New

Southerners, Hill admitted the "abuses" of slavery and the timeliness of its demise. Although a noxious institution, the "tutelage" of slavery wrenched blacks out of the "condition of the savage" and set them on the path of racial progress. The education gained from slavery was not in books but in the rigors of labor and "practical ethics." Just as industrial education was designed to inculcate moral virtue, so the discipline of slavery taught the "virtues of order, fidelity, temperance and obedience." Yet the architects of Reconstruction "blundered" by assuming that book learning could be foisted on a backward race unprepared for the rarefied atmosphere of Anglo-Saxon culture. With the recognition that traditional education was "spoiling" black labor capacity, southern whites decided that the education conducted under slavery should not be abolished but "supplemented." While blacks should be taught the educational rudiments, reformers postulated that education "should be largely manual, industrial and agricultural, so as to be adapted to the real needs of the masses."[27]

Just as Hill considered the Blair bill a legacy of the Reconstruction crusade, so too did he place the impetus for industrial education in the waning of northern interest in southern affairs. For northerners who retreated from Reconstruction, southern white management of race relations was an acceptable alternative. Also palatable was the Hampton-Tuskegee model of industrial education. As Hill explained, the work of these two schools was under way while the Blair bill was before Congress, "but these institutions had not then made the impression upon the national consciousness which they have now made." Hill explained to the northern readership of the *Annals of the American Academy* that the problem of education in the South had been entrusted to the South. Although differences of opinion about public education persisted, the success of the Hampton idea cleared the way for a reconsideration of federal support for state education.[28]

If Hill believed industrial education was the remedy for black indigence, he at least admitted some place for traditional learning in the curriculum. As he wrote to George Foster Peabody, "You know I have no narrow views about industrial education being the only education for a negro." Alone among the educators examined here, Hill endorsed liberal higher education for the limited number of blacks privileged enough to take advantage of it. A traditional college education was necessary for the professional training of lawyers and physicians. Yet like Washington, Hill believed that universities should train black exponents of practical education rather than critical thinkers who might entertain ideas of social equality. University education was necessary "in order that the 'lower' education suitable for the masses may be rationally planned and conducted." Like white universities, black colleges would train technical experts to administer a subtly coercive system of education.[29]

Despite Hill's comparative ideological latitude, his ideas about black education were hemmed in by the racial assumptions endemic to the southern education movement. Although he allowed some instruction in the three *R*s, he prescribed industrial training for the majority of southern blacks. According to Hill, blacks needed education "specialized to meet actual conditions," and it should be "adapted to meet industrial and agricultural needs." He lamented the "pathetic significance" of a large occupational force deficient in the type of education related to their "life-work." But the chancellor was encouraged by the South's embrace of practical education, which would see "Uncle Tom in His Own Cabin." Under the leadership of Booker T. Washington, Chancellor Hill reported that "the negro is becoming a home-maker, bound to the soil, a good citizen." Again, in an article for the *Atlanta Constitution* in 1905, Hill postulated that education offered the only sensible solution to the "race problem"—education not from books, of course, but "the education that means life, that in the language of Booker T. Washington fits the negro for agriculture and the making of a home." At least Hill admitted that practical education would result in "the diminution—for the present—of his political activities."[30]

Although Hill hoped that technical education would train blacks in subservience, he also wanted schools to reinforce southern commercial agriculture. In company with Charles Dabney, Hill encouraged an education that would bolster the agrarian economy and the largely black agricultural class that supported it. The chancellor disparaged the tendency of traditional education to lure children away from the soil. Technical instruction would reduce rural depopulation and ensure a steady supply of labor for the agricultural sector. Education should "fix the affection upon the soil." Hill was certain that the priority for educators should be the adjustment of education to "the life and work of the agricultural masses."[31] Even while Hill's ostensibly liberal voice permitted educational flexibility, it was muffled by his persistent commitment to racial control and white dominance.[32]

The chancellor's emphasis on agricultural training harmonized with the northern industrialists' desire for a steady supply of tenant labor. During a period of rural out-migration, philanthropists such as Robert Ogden considered technical education a reliable method for maintaining a stable supply of black agricultural labor. Hill would have agreed with Ogden's assertion that "Our great problem is to attach the Negro to the soil and prevent his exodus from the country to the city." For all of their talk of industrial education, they generally believed that Hampton and Tuskegee should train blacks for agricultural work. Most shared Samuel Mitchell's conviction of the "providential" existence of two occupations suited to the racial characteristics of the region's inhabitants: "The field gives the Negro his opportunity, while the factory requires all the skill of the white man." The assortment of blacks and whites into racially determined spheres of work would maximize productivity and minimize racial tension. "Such is the true economical relation of the two races in the South. It is one of inter-dependence." Mitchell was certain about education's role in the division of southern labor: It would make blacks "more useful in industry" by providing training in "very practical things."[33]

Edwin Alderman also played propagandist for industrial education. Like Hill and Dabney, he built his case for industrial education on a foundation of moderate racial prejudice. Alderman catalogued his racial beliefs in an address he gave while president of Tulane University. According to a local reporter, the president's remarks "accurately and completely" reflected "intelligent public sentiment" on race relations. Blacks, he boldly asserted, were an inferior race that needed the control and leadership of the "more civilized whites." Racial development depended on a recognition of the "disparity" between the two races. Concomitantly, racial progress meant preserving "Caucasian" integrity. The white South, having decided that social equality was "unthinkable," was determined to enforce social separation. "God made us white, and it is our business to stay white."[34]

Yet Alderman suggested that the spirit of racial conciliation was moving across the South. Although the region's whites were decided on racial subordination, they were equally committed to "do justice to the negro." Whites, in fact, had given to blacks "generously," ruled them "fairly," and treated them "leniently." There was no better example of southern benevolence than the treatment of blacks in judicial proceedings. With the self-assurance of a racial moderate, Alderman submitted that, "as every one knows, justice, when a negro is on trial, is in every Southern court tempered with mercy by every judicial officer from the juryman who weights [*sic*] the evidence . . . to the judge who passes sentence." He also suggested that the better sort preferred less violent means of enforcing black compliance. Neither slavery nor Reconstruction had worked to control blacks. Like Mitchell, he rejected annihilation and deportation, the latter of which had gained some currency among southern conservatives. Alderman described both options as tantamount to "crime and stupidity." Education, he suggested, was the answer.[35]

But the education Alderman had in mind was worlds away from the sort that had developed under the wing of missionary philanthropy in the postwar period. Northern-financed schools had failed by emphasizing the acquisition of culture rather than skills. "The dignity and necessity of labor were not pressed upon the consideration of the race as vividly as they should have been." Alderman rejected the traditional curriculum, but he argued that the guiding principle of the race question should be the training of black workers. The "thoughtful" men of the South could not deny the humanity of blacks or their "economic value."[36]

Given this assumption, the race issue could not be solved by repression but by "social adjustment," to which education was peculiarly suited. "It has been settled," Alderman wrote in an address to the Conference for Education in the South that was published in the *South Atlantic Quarterly,* "that the emphasis laid by the leaders of the negro race upon training in the industrial arts promises the best returns in the development of the capacities of that race as workers and as elements in civic life."[37] In a 1908 article, Alderman recited his conviction that the white South had settled on industrial education for the development of blacks "as useful factors in economic life."[38] The success of the Hampton and Tuskegee Institutes provided "sociological" evidence of black enthusiasm for education, the willingness of blacks to endure hardships to acquire education, the potential of "gifted leaders" among the race, and, of course, the "sympathy" of the white race for black advancement. It was not in Alderman's interest to discuss the resilience of the traditional curriculum at most private black colleges. Instead, he and other educators promulgated Booker T. Washington's assurances that the black South uniformly endorsed industrial education.[39]

Samuel Mitchell joined his voice to the industrial education chorus. Thrift, education, religion, and politics were the four doors to progress for the region's blacks. According to Mitchell, the enfranchisement of blacks was a mistake. Yet blacks were correcting their mistakes by accepting the white dictum that "property and intelligence" preceded the suffrage. Education would teach blacks the virtues of frugality and hard work, essential for even modest racial advancement. "Fitness for life is the thing desired. His education must look toward thrift and his religion toward conduct." The progressive school would provide the democratic lever for the uplift of the masses. But in elevating the masses the modern school would also promote racial adjustment, the "deeper nerve of southern life." Industrial education was not flourishing spontaneously in the South, however. Instead, the education offered by schools such as Hampton and the Virginia Normal and Industrial Institute at Petersburg reflected the "common sense aim of the Southern Education Board, which along with other agencies is ushering in a new era in the South."[40]

The SEB's "common sense" policy of support for black technical institutes was forged at the expense of public schooling for black children. Although the connection between white philanthropy and colleges such as Hampton was well established before the education movement, the SEB's endorsement of black technical instruction grew in inverse proportion to its support for black common schools. Southern progressives and northern philanthropists consoled themselves with the belief that the success of the Hampton idea would fulfill the objective of universal education.

To be sure, educational progressives were not solely responsible for the inequitable distribution of public funds between white and black schools. Hill and others opposed efforts to divide the educational taxes in proportion to the relative contributions of blacks and whites. Yet shortly after the SEB's founding it resolved to downplay black education. Dabney and the others agreed that "we would not emphasize the *negro* too much. . . . In the excited state of public sentiment, this was considered wisest."[41] At an SEB meeting in 1906, Alderman claimed that Booker T. Washington's dinner with President Roosevelt had made the discussion of black education imprudent. "It has been like touching a sore tooth," he told the board. In response to George Foster Peabody's suggestion for a crusade on behalf of black education, Alderman argued, "Progress does not lie that way. We want now to influence public sentiment: stop being silent but be wise; go forward, but with forethought." The SEB stressed the idea that white education would inevitably benefit black education. Progressives rarely explained this calculus but continued to make perfunctory overtures toward black instruction. Progressive educators also agreed to avoid any unorthodox pronouncements on the doctrine of "separate but equal." The SEB would then privilege the improvement of white education in its crusade.[42]

Far from abandoning industrial education, progressives considered it the hope for racial accommodation. They were surprised by the tenacity of both black and white resistance to the Hampton idea. Some of this resistance came from within the state universities. In 1900 Paul B. Barringer, then chair of the UVA faculty, advocated terminating public support for black schools on the grounds that blacks were using education as a "weapon of political offence." Barringer also accused schools of encouraging black indolence and competition with whites. Richard Heath Dabney, professor of history and economics at Virginia, ridiculed the idea of levying taxes to educate the disenfranchised. Evidently, not all progressives shared the enthusiasm for industrial education expressed by the leading members of the SEB.[43]

Southern white opposition to black education was mounted by a coalition of rural politicians, state school superintendents, industrialists, academics, and newspaper editors. Resistance was spearheaded by some of the region's leading papers, including the *Charleston News and Courier*, the *Charlotte Observer*, and the premier organ of the New South, the *Manufacturer's Record*. Educational reformers were frustrated by the South's inability to understand the social and economic benefits of industrial education. The educational crusade was not aimed at transforming southern society, they argued, but at achieving social stability for economic growth. To the frustration of progressives, opponents of the movement did not differentiate between academic and industrial education, however.[44]

Educational progressives and northern philanthropists retaliated by accusing the opposition of demagoguery. Yet southern white opponents of black education were aware of the nature of the caste system and they "understood better than the philanthropic northerners what was required to hold it intact." White opponents believed that black education would stimulate demands for political and civil equality. States with black majorities, such as South Carolina, and states where blacks made up the bulk of agricultural laborers consequently mounted a stiff opposition to universal education. Opponents also argued that educated blacks would compete with whites for nonagricultural jobs. What was at stake were differing conceptions of racial control, not divergent ideas about the status of blacks in society.[45]

Black opponents of the Hampton-Tuskegee program denounced it as an instrument of racial subordination. They also argued that it was premised on an obsolete form of technical instruction. John Hope, president of Atlanta Baptist College, criticized the Tuskegee program and defended liberal higher education for blacks. A member of the Niagara movement, Hope's ideas on education grew logically from his racial philosophy. Writing to Du Bois, he claimed that he had "dared to live up to my views even when they threw me in the midst of the most radical." He translated this militancy into his administration of Atlanta Baptist College: "Furthermore, every man on our faculty does the same and will as long as I am head of the institution."[46]

For many opponents of the industrial model, Booker T. Washington became the focus of their attacks. While a professor at Roger Williams University in Nashville, Hope traveled to Atlanta in 1895 to hear Washington's address at the Atlanta and Cotton States Exposition. A year after hearing Washington's "Atlanta Compromise," Hope assailed it in an address at Roger Williams: "If we are not striving for equality, in heaven's name for what are we living?" It was a gross misrepresentation "for our colored men to tell white people or colored people that we are not struggling for equality. . . . Yes, my friends, I want equality."[47] At an Atlanta University conference in 1899, Hope disputed Washington's contention that black poverty could be explained by deficiency in industrial skills. He also rejected his assertion that disfranchisement could be reconciled with black advancement. President Hope argued that political rights were indispensable to social progress. Social mobility would come not through courses in gardening and crafts but through competition with whites on a level economic playing field.[48]

University education was not simply a mechanism of social mobility but a source of racial pride. Hope argued that the "mere wealth" promised by industrial education would be insufficient for achieving equality with other races. Original research and the higher disciplines would encourage "progress, dignity and respectability." Ultimately, racial pride was connected to the search for "truth." Under his administration Atlanta Baptist College continued to focus its efforts on liberal higher education. It paid the price of emphasizing the traditional curriculum in financial neglect from the major philanthropic agencies.[49]

Hope's critique was bolstered by the vigorous antiaccommodationism of W. E. B. Du Bois. A professor at Atlanta University and a leading black intellectual, Du Bois excoriated Washington's "attitude of adjustment and submission" and the industrial education it justified. Du Bois admitted Tuskegee's contributions to black education and accepted a program of industrial education for "the masses." What he challenged was the disparagement of black liberal education by white and black exponents of industrial education. In a chapter titled "Of Booker T. Washington and others" in his book *The Souls of Black Folk,* published in 1903, Du Bois included industrial education as one of the elements in Washington's policy of "silent submission to civic inferiority."[50] Du Bois believed that industrial education was in complicity with New South materialism and white supremacy. "And men ask this today [the merit of industrial education] all the more eagerly because of sinister signs in recent educational movements. The tendency here is . . . to regard human beings as among the material resources of a land to be trained with an eye single to future dividends."[51]

Educational thinking of this sort was harmonious with the policy of keeping blacks "in their place." While reform enthusiasts broadcasted the ennobling effects of education, blacks were told that colleges were exclusively for whites. But emancipation and the black schools that arose in its wake stirred the ambitions of a "Talented Tenth" to pursue the highest educational opportunities. Fisk, Atlanta, Atlanta Baptist College, and Spelman were fulfilling these aspirations. Yet at the same time they were graduating professional teachers, doctors, lawyers, and ministers to meet the needs of black people throughout the South. "By taking away their best equipped teachers and leaders, by slamming the door of opportunity in the faces of their bolder and brighter minds, will you make them satisfied with their lot?" Practical education had its place, Du Bois argued, but social leadership and cultural ferment, not to mention genuine economic development, required higher education.[52]

The greatest benefit of higher education was the intellectual development of southern blacks. Colleges such as Atlanta, Fisk, Howard, and Lincoln were established to protect the standards of common school education. By training teachers in "human culture and lofty ideals" as well as normal school techniques, the colleges provided the foundation for a black school system. Du Bois echoed white educators who advocated creating an integrated, hierarchic system of education with the university as the capstone. Strains of elitism emerged in his conviction that black progress required the educated to hoist their brethren out of ignorance and into the light of middle-class culture. But Du Bois entertained a meritocratic ideal of social mobility. For him, it was necessary to "teach the worker to work and the thinkers to think." He was unclear about how or when workers would be distinguished from thinkers. Still, he insisted that education should not become a mechanism for sorting black Americans into inescapable class categories.[53]

In striking contrast to white progressive educators, Du Bois maintained that the principal function of the university was not to promote economic progress or social uplift but to extend liberal culture. "The university should be the organ of that fine adjustment between real life and the growing knowledge of life . . . the secret of civilization." Rather than conduits of New South boosterism, the black universities of Atlanta were the amulets against the allure of cheap materialism. By teaching the higher disciplines, Du Bois hoped to train a cadre of social leaders who would challenge the philosophy of racial submission embedded in industrial education. Against the grain of progressive specialization, Du Bois proposed an education that broadened the mind and connected people to the ethical universals that might serve as a foundation for justice.[54]

Far more sympathetic to industrial education, Kelly Miller, dean of Howard University, also defended the need for black higher education. Miller endorsed the general trend toward practical education, exemplified by the expansion of the elective system. Practical education had given rise to the growing pedagogical emphasis on method rather than subject matter. But methodical research and investigation should not be limited to "dead languages." Instead, it should be applied to complex social problems such as those related to "the population of Alabama or Florida." Courses in chemistry and physics were as useful in fostering practical skills and coordinating mental and physical faculties as the courses taught under the rubric of industrial education. Countering the southern white criticism of Reconstruction-era schools that offered a classical curriculum for blacks, Miller suggested that the universities had turned their attention to practical matters. Considering the practical focus of education, he concluded that the primary function of the educated black person was to instruct the masses in rudimentary knowledge. Regrettably, the opportunities for blacks to undertake "productive scholarship" were limited by circumstances. Educated blacks should not "explore"—the white criticism of black colleges—but should instead "interpret and apply," which harmonized with the Tuskegee philosophy. Why, then, the need for higher education?[55]

Using Aristotelian logic, Miller argued that to apply a theory, one needed to understand its underlying principles. He likened a teacher deficient in theoretical knowledge to a captain ignorant of the rules of navigation. There were less esoteric justifications for black higher education. Echoing Du Bois, he argued that racial segregation required institutions that could train a black professional caste. Industrial schools could not provide the necessary training, and Miller boldly rejected the suggestion that blacks should have to tolerate a poorly trained physician or lawyer. Paying obeisance to white accusations of an exceedingly classical curriculum at black colleges, Miller, in the next breath, "dare[d] to affirm" that the study of classics encouraged blacks to pursue "lofty ideals" and "noble aspiration[s]." To Miller, Du Bois, and Hope, the classics were a repository of cultural riches that civilized and humanized.[56]

The unique function of the black university was to give blacks a voice in the management of race relations. Analogous to the white-only universities, black colleges would sponsor the investigation of concrete social issues, "for knowledge which ultimates in social service reaches its highest effective level." The most important new discipline was sociology, which could be wielded effectively in the analysis of the "Negro problem." It was incumbent on black leaders to gain the empirical, scientific understanding of race relations that sociology provided. Reaching out to white progressives, Miller cited Edwin Alderman's endorsement of sociology for southern white students. But he categorically rejected Alderman's assertion, in fact the guiding assumption of the progressive education campaign, that blacks derived some residual benefit from the education of whites: "It devolves upon Dr. Alderman to point out any particular white man whose scholastic training would be worth more to the Negro race than that of R. R. Wright or W. E. B. Du Bois." It was Atlanta University, not UVA or UGA, that Miller held up as a model of sociological scholarship.[57]

Here, Miller seemed to suggest, blacks would find intellectual credibility to contest the racial discrimination that progressives wrapped in the idiom of scientific objectivity.

Although not a southerner, William Monroe Trotter, editor of the *Boston Guardian* and founding member of the Niagara movement, joined Du Bois as a vehement critic of the "Tuskegee Machine." Echoing Du Bois's indictment of the Hampton-Tuskegee program, Trotter asserted that "the idea lying back of it is the relegating of a race to serfdom." Racial prejudice and economic self-interest underlay white support for industrial instruction. Although always a minority, Trotter, Du Bois, and Hope were not alone in criticizing industrial education. Joining them was a coterie of northern and southern black intellectuals, including Charles Chesnutt, Bishop Alexander Walters, Calvin Chase, and Ida Wells-Barnett. All were members of the Niagara movement and some edited prominent black newspapers, such as the Chicago *Conservator,* the *Washington Bee,* and the *Chicago Broad Axe.* Influential voices among the black middle class, they challenged a system of education that for many symbolized black submission to white authority.[58]

Despite the objections of Du Bois and others, black industrial institutes secured a strong foothold in the New South. Relying largely on the advice of Booker T. Washington, northern philanthropists such as Carnegie and Rockefeller channeled substantial sums of money into the development of Tuskegee-like institutions. Between 1900 and 1910 Andrew Carnegie devoted his entire budget for black education to supporting Tuskegee and Hampton. By 1915, philanthropic appropriations to industrial schools far outweighed those for liberal arts colleges. That year, the Hampton Institute's endowment stood at $2.7 million, and Tuskegee's had risen to $1.9 million. Cumulatively, these funds accounted for more than half of the total endowment of private black colleges in the United States. By comparison, Lincoln University, the most generously funded black liberal arts college of the period, could claim only $700,000 for its endowment. As one historian has commented, the consequences of the philanthropists' "primarily industrial orientation was fiscal disinterest in Negro colleges that promoted liberal education and more generous attention to the recognized industrial institutions."[59]

Despite progressive optimism, industrial education failed to achieve uncontested dominance in the late nineteenth-century South. Samuel Chapman Armstrong, Hampton's founder, was encouraged by the adoption of industrial courses at several black colleges in the 1880s. Schools operated by northern mission societies offered practical training courses at the secondary and college level, often financed by the Slater Fund. Yet, as historians James McPherson and James Anderson have discovered, industrial education at most black colleges was of marginal significance. Colleges supervised by black religious organizations, such as the African Methodist Episcopal Church and the Colored Methodist Episcopal Church, were even more adamant about assigning industrial training an inferior position in the college curriculum. Unlike the Hampton Institute, the leaders of the missionary colleges maintained a traditional education that would produce engineers, architects, and factory supervisors. Whereas the Hampton program was predicated on racial control, private black colleges promoted liberal and professional education favorable to black social mobility.[60]

Only in 1898 did the Hampton model begin to achieve favored status among northern philanthropists and white middle-class educators. By the end of the century, advocates of the Hampton model realized that industrial training had not supplanted liberal education at most black colleges. They also understood that missionary educators would oppose the advance of technical education at black schools. In the face of opposition, proponents of the Hampton program began to disseminate industrial education with "dogmatic determination."[61] Educational progressives collaborated in the effort to attract northern financial support for the program and expand its reach throughout the South. While northern philanthropy underwrote industrial education in the South, progressives such as Alderman and Mitchell provided it an ideological framework.

To be sure, northern educational modernizers extolled the virtues of vocational instruction for southern blacks. Yet university progressives provided the intellectual medium between northern dollars and southern opinion. Addressing northern audiences, they offered their ideas as representative of the region's better sort. They lent the prestige of their institutions to the movement for a segregated system of education that was anything but equal. Northern reformers applauded people such as Alderman, Dabney, Mitchell, and Hill for promoting the realignment of southern schools according to "northern standards of efficiency and social organization."[62]

Simultaneously, university progressives established themselves as authorities on the race question. Cloaked in pseudoscientific language that appealed to the sensibilities of the era, university progressives marketed industrial education as a rational method of racial control. Industrial training was not the brainchild of university progressives; the Hampton Institute had been preaching it since 1868. But university-based progressives cemented the association between the southern education movement and the Hampton-Tuskegee program. At a crucial point in the development of southern education, university progressives became the advertising agents of an educational philosophy premised on black subordination. Industrial education joined sharecropping, the crop lien, low-wage extractive manufacturing, illiteracy, and disfranchisement as pillars of an impoverished and racially stratified New South.

The pedagogical opinions of the state university progressives stood in stark contrast to those of white administrators of black colleges. Henry S. DeForest of the American Missionary Association's Talladega College argued that "while all should have the lower education, a great many should receive the higher." The college offered industrial instruction, but its primary purpose, DeForest pointed out, was to extend "choice scholarship" to black students. George Sale, president of Atlanta Baptist College, told the Georgia Teacher's Association of his opposition to "the idea that the education of the Negro should be exclusively or distinctly industrial." Sale asked the assembled teachers why classical education would be any less edifying for blacks than it was for whites. E. C. Mitchell of Leland University in New Orleans registered an eminently practical criticism of industrial education. Training for the trades at black colleges was pointless, he argued, because "every village has its Negro mechanics who are patronized both by white and colored employees, and any who wish to learn the trade can do so."[63]

Administrators of southern black colleges were not the only white opponents of the Hampton-Tuskegee program. William T. Harris, United States Commissioner of Education, reprimanded the Lake Mohonk Conference for its endorsement of pedagogical discrimination. Sponsored by philanthropist Albert K. Smiley and attended by leading white educational activists, the conference was meant to foster discussion of racial issues. In 1890 and 1891 the focus was primarily on questions of education. The Hampton idea was met with enthusiastic approval by those assembled. Harris excoriated the conference's assumption that it was "in the power of one class to determine the metes and bounds of another class." The commissioner championed instead "the Negroes' right to an education from a, b, up to Syriac. . . . Or, if there is anything higher than that, that higher thing, whatever it may be."[64] White educators at black colleges may have shared the racial prejudices of educational reformers, but they refused to throw barriers up between blacks and the highest forms of education. Progressive administrators had little interest in jeopardizing public funding for their institutions by approving a form of education that implicitly endorsed black social equality. Unfortunately, for the progressives, the educational horse they bet on caused almost as much controversy as support for black higher education might have generated.

Yet if southern progressive educators were apologists for racial stratification, to many of the region's blacks they represented the harbingers of a more humane, if not just, racial order. The advancement of the social sciences that accompanied academic professionalization was part of a larger intellectual shift in the early twentieth-century South. The study of cultural anthropology, economics, and sociology at universities such as Georgia encouraged the emergence of a "Modernist" temperament that eschewed rigid definitions of culture and morality dominant in the late nineteenth century. In its place, modernists cultivated intellectual sensibilities tolerant of cultural relativism and moral uncertainty. Southern modernists gained new insight into the power of the irrational and the structural determinants of social behavior. This intellectual framework permitted educated southerners to analyze in a critical manner the social disorders that gripped southern society.[65]

Although progressive educators believed that industrial education was perfectly suited to racial control and economic productivity, it fit equally well into the pedagogical template at the center of the ideology of southern progress. Industrial education complemented university-level technical instruction. In the progressive worldview, technical experts would construct the modern, efficient state using pliable black and white laborers. In effect, educational progressives extended their philosophy of service-oriented, practical education to black schooling. Liberal education still had some merit as a source of cultural refinement among white college students. With their functionalist approach to education, though, it was easy to proscribe classical instruction for blacks.

Progressive educators wanted to transform the social order from one mired in poverty and racial conflict to one built on industrial productivity and racial harmony. Central to their scheme for a New South, however, was an insidious program of social engineering and racial control. Cloaking their ideas in the language of objectivity and evangelical uplift, they clouded the elements of coercion and racism inherent in progressive education. Southern higher education became entangled in the cross-sectional crusade to educate blacks in subservience. Its history was inseparable from the chronicle of the Jim Crow South.

Notes

1. Cell, *The Highest Stage of White Supremacy.* Consistent with Cell's thesis, university progressives, ensconced in predominantly urban environments, contributed to the institutionalization of racial separation in the New South.

2. Alderman, "The Growing South," 10377; also see Grantham, *Southern Progressivism,* xvii, 126–27; Daniel, *Standing at the Crossroads,* 37–39.

3. Mitchell, "The Nationalization of Southern Sentiment," 109.

4. Alderman, "The Growing South," 10377–78.

5. Mitchell, "Proposed Solutions of the Negro Problem"; also see untitled address, *Proceedings of the Conference for Education in the South,* 162; Fredrickson, *The Black Image in the White Mind,* 283–86.

6. Dabney quoted in Anderson, *The Education of Blacks in the South,* 85.

7. Fredrickson, *The Black Image in the White Mind,* 207, chapters 7 and 9.

8. Mitchell to Reverend P. P. Watson, December 29, 1911, in folder titled "Colleges and Universities, 1911," Mitchell Papers, USC.

9. Mitchell, "Proposed Solutions to the Negro Problem," 549.

10. Mitchell to Reverend P. P. Watson, December 29, 1911, in folder titled "Colleges and Universities, 1911," Mitchell Papers, USC; "Proposed Solutions of the Negro Problem," 548–49.

11. Mitchell, untitled address, *Proceedings of the Conference for Education in the South,* 166.

12. Hill, "Negro Education in the South," 81–82.

13. Alderman,"The Achievement of a Generation," 239.

14. Alderman, "The Growing South," 10378.

15. Anderson, *The Education of Blacks in the South,* 80–81.

16. Anderson, "The Hampton Model of Normal School Industrial Education," 62–64, including quote. Although vocational training became a vital component of the Hampton curriculum, the institute was designed primarily as a normal school for training black teachers. Clearly, the school's objective was to train teachers who would propagate the industrial model of education.

17. Washington, "Chapters from my Experience," 14232–34.

18. Ibid., 14234–35.

19. Washington, "Chapters from my Experience," 14238; see also Meier, *Negro Thought in America,* 87–89; Washington, "A University Education for Negroes," 613–18.

20. Moton, "Hampton's Gift to the Negro," 297–98.

21. Meier, *Negro Thought in America,* 92–93, 98; Ayers, *The Promise of the New South,* 324–25.

22. Meier, *Negro Thought in America,* 92–93, 98; see also Walter Barnard Hill to George Foster Peabody, July 28, 1904, box 3, Hill Collection, UGA.

23. Anderson, *The Education of Blacks in the South,* 85.

24. Ibid. First articulated by Samuel Chapman Armstrong, founder of Hampton, the emphasis on black cultural inferiority and the consequent need for gradual improvement "resulted in a curriculum that placed more emphasis on manual and industrial training than was the case with other missionary models of black education," in Adams, "Philanthropists, Progressives, and Southern Black Education," 103.

25. Hill, "Southern Education a National Responsibility."

26. Hill, "Negro Education in the South," 78–79.

27. Ibid., 77–79; Hill, "Southern Education a National Responsibility."

28. Hill, "Southern Education a National Responsibility."

29. Hill to Peabody, December 27, 1904, box 4, Hill Collection, UGA; Hill, "Negro Education in the South," 82–84.

30. Hill, "Negro Education in the South," 85; Hill, "Uncle Tom without a Cabin," *Chautauqua Assembly Herald* (July 1902), box 7, Hill Collection, UGA.

31. Hill, "Negro Education in the South," 83–85.

32. Ibid., 82–83.

33. Anderson, *The Education of Blacks in the South,* 88–89, including Ogden quote; Mitchell, "Proposed Solutions of the Negro Problem," 547, 549.

34. "Dr. Alderman on the Race Problem," undated newspaper report of speech, Alderman Collection, UVA.

35. Ibid.

36. Alderman, "Education for White and Black," 2648.

37. Alderman, "The Achievement of a Generation," 249–50.

38. Alderman, "The Growing South," 10378.

39. Alderman, "The Achievement of a Generation," 250. Although disapproving of the kind of education supported by the first wave of northern educational philanthropy, which lasted from 1868 until 1895, Alderman exempted the Hampton and Tuskegee Institutes from censure: "I did not include in my remarks Hampton Institute or Tuskegee. . . . These schools under the sane, large minded leadership of General Hampton, Booker Washington, and Dr. Frissell, have done much to change the state of affairs and to relate the schools all over the South to their real needs at this stage of their development," in "Education for White and Black," 2648.

40. Mitchell, "Proposed Solutions of the Negro Problem," 549–50.

41. Harlan, *Separate and Unequal,* 92–93, 97, including Dabney quote.

42. Minutes of the Summer Meeting of the Southern Education Board, August 6–8, 1906, box 17, Ogden Papers, LOC.

43. Quotes from Anderson, *The Education of Blacks in the South,* 96.

44. Ibid., 97–100. Of course, the progressive program for industrial education won white supporters as well as detractors. The reformers' most formidable support came from the *Atlanta Constitution,* the *Birmingham News,* the *Richmond Times,* the Columbia *State,* and the *Raleigh News and Observer.*

45. Ibid., 96–100.

46. John Hope to W. E. B. Du Bois, January 17, 1910, quoted in Dittmer, *Black Georgia in the Progressive Era,* 158.

47. Quoted in Lewis, *W. E. B. Du Bois,* 256.

48. Meier, *Negro Thought in America,* 212–13.

49. Torrence, *The Story of John Hope,* 115–116.

50. Du Bois, *The Souls of Black Folk,* 42–43.

51. Ibid., 71–72, 79–82.

52. Ibid., 71–72, 79–82.

53. Ibid., 67, 74–77.

54. Ibid., 65, 74.

55. Miller, "The Function of the Negro College," 267–69.

56. Ibid., 268–69.

57. Ibid., 269–70.

58. Anderson, *The Education of Blacks in the South,* 105.

59. Peeps, "Northern Philanthropy and the Emergence of Black Higher Education," 261–63.

60. Anderson, "The Hampton Model of Normal School Industrial Education," 84–86.

61. Ibid., 89–91.

62. Ibid., 99.

63. Ibid., 87–88.

64. Ibid., 88.

65. Singal, *The War Within,* 6–10, 261. During the Barrow administration, for instance, professors Robert Preston Brooks and R. J. H. DeLoach participated in the University Commission on Southern Race Questions, an organization dedicated to racial reform. An adjunct of the Southern Sociological Conference, the University Commission whittled away at the popular belief that black transgressions were at the root of lynchings. Instead, they attributed group violence against blacks to poverty, illiteracy, and rural conservatism. A recipient of a grant from the Phelps-Stokes Fund in 1912, Alderman's UVA endowed a chair in sociology for the study of race relations. For Alderman and others the grant signified the advent of a more rational approach to race issues: "The thing to do is to take it out of the nervous system of our people and their emotions, and to get it set up before them as a great human problem—economic in nature, scientific in character," in "For the Study of the Negro," unidentified newspaper report, in folder titled "Stokes Lectureship, 1911–1914," Alderman Collection, UVA. See also Brough, "Work of the Commission of Southern Universities on the Race Question," 47–57.

4

Lessons of the New South: Charles Dabney and the University of Tennessee, 1887–1904

Perhaps more than other school reformers, Charles Dabney exemplified the educational pragmatism of the New South. Convinced that higher education should meet current economic demands, Dabney worked vigorously to infuse the University of Tennessee with the creed of practical education. He believed that the university was in a position to galvanize the forces of southern progress by applying technical expertise to industry and commerce. Paying lip service to liberal education, Dabney aggressively promoted a utilitarian pedagogy that hinged on technical instruction. Whereas Samuel Mitchell might be classified as the progressive activist, Dabney was the philosopher of service-oriented education for the South. But like Hill, Alderman, and Mitchell, Dabney confronted the disparity between the promise of educational uplift and the economic realities that hampered university modernization. His administration left the imprint of the New South on the University of Tennessee.

Dabney was born in 1855 in Hampden-Sydney, Virginia, and his earliest recollections were of the war. His father, Robert Louis, a Presbyterian minister, served as the chief of staff in Jackson's army, while at home "everything was desperately tense and that excitement ran high." Like that of his contemporary Woodrow Wilson, whose father also served as a chaplain to Confederate forces, Dabney's home became a hospital for wounded and dying soldiers. Despite wartime deprivation, he was able to attend Hampden-Sydney College at Farmville after the war. From 1874 to 1877, he attended the University of Virginia. Beyond what Dabney wrote in his often self-aggrandizing memoirs, we know little about his personality, particularly his pre-Tennessee years. On an impressionistic level, Dabney appeared confident, even smug in his photographs. He was a heavy-set man with a stern countenance, one who no doubt commanded respect but probably little affection. If the comparison is fair, he had none of the warmth and humor of Walter Hill. Before dismissing him as a starched Victorian, however, one should look through Dabney's correspondence surrounding the death of his seventeen-year-old daughter. Beyond the stylized language that laced Victorian accounts of death, his letters suggest that her death was a tragic, personal loss for him. Perhaps, too, it explains the rigidity he seemed to project.[1]

Not unlike many young, middle-class southerners whose formative years were shaped by the experience of Reconstruction, Dabney believed that the region's talented white men were responsible for revitalizing the South. "My father and Professor Holladay had impressed me deeply with the idea that the educated young men of the South should devote themselves to the reconstruction of their land, and I was impressed with the idea that this must be done by the development of its resources and industries." Dabney eventually added education to his scheme for southern recovery. Reflecting the pedagogical conflict that seized universities in the late nineteenth century, he and his father were divided over what Dabney would study at the university. Although his father insisted that he study the classics, Charles's own interests led him toward science. As a compromise, he took Latin and Greek in his first year but spent most of his time and energy on math, physics, and chemistry.[2] Pursuing his interest in science, Dabney studied for a Ph.D. in industrial and organic chemistry at Göttingen, Germany. There he imbibed the spirit of rigorous scientific investigation that distinguished the German ideal of scholarship from the hidebound traditions popular at most American colleges of the period. It was his experience at Göttingen, contends one University of Tennessee historian, that had the most significant influence on his vision for university modernization in the South.[3]

In 1880 Dabney accepted the position of state chemist in North Carolina. Appointed originally to teach chemistry at the University of North Carolina, he elected instead to take a position at the experiment station after examining the department's shoddy laboratory. The state chemist's equipment was by no means first rate, but it seemed to offer a better opportunity for "practical work." As state chemist, Dabney was responsible for analyzing fertilizers used by the Department of Agriculture, conducting experiments on plant nutrition and growth, suggesting which crops were best suited to conditions in North Carolina, and overseeing the general operation of the experiment station.[4]

In company with educational progressives such as Walter Barnard Hill, who called for fulfillment of the obligations set out by the Morrill Land Grant Act, Dabney advocated establishing an authentic agricultural college at Chapel Hill. Like the University of Georgia, UNC faced a concerted movement under the leadership of Leonidas K. Polk to create an agricultural and mechanical college separate from the state university. President Kemp Plummer Battle, like

Hill, responded by insisting correctly that the Morrill Land Grant Act envisioned the establishment of colleges that balanced industrial training with instruction in the liberal arts. According to his memoirs, Dabney became one of the president's most devoted supporters. Relentlessly agitating for state funding to comply with the act, he also urged faculty members to support Battle's efforts to improve agricultural instruction. Farmer demands for an independent agricultural college eventually scuttled efforts to bring the university in line with the requirements of the Morrill Act. Accepting the inevitability of a separate A&M college, Dabney, together with Augustus Leazer, chair of the House Committee on Education, drafted the bill for its establishment.[5]

In Dabney's campaign for agricultural instruction at UNC, a rehabilitated Robert E. Lee served as a convenient model of educational wisdom for the New South. "In vain," Dabney reminisced, "did I quote the advice General Lee had given the people of the South and had carried out in Washington College." Dabney found the essence of this advice in a quote from a book by John Latane titled *Lee's Educational Policies:* "But General Lee realized . . . that a new kind of education was needed for the young men of the South; that wholly new conditions confronted them, that the hope of the future lay not in political agitation but in economic and industrial development, and that the College must lead in this work."[6] Lee's ideas offered Dabney a blueprint for higher education in the South. Lee's prototype included a School of Agriculture, a farm for agricultural demonstration and experiments, a School of Commerce, a School of Applied Chemistry, and a School of Civil Engineering. Chapel Hill, preoccupied with cultivating oratory at the expense of practical training, did not compare favorably with Lee's majestic college.[7]

But to Dabney the state university was no bastion of classical education, either. Battle's efforts to improve industrial and mechanical education were commendable. So too was his successful establishment of the first summer school for teachers in North Carolina in 1882. In fact, the UNC summer school became a model for the Summer School of the South that Dabney established at Tennessee several years later. The school gave him a forum for his doctrine of technical education. It also featured lectures by Walter Hines Page, the most famous of the South's educational crusaders, as well as Edward P. Moses, who, according to Dabney, converted the redoubtable Charles McIver and Edwin Alderman to the gospel of public education.[8]

Dabney was pleased with his accomplishments in North Carolina. Almost single-handedly, if we are to take his account at face value, he created the office of state chemist, building the Raleigh laboratory and assembling for it a "fine staff." He explored state resources and prepared agricultural exhibits. He also conducted several farmers' institutes, which convinced him of the need to improve rural education. His most significant accomplishment, though, was the transformation of the state chemist's office into an agricultural experiment station. Again, Dabney's tendency for self-adulation might diminish the accuracy of his account, but it seems that he played some role in securing funds under the provisions of the Hatch Act to establish a legitimate experiment station. Most importantly, his experiences in North Carolina crystallized his utilitarian, service-oriented view of higher education for the South.[9]

In July 1887, James Comfort, trustee of the University of Tennessee, wrote to Dabney to ask whether he would consider the position of experiment station director at Tennessee. Dabney's response to Comfort became a manifesto for service-oriented education. Dabney told Comfort that his experience on a planning committee for a North Carolina College of Agriculture and Mechanic Arts convinced him of the need for the "right kind of technical schools." Citing Tennessee's proximity to the South's iron and coal belt, Dabney expressed his hope that the university would soon be "placed upon a plane of usefulness equal to the demands of the hour" by becoming a "great central industrial school" of the South. Impressed by the university's opportunities for practical education, he was disillusioned by what he considered the decay of most southern colleges under the dead hand of classical pedagogy: "We have not a single true polytechnic institute in the South. The land-scrip funds which should have been sacredly dedicated to this kind of education, have in nearly all instances fallen into the hands of the old-foggy, leterary [*sic*] institutions." Southern youth had been deprived of an education that would train them to meet the challenges of the New South. Denying crass intolerance for education that was not solely "practical," he advocated a system of education "modified to suit the new order of things." His decisions as president would belie his professed sympathy for liberal education. At least in the early stages of his association with Tennessee, though, Dabney sponsored a balanced education that included technical instruction.[10]

Not content to convince Comfort of his utilitarian credentials, Dabney went on to critique the traditional system of southern higher education. Antebellum colleges strove above all else to ensure that graduates would not have to suffer the indignity of manual labor. This was the incentive that every two-bit high school and college held out to parents of southern children. Literary education had simply become an excuse for "idleness." The disdain for manual labor encouraged by classical education was destroying the region's agricultural system. Dabney's celebration of polytechnic instruction made no mention of the black majority shackled by debt in sharecropping arrangements that largely benefited white landowners. For him, as for many others, agricultural revitalization depended on a rural white yeomanry awakened to the potential of scientific agriculture. To the chagrin of New Southerners, however, poor whites often found the mill and town more appealing than the debt-ridden plantation. In any case, the "smart boy" was convinced that he must leave the farm to become a doctor or a lawyer, professions requiring "varied knowledge" and training. But if agriculture was the South's dominant industry, Dabney argued, polytechnic schools were needed to expose farmers to scientific knowledge as advanced as that required of any urban professional. In a perfunctory gesture of deference to the antebellum college tradition, Dabney suggested that the study of mathematics and chemistry would impart mental discipline just as well as the study of "Greek roots and Latin particles."[11]

Advocating the education of "the whole man," Dabney attributed the inadequacies of southern higher education to the administration of mechanical colleges by hidebound classicists. Antagonistic to the "new education," they "dwarfed the pretended industrial features or allowed them to become a mere sham." The South required skills that would enable it to exploit its resources for "profit and fame." As rhetorically shrewd as any New South booster, Dabney asked, "Shall we continue to get most of our Engineers, miners, mechanics . . . the skilled workers of all kinds, from the North? Shall our boys have to go to ther [*sic*] Northern schools to get the best technical training?" Dabney would accept the position only on the condition that the university commit itself to promoting technical and agricultural education. He feigned ignorance of the internal situation at Tennessee, but his letter to J. M. Heck of Knoxville suggested otherwise. "I hear a rumor," he wrote, "that they are not altogether satisfied with the college in its present form. If they are going to reform it and make it a genuine technical institution I can take more interest in it." Yet Dabney expanded his conditions to include "sufficient authority" to carry out his program. Recognizing that entrenched interests might obstruct change, he refused to accept a subservient position in "an institution which does not conform to my ideas of what an agricultural and mechanical college ought to be." Impressed by Dabney's ideas, Comfort and fellow board member O. P. Temple invited him to consider the executive position, which had been vacant for the past four years.[12]

Interested in the offer, Dabney visited the university for an on-site inspection. What he found was a destitute college staffed by mediocre professors and administered by a Board of Trustees divided over the issue of classical versus mechanical education. "Horribly mismanaged," he said of the university in a letter to his wife; "there is no state pride in it—quite the reverse. Educated people are ashamed of it." Its annual income, derived solely from state bonds, amounted to a paltry $31,000. Dabney was appalled by the school's financial situation: "Surely the Legislature can be shoved into doing *something* for it. Perhaps they would, if properly approached, do a good deal." The faculty, he observed blandly, was "decent enough, but quite ordinary." The city of Knoxville, on the other hand, appealed to Dabney's New South sensibilities. Business-minded and "progressive," Knoxville's residents acknowledged the university's dismal condition. He speculated that they would firmly support a program of institutional revitalization. In addition, he was convinced that the people of the city would demonstrate a "fair appreciation of technical education" if given pedagogical priority under a vigorous new administration.[13]

Despite its inadequacies, Dabney, like Mitchell, welcomed the opportunity to play a leading role in the reconstruction of southern higher education. Like other progressive educators, Dabney greeted the prospect of educational improvement with evangelical zeal. He confided to his wife that he knew "how to go about it. But it will require a fearful amount of work and a great responsibility. It will take the best part of my life and health to do it." He warned solemnly that "I may expect to spend my whole energy in it. Perhaps it will use me up." But if Dabney was to assume the helm at the struggling provincial college, he would require breathtaking executive latitude.[14]

He would first demand the right to nominate faculty after his first year in office. He would then require absolute control over curriculum and university management, unquestioning faculty compliance, the authority to review all faculty requests for money, as well as the right to "control expenditures under these appropriations." He also expected to be appointed both president and director of the experiment station. In addition to these demands, Dabney insisted on organizational jurisdiction over all departments. Admitting that his conditions were "very bold," he justified his bravado by insisting that "these Trustees are sick of their job."[15]

He was probably encouraged to make such sweeping demands by a letter that Temple had written to him a week before his trip to Tennessee endorsing the principle of executive authority over faculty appointments. Observing that board members often were unqualified to evaluate the qualifications of prospective faculty, Temple made it clear that Dabney's nomination enjoyed the support of a majority of trustees. Although the task of infusing life into the moribund college was daunting, Dabney, unlike Walter Hill of Georgia, had the approval of a board generally favorable to executive management. However, the board was hesitant to grant the untried Dabney dictatorial powers. Acknowledging their tendency for intrusive management and committing themselves to Dabney's utilitarian program, the trustees drew the line at conceding him absolute control over faculty appointments. Despite this limitation, the board included a clause in Dabney's contract ensuring that professors elected in 1887 before the new president's term would be required to renew their appointments in 1888, thus giving the president authority to reorganize the faculty after his first year.[16]

Dabney's demands highlight his managerial vision of university leadership. He insisted on rationalizing departmental development and defining the administrative chain of command. By controlling university finances, the president could allocate resources to promote industrial and technical education. Control over curriculum would allow him to encourage agricultural education. At the same time, a tight grip on faculty appointments would give him the freedom to advance professionalization. Although historians have acknowledged the tacit understanding that bound the board and Dabney to a policy of practical education (often without explaining what that meant), they have paid less attention to the model of executive leadership that guided his administration.[17] Like his northern counterparts at Michigan and Chicago, Dabney considered himself above all an academic manager. As an administrator, mediator between conflicting interests, solicitor of financial support, and architect of departmental specialization, Dabney claimed that he would finally have the executive latitude needed to transform the university into an instrument of public service. Above all, university modernization required a vigorous executive who would challenge trustee complacency and legislative hostility.[18]

In an acceptance letter that was released to the state's papers, Dabney recapitulated his commitment to practical education. Sensitive to the Zeitgeist of progress, Dabney claimed that the demand for practical education "is in the air, we all it feel. An epoch of vast development is upon us." Reciting his indictment of traditional education as a deterrent to industrial pursuits, he extolled the virtue of an education that developed "the whole man," one that taught "the hand to hew the line, as well as the brain to reason and remember facts." In a rhetorical qualification that Dabney attached to almost every defense of technical instruction, he insisted that "we must not be understood to depreciate classical education." Of course, as a recipient of funds under the Morrill Act of 1862, the university was obligated to cultivate practical education: "This is the idea: Let our agricultural and mechanical college be faithful to the purposes for which its funds were given, faithful to the present needs of our country and it will be sustained." Careful not to discredit classical education entirely, the president made it clear that he would privilege agricultural and technical education.

Moved by the spirit of practical education, the board's executive committee resolved to realign the university according to the principles of the Morrill Act. They asked the new president to prepare a plan for organizational reform. Dabney drafted a report calling for a review of existing faculty and the school's curriculum. He also requested that the board comply with the Land Grant Act by selling off surplus land to generate funds to build facilities for technical instruction. The strongest impetus to developing agricultural instruction at Tennessee came from federal support under the Hatch Act of 1887. The bill allocated $15,000 to each state for establishing experiment stations in connection with the country's agricultural colleges. The Tennessee legislature accepted the gift and Dabney was made experiment station director. He set out quickly to find a permanent director.[19]

Much like Walter Hill and Samuel Mitchell, Tennessee's new president attempted to rationalize university resources by consolidating faculty positions. To this end he hired Charles Plumb, director of the New York experiment station, as both assistant experiment station director and professor of agriculture. By using faculty members from the agriculture and science departments as researchers at the experiment station, Dabney hoped to save the university more than $10,000. The money could be used for a new department of mechanics and physics. In acquiring Plumb, the president illustrated that he, like other educational progressives, could espouse an updated sectionalism even while recruiting qualified northerners to fill key positions in southern colleges.[20]

Although the Hatch funds were not available until the spring of 1888, Dabney and Plumb threw their energies into the experiment station. In the latter part of 1887 they devised a system of field and feeding experiments, made headway in improving horticultural instruction, and bought rudimentary equipment for the new station. More importantly, they initiated construction of a $6,800 addition to the agricultural hall to accommodate the experiment facilities. The new arrangement would combine agricultural instruction and experimentation under one roof. The building included a museum, laboratories for the study of botany, biology, and chemistry, lecture rooms, and a library. During his three years at the University of Tennessee, Plumb advanced forage and field crop studies, soil conservation, animal husbandry, and dairy farming. Like Samuel Mitchell's efforts to advertise university extension, Tennessee's experiment station began to publish regular reports of its activities. In addition to quarterly and annual reports, the station published bulletins on "Weeds of the Farm," "Diseases of the Irish Potato," and "Points about Country Roads."[21]

To prevent the new station from degenerating into another example of misplaced federal largesse, Dabney insisted that it function as a bureau of information for the state's farmers. The experiment station would promote crop diversification as well as industrial and resource development. It would illustrate the university's dedication to social service and practical knowledge. As Dabney wrote to a prospective candidate for the dual position of station entomologist and head of the biology department, "We want an investigator first; and a teacher second."[22] Dabney's priorities for the experiment station exemplify his program for university development. At the same time, they encapsulate the values articulated by progressive educators at southern universities.

In the effort to advance the research ideal at Tennessee, Dabney sought to lighten the teaching loads that weighed down even the most ambitious scholars. In 1902 Dabney brought a proposal for faculty sabbaticals to the board's attention. The president prefaced his appeal for sabbatical time by reinforcing the public service theme of academic work. "They are devoted not alone to their work in the University and for the students," he wrote to the board, "but to the advancement of knowledge, the improvement of the school, and the general betterment of society about them." Scholarly research and personal rejuvenation from tedious classroom demands required time allowances, especially considering that the board could not increase faculty salaries. "A man who is constantly in the treadmill of college work year after year soon loses all freshness and will in time lose all vitality." Dabney also recognized that research and the introduction of teaching assistants to handle the "brain-consuming labor" of grading would augment the faculty's and the university's credibility.[23]

The experiment station signaled a move toward practical instruction. But recasting Tennessee in the mold of social service meant overhauling the faculty and the curriculum. Again, Dabney explained these reforms in terms familiar to most proponents of university modernization. Rather than an isolated asylum for poet-philosophers, the university was the capstone of the public education system. Unanimously approved by the board, Dabney's 1888 plan for departmental organization was simply "designed to meet the requirements of the laws," including the Land Grant of 1862, hitherto neglected by the state legislature. The university was to be divided between three departments: the academic, the professional, and the postgraduate. The academic department, which housed the College of Agriculture, Mechanic Arts, and Sciences, featured courses in agriculture, civil, mining, and mechanical engineering, chemistry, and the "general" or literary course. Balancing tradition and innovation, Dabney and the trustees preserved military training as a method of inculcating student discipline. The assimilation of the classical courses into an academic department that included engineering and agriculture placed the emphasis on technical education.[24]

Of equal importance to Dabney's utilitarian agenda was the creation of an independent professional school. The new school would include departments of medicine, dentistry, and graduate studies. The president also made it clear that the administration was devoting public funds exclusively to maintaining the College of Agriculture and Mechanic Arts. Conformity with the provisions of the Land Grant Acts left the responsibility for developing the other departments to the state government. Following the de facto pattern of segregated educational institutions already pervasive throughout the South, the university "accommodated" blacks studying agriculture and mechanic arts at the separate Knoxville College. Racially stratified, administratively rationalized, and committed to using Hatch Act funds for the scientific study of agriculture, Dabney's school was on the way to becoming a university for the New South.[25]

Crucial to the president's program for elevating the university's credibility was eliminating the preparatory department. A longtime fixture of higher education, preparatory departments functioned as surrogate high schools for students unable to meet the southern university's already lax standards. In his report to the legislature, Dabney claimed that the preparatory department was an anomaly that had "no place in a University. A department of this kind, with a special head, would scarcely find place in a good college." Dabney's optimism may have outdistanced his grasp of the realities of southern higher education. Even so, his plan to abolish the preparatory department suggested his sincere desire to improve university standards. But noble intentions could not ensure a steady supply of students. Understandably concerned about maintaining an acceptable level of attendance, the administration transferred the burden of preparatory work to M. G. Baker and Charles Himel of Knoxville, who established a University School that prepared candidates for the study of Latin, Greek, and mathematics. The relationship between Tennessee and the University School is unclear. Even if it received no financial support from the university, the University School highlighted the constraints on efforts to improve admission standards at state universities.[26]

As the president eliminated one department, he created and rationalized others. Separating mechanical engineering from mathematics and combining it with physics, which had been detached from chemistry, he created the School of Industrial Mechanics and Physics. To promote specialized agricultural research, Dabney created the Chair of Agricultural and Organic Chemistry and separated it from the School of General and Analytical Chemistry. The president's intentions grew unmistakably from his utilitarian pedagogy: "In an agricultural college these subjects should receive special consideration, and this is not likely to be secured in any other manner." The clearest illustration of

Dabney's program for academic specialization was his realignment of the School of Agriculture. Previously, this school had existed merely as a polyglot "dumping ground for all the subjects not otherwise provided for." Botany and horticulture were excised from the agricultural school and made into an independent department under the direction of yet another northern star, professor Lamson Scribner, a graduate of the Maine Agricultural College.[27]

Like his scheme for departmental realignment, the president's plans to revitalize the faculty reflected his scheme for practical education. It also provoked resistance from the board. Cautioned by the trustees to adopt a gradualist approach to faculty improvement, Dabney cited his authority over recommendations for teaching positions. Just to ensure that the board understood his determination, he threatened to resign. Reluctantly, the trustees accepted Dabney's plans. The president's scheme amounted to an evisceration of the 1887 faculty. Of the ten faculty members hired before his reorganization plan, only William W. Carson, professor of mathematics and civil engineering and a graduate of Washington and Lee, and Thomas C. Karns, professor of English and a graduate of Tennessee, remained. The casualties either found other positions or returned to graduate school. Emphasizing his commitment to professionalizing Tennessee's faculty, the president, with the board's approval, hired faculty on the basis of year-long contracts, not tenure.[28]

Northerners were in conspicuous abundance on the president's new teaching staff. As a result of his interest in technical instruction and the scarcity of qualified southerners, he hired northerners for the majority of his agricultural and mechanical positions. In the vital positions of agriculture, botany, and horticulture, he placed northerners. Similarly, the newly organized chair of mechanical engineering and physics was filled by J. S. Coon from Cornell University; biology and zoology was occupied by Henry E. Summers, also from Cornell; and the position of instructor in drafting was filled by David B. Oviatt, another former Cornell employee. From the United States Navy the president acquired the services of Theodore Burgdorff as associate professor of mathematics and engineering, and Winthrop E. Stone, who had completed graduate studies in Germany, occupied the position of chemist in the experiment station.[29] Governor Robert Taylor took notice of the northern bias in Dabney's appointments and roundly criticized him for not hiring more Tennesseans. Submitting to political pressure, Dabney hired C. F. Vandervord as assistant professor of agriculture. According to Dabney, Vandervord subsequently proved himself an incompetent researcher and a subpar professor.[30]

Faculty improvement and course rearrangement were two components of Dabney's plan to make the university an instrument of state service. Prefiguring Walter Hill's critique of Georgia's negligence, Charles Dabney outlined in his first report to the legislature a scheme for university reform set squarely against the backdrop of state mismanagement of higher education. The university was created in 1807 as a state institution, Dabney observed acerbically. Amazingly, though, "the State itself has never once put its hand into its own vaults and drawn hence a gift for this child of its creation." The only state support that the university received was interest paid on money borrowed from the school and held in the form of bonds. In 1888–89 this, together with interest accrued from the Morrill Act of 1862, amounted to a dismal $26,000 a year.[31]

More egregiously, the state accepted the Morrill funds, which were designed to promote industrial and mechanical education, but failed to fulfill the conditions of the act. At the same time the state imposed obligations on the university that made it virtually impossible for it to advance technical instruction. Conditions in the legislation appropriating the Morrill funds required that the university trustees provide furnished buildings to accommodate 275 students tuition-free, the candidates to be determined by state senators and representatives in proportion to their respective constituencies. Also, the school was required to provide at least 200 acres of land valued at no less than $175,000 before the university could lawfully claim the state bonds representing the revenue from the sale of the agricultural scrip. But as Dabney pointed out, "it took all of the slender resources of the University of that day, with the exception of about ten thousand dollars, to acquire the additional land and put up the additional buildings to meet the terms of the proposal." The state's proposal placed the responsibility for the dormitories and land—including an experimental farm—on the shoulders of the trustees. However, it did not provide the equipment, library facilities, instruments, machinery, barns, implements, and scientific apparatus needed to establish a genuine college "for the benefit of agriculture and mechanic arts." The trustees, having "stripped themselves of everything they had in order to provide the land and dormitories required," were left without means to furnish the school. Reviewing the disparities between Tennessee's appropriations for agricultural instruction and those of other states, Dabney concluded indignantly that the legislature may have met "the technical requirements of the act of Congress, but it has certainly fallen far short of its duty under the act."[32]

The answer was to develop an authentic polytechnic institution that would educate southerners to meet modern economic demands. Rather than a vocational school offering training available on the farm, Dabney proposed an institution that would produce "the future scientific agriculturist, the mining engineer and metallurgist, the mechanical engineer and the manufacturers of our country." Instead of a broad education that stressed mental discipline or liberal culture, students would be channeled into the schools providing professional and technical training. Like Mitchell, Dabney was certain that forming a technical elite was essential for southern revitalization. "We are more weary still of this wretched twaddle about the 'need of the immigration of skilled labor and of capital' to the South. Our best 'resources' are our robust young men and women. We want to 'develop' the power that is in them. This can only be done by education. . . . We must educate our youth in the sciences and the useful arts." Dabney highlighted the dangers of the South's reliance on foreign capital, labor, and technical expertise. In a critique of capitalist consolidation that might have won the approval of the Populists, he excoriated the "Great combinations of capital" that "choke out the small ones" and make an "agricultural section more and more dependent and helpless." But instead of reforming the financial system and the myriad railroad laws that injured the agricultural class, the president endorsed industrial expansion to meet the threat of northern corporate hegemony.[33]

While economic opportunity beckoned, the tradition of classical education prevented schools from responding. "In a scientific age and an industrial section an exclusive education in the dead languages is a curious anomaly." Espousing the materialistic optimism of Edwin Mims and Edgar Gardner Murphy, Dabney linked technical instruction to southern prosperity and ridiculed the classicists' "bigoted veneration for the supposed superlative wisdom of their fathers" that would keep the South interminably in a "state of barbarism and wretchedness."[34] What the one-crop, low-wage, credit-starved South demanded was practical education, which only a state university could provide. Yet the utilitarian program Dabney espoused took as one of its central assumptions the creation of a class of technical experts driven by a missionary sense of social leadership. Promoting what he assumed was value-neutral "practical education," Dabney also helped transform the University of Tennessee into an agent of middle-class formation.

Like other progressive educators, Dabney called on the legislature to remold Knoxville's destitute college into an instrument of state service. Reciting a litany of state-supported agricultural and mechanical colleges in the South, the president castigated Tennessee's neglect of higher education. He chided state representatives to elevate the college from a groveling solicitor of private charity to a credible institution of higher learning dignified by regular state appropriations. His recommendations for improvements over the following year reflected his determination to promote technical and professional education. In addition to an assembly hall and lecture rooms, the college needed a chemical laboratory, $10,000 to equip the Mechanical Department, $8,000 for farm buildings and barns, funds for a physics laboratory, and a separate chair of pure mathematics. No doubt, the $50,000 request to build "academic buildings" would benefit both the sciences and the liberal arts, but Dabney's concerns were clear: Tennessee would be revitalized under the aegis of practical education, not the "barbarism" of the classics.[35]

Although the relationship between the legislature and the university did not improve appreciably by 1890, the school's financial status did. In his 1890 report to the General Assembly, Dabney, on behalf of the board, was able to boast that by 1891 the school's income would reach $50,000. This handsome figure did not even include the annual appropriation of $15,000 to the experiment station courtesy of the Hatch Act. The fiscal infusion came in the form of funds appropriated under the second Morrill Act of 1890. The new law gave $15,000 in the first year to the country's land grant colleges and increased the yearly grant by increments of $1,000 until the total appropriation amounted to $25,000. The income was "due entirely to the bounty of the United States, Dabney pointed out. The president asked the legislature to accept the funds, once again pointing out the state's responsibility to provide the lands and buildings for the college's permanent equipment. The federal funds were to be used solely to defray the school's operating costs and facilities. Once again, the president drove home the idea that the Morrill Act was meant to provide an impetus to state support for agricultural and mechanical education.[36]

The money certainly stimulated the expansion of the university's agricultural program. Dabney reported hiring additional instructors in practical agriculture, horticulture, and economic science, and he planned to augment instruction in practical mechanics, mineralogy, and geology. Expanded departments required larger, modernized buildings able to accommodate increased enrollment. The college's dilapidated halls were "entirely out of harmony with the progressive work of the institution, the substantial city in which they are located, and the spirit of progress now everywhere felt in our State."[37] The implication was clear: A state university dedicated to socially beneficial education needed financial support beyond the federal grants propping up the South's polytechnic colleges.

The promotion of farmers' institutes also illustrated Dabney's program for university-sponsored social service. Farmers' institutes grew from the efforts of proponents of agricultural science to garner prestige for agricultural colleges and the specialists who staffed them. The first institutes appeared in the Midwest after 1870 and were supported initially by the agricultural colleges. Featuring addresses by agricultural college professors, the institutes traveled throughout the states, stopping briefly at different locations to proselytize farmers in the methods of scientific cultivation. However, their very success undermined their effectiveness in promoting agricultural colleges. Gradually, they were elbowed out by competing organizations and absorbed by bureaucratic state agencies.[38]

Nevertheless, the institutes enjoyed enormous popularity as a medium for communicating modern agricultural techniques to interested farmers. With this objective in mind, in 1899 Dabney recommended developing a system of farmers' institutes in conjunction with the work of the agricultural experiment station. Like the Agricultural and Mechanical College, the farmers' institutes would exemplify the university's commitment to public service. "The object of these institutes is, as is well known, to educate and stimulate farmers and especially to give them the results of the experiments made at the Experiment Station. . . . It is our desire and purpose to serve all the people of the State to the utmost of our resources."[39] The president made explicit the connection between agricultural extension work and university modernization. Both were predicated on the expansion of practical and socially beneficial education. As contributors to the commonweal, both also needed public support.

With the board's endorsement of the farmers' institutes, the faculty, aided by the efforts of the state commissioner of agriculture and the experiment station staff, began to plan extension programs. The agricultural professors generously offered their unpaid services to the institutes, eight of which were held between 1898 and 1899. Although the faculty and the president celebrated the virtues of the institutes, the states' farmers were ambivalent. Responding to an offer from Charles Plumb of the experiment station to give a lecture at an upcoming institute, P. F. Kefauver, secretary of the Farmers' Alliance of Monroe County, read the assistant director's letter at an alliance meeting, only to be greeted by overwhelming hostility. "I am opposed to the Institute," shouted one member, "and I hardly think it necessary for the [Farmers' Alliance] to go outside of our order to get anybody to instruct us in Agriculture." Even so, according to historian James Riley Montgomery, the animosity of some Tennessee farmers for ivory tower sages did not prevent the institutes from attracting extensive support.[40]

Professionalization was equally prominent in Dabney's pedagogical mandate. In 1890 the president cooperated with Thomas J. Freeman, former Supreme Court justice, to establish a law department at Tennessee. Freeman offered to teach the law course, asking only that the school provide office and classroom facilities. His own salary would be paid directly from student tuitions. Following Dabney's program for academic specialization, the school would belong to the professional department, independent of the Agricultural and Mechanical College. The program allowed students who had already studied law under an attorney to graduate after one year with a bachelor of laws degree. Others would complete the degree in two years. When Freeman died in 1891, he was replaced by judge Henry Ingersoll, soon joined by associate professor George E. Beers. Starting in 1890 with a humble enrollment of eight students, the law department had sixty-one students by 1902.[41]

The administration also established the teacher's department to help the state acquire a sufficient number of qualified teachers. Better teachers were needed to improve common school instruction, and the state university was obligated to provide them. "As the finishing school, and in this sense the head of the public educational system of the State, the University has a duty to discharge in regard to the public schools." But the university program was not meant to duplicate the normal school instruction offered at institutions such as the Peabody College in Nashville. Students in the two-year teaching program at Tennessee were expected to acquire normal school training as well as experience in the classroom. But rather than simple pedagogical instruction, the department would promote a comprehensive university education. Courses included the philosophy and history of education, educational systems, supervision, and pedagogical practices in various countries. By 1893, the teacher's department was able to boast forty-seven students. Despite the department's growth and ostensible benefit to the state, Dabney's request for an appropriation to continue its work was met by legislative indifference. When T. C. Karns, who had taken over the bulk of the teaching assignment in the department, resigned in 1899, the department folded.[42]

But circumstances conspired to rehabilitate the university's department of education. Stimulated by the formation of the Southern Education Board (SEB) in 1901 and by the promotional work of its Bureau of Investigation and Information, which was administered by Charles Dabney and Philander P. Claxton, the educational crusade of 1902 created an atmosphere favorable to reviving the teacher's department. In collaboration with Claxton, Dabney launched the Summer School of the South in 1902. The school's regionwide popularity impressed on the trustees the demand for professional pedagogical training. In the glow of the Summer School's success, the board decided to restore the department of education. Their only condition was that the president find an external source of funding for the venture. Deprived of any state support, the president turned to the General Education Board (GEB).

The GEB agreed to grant Tennessee $5,000 for three years on the condition that the university raise $4,500 from another source and establish a practice school for teachers in training. Following a pattern familiar to most administrators of indigent southern state colleges, Dabney turned to George Foster Peabody for help, who agreed to give Tennessee $3,000 to furnish the training school. Having secured the funds, Dabney opened the new department in January 1903. Although the department would train teachers for the state's rural schools, its primary function was to produce administrators for the South's rudimentary educational system: "It aims to prepare men and women," Dabney wrote in his annual report to the Board of Trustees, "of good scholarship for responsible positions as teachers in public and private schools . . . but it aims especially to train superintendents, principals and supervisors." Providing efficiency experts for a standardized education system, the department would also foster expansion of the South's new middle class.[43]

Featuring courses in the history and philosophy of education, psychology, ethics, and literature, the curriculum also reflected the utilitarian impulse remaking the wider university. In addition to the liberal arts, students would take classes in manual training and domestic economy, school organization, general agriculture, and horticulture. Teachers were to be educated in "sound scholarship" and "accurate knowledge," but they would also acquire a firm grounding in the manual and agricultural arts. Reinforcing the technical character of the new pedagogy was the positivist claim that students could learn the "science" of teaching. Education students did not simply conduct library research; they used a laboratory of psychology and a laboratory of manual training, while they studied the "science and art" of teaching and "domestic science."[44]

The imperatives of utility and professionalism also redefined the function of the school's faculty. Along with their work in the classroom, faculty members were expected to participate in university extension, give lectures and teachers' institutes, and investigate the state's rural schools. The faculty's new role as activist experts reflected the nexus of southern progressivism and educational pragmatism. Just as teachers were to function as pedagogical engineers for the rural South, faculty were expected to disseminate technical wisdom to farmers and teachers.

The department of education represented a high-water mark for professionalization at the university during Dabney's tenure, but it was the Summer School of the South that symbolized university extension. In his annual report for 1898, Dabney called for a permanent summer school for teachers unable to attend the university during its regular session. Nothing came of the proposal until 1902. That year, buoyed by the enthusiasm for educational reform stimulated by the Conference for Education in the South and the SEB, Dabney asked the Board of Trustees to authorize a summer school. The president recruited Philander P. Claxton, head of the SEB's Bureau of Investigation and Research, to design a program and run the school. Claxton became the linchpin of the summer school. An employee of the SEB, Claxton organized the summer school program and eventually served as a faculty member in the department of education.[45]

Claxton's role reflected the interorganizational character of the summer school. The school was the product of the coordinated efforts of the GEB, the SEB, the state university, private philanthropy, and the region's elite. "Thus all the interests and forces of the whole movement for which the General and Southern Education Boards stand were for the time merged" in Tennessee's summer school enterprise. Combining practical education with an ethos of social reform, the school offered courses ranging from horticulture to physiology, from manual training to economics and sociology, all designed to produce teachers who would "translate material appliances over into more abundant life and power and social efficiency."[46]

Although its program was directed at the minds of southerners, progressivism sought to stir their hearts with emotional appeals that celebrated the educational cause. Combining elements of evangelical revivalism and civic ritual, the summer school held a Fourth of July parade filled with martial imagery. The parade fostered the conviction that the summer school participants were legionnaires in a crusade for southern revitalization. After a discussion of educational issues, the assembled joined in a "patriotic demonstration of great interest and power." Marching in formation from the assembly hall, the various state organizations bore "banners and mottoes expressing their opinions on Southern educational problems." Each state delegation sang songs and delivered messages vividly expressing its dedication to the cause of school improvement. After the presentation and endorsement of resolutions, the state delegations "presented their banners at the front of the platform and grouped them around the national emblem, while the audience sang 'America.'"[47]

Perhaps the demonstrative nationalism of the Fourth of July ceremony reflected eastern Tennessee's traditional Union sympathies. It almost certainly expressed the New South conviction that southern regeneration required sectional cooperation. Indeed, the celebration assured the School's northern supporters that despite the tenacity of sectional consciousness, the South's leading reformers welcomed northern financial assistance. Considering that most northerners accepted the southern claim that only they could manage the region's race "problem," agreement on nationalism was hardly a stumbling block to reform.[48] Equally important, the celebration illustrates the formation of a political culture that fused education, social reform, and elite leadership. Participants celebrated not only a renewed nationalism, but the crystallization of an ideological compound that expressed their deepest desires for social leadership and social order.

A vehicle of progressive reform, the school provided a forum for discussing education reform and disseminating movement doctrine. The school drew more than 2,000 people from twenty-nine states, 1,500 of whom were teachers. Participants were treated to the elite of the education reform movement. Among the notables were Walter Hines Page, Edwin Alderman (then at Tulane University), Charles McIver of the North Carolina Normal and Industrial College, Wickliffe Rose of the Peabody Normal College, Wallace Buttrick of the GEB, and psychologist G. Stanley Hall of Clark University. The school even enlisted the services of superintendent James E. Hughes from Toronto, Canada. The summer school was a remarkable success, attracting 11,000 students to Knoxville between 1902 and 1907. The SEB considered the enormously popular venture a "crusading weapon for the advancement of southern education." It became the model for those that sprang up on college campuses throughout the South, including Walter Hill's University of Georgia.[49]

The intellectual atmosphere of the summer school was heavy with progressivism, and its guiding axioms resonated through the school's inaugural "Declaration of Principles." Citing statistics from 1900, the drafters of the declaration claimed that although 25 percent of the country's school population was in the South, it owned only 4 percent of the public school property and spent a mere 6.5 percent of the available public school funds. Echoing the cries of Hill and Mitchell for state support of higher education, the school's participants declared themselves "in favor of a public school system, State supported and State directed," and dependent on local taxation. But if the participants espoused the progressive tenet of government expansion, they linked it to a program of educational utilitarianism. Evidently bearing Charles Dabney's prints, the sixth declaration trumpeted, "The lines in the South must be both agricultural and mechanical: Our people must bring a trained brain and a trained hand to the daily labor. Education should be a means not of escaping labor, but of making it more effective."[50]

Reflecting the progressive dream of a rural South enlightened by modern education, the declaration expressed the hope that the school would become "the social center of the community . . . sympathetically touch[ing] all the social and economic interests of the people." In company with advocates of social regulation, educational progressives extolled the virtues of professional leadership. Teaching, the declaration proclaimed, "should be a profession, and not a stepping-stone to something else." Bent on rationalizing southern society, southern progressives were equally committed to depoliticizing it by extirpating small town partisanship. This could be accomplished only through disinterested and efficient administration. "We call upon the people to banish forever politics and nepotism from the public schools, and establish a system in which . . . merit shall be the touchstone."[51] In large part, the declaration encapsulated the reformer's vision of southern progress. Sanitized of partisan intrigue, administered by efficiency experts, supported by public funding respectful of racial orthodoxies, and predicated on a practical model of education, the region's schools would create the intellectual and material environment favorable to economic growth.

Whereas the summer school exemplified university outreach and educational professionalization, Dabney continued to point out the university's obligation to develop technical education. In the trustees' report of 1901, he reiterated that the Morrill Act required the expansion of mechanical engineering: "The laws under which we are operating make the subject of mechanical engineering, mechanic arts and the sciences pertaining thereto coordinate with agriculture." Lacking any state appropriation, the board constructed Reese Hall to accommodate the mechanic arts. Like many of the school's other departments, the growing department soon outstripped Reese Hall. To solve this predicament the board began the construction of Estabrook Hall in 1898, yet another building project lacking a state appropriation. The new building, Dabney reported, was a "model of its kind," with electric machinery, shops for machine work and woodworking, hydraulics, coal- and oil-testing laboratories, and engine and dynamo rooms featuring the "best appliances for testing."[52]

A good measure of the importance of practical instruction in Dabney's administrative agenda are his requests for university improvement. His first biennial report of 1887–88 called on the legislature to provide the school with a building for general purposes. The school's "urgent needs" included a chemical laboratory, a physics laboratory, $10,000 to equip the mechanical department, and farm buildings and barns for the agricultural students. Despite the infusion of federal money, the university's "pressing needs" in 1890 were better farm buildings and accommodations for the agricultural professors and students.[53]

By 1893 Dabney was alerting the Board of Trustees to the need for equipment for the science departments, including the Schools of Physics and Electrical Engineering, Zoology, and Geology. Once again, he called on the board to provide a new barn and other buildings for the School of Agriculture. At the same time he asked the board to acquire new lathes and a foundry for the School of Mechanic Arts. Fearing the proliferation of inadequately equipped scientific departments, Dabney advised that the university focus on developing existing schools rather than adding new ones. In his 1894 report to the Board of Trustees Dabney made building a new academic building, which would provide classrooms for instruction in the classics as well as agriculture, the priority in his list of university needs. (The president was still calling on the legislature to provide the funds for a new academic building in 1903.) Soon after, however, he asserted a "great demand for better equipment for the engineering and scientific schools."[54]

Conspicuously absent from Dabney's requests was any discourse on the value of liberal education. His appeal for scientific equipment was joined to a regionalist defense of pedagogical utilitarianism. The industrializing South, with its network of railroads, factories, and mines, demanded competent and trained workers, which only the North could then provide. "It is needless, therefore, to say that Tennessee ought to have a great school of natural science and engineering, with buildings and equipment equal to the best in the land." The South's greatest need was for trained technicians to manage economic growth. Dabney maintained that only the university could produce them. These efficiency experts would be the product of the academic division of labor that, despite the president's rhetoric, was rapidly separating the practical sciences from the arts.[55]

Admittedly, Dabney also made appropriation requests that had little to do with scientific education. Periodically, he requested funds to hire new instructors, buy books for the library, purchase new textbooks, and construct new buildings for the liberal arts department. In an address before the Association of Southern Colleges and Preparatory Schools in 1900, the president applauded the traditional curriculum: "The union of the liberal arts college and the scientific and technical department promotes a broad mindedness among professors and students, which is greatly to be desired."[56] And despite the tone of his administration, the University of Tennessee remained a predominantly liberal arts college during his tenure. But this was precisely the point. Like Hill, Dabney was a conscious agent of university modernization who promoted a utilitarian model of higher education. Although pushed by the winds of New South pragmatism and educational positivism, Dabney chose to follow a course that loosened the university from its classical moorings and set it in the currents of economic progress.

Commenting on the Dabney administration in 1893, Lucius S. Merriam suggested that the president "bent every energy in the direction of science and industrial lines. Latin and Greek were still retained, but they were made far less prominent than formerly. . . . The work in all departments was made largely practical in character."[57] The turn toward practical instruction impressed not only the Board of Trustees, but also observers far removed from east Tennessee. J. Sterling Morton, editor of the Nebraska City's *The Conservative* and secretary of agriculture in the second Cleveland administration, declared his approval of Dabney's "judicious management" of the university. "The fact that you have completed a new mechanical building and will open it with a celebration is evidence that you are going to teach something quite utilitarian and practical."[58] Classical education, though not abandoned at Tennessee, was subordinated to a program of practical instruction.

Extracting practical education from the New South ideology, Dabney used its quantitative, concrete standards to measure university progress. Expressing it numerically, Dabney claimed that the university offered "five excellent, large buildings used exclusively for lecture halls, laboratories etc; seven commodious structures used for dormitories and similar purposes." In the president's mind, one had only to count the bricks to gain an appreciation of Tennessee's progress. An expanding faculty and growing student enrollment represented equally reliable indicators of university development. From a faculty of 7 in 1888 the teaching staff had grown to 22 in 1898, and over the same period the school's student body had multiplied from 125 to 318 attending both the academic and law departments. As the number of staff and students increased, the school's departments proliferated from one in 1888 to five in 1898.[59]

For Dabney, the growing numbers of students, faculty, and departments represented "in a general way the growth of the organization of the University during the last ten years." Perhaps more importantly, the students were preparing themselves for service to the state and country in "the most efficient manner." Missing from Dabney's encomium was any mention of the development of "mental discipline," "liberal culture," or moral rectitude. Absent too was any attempt to assess the qualitative dimension of education. Were students better educated (however defined) in 1898 than they were before 1887? Were students equipped with the analytical skills necessary to critique southern social institutions, regional problems, and political economy? For that matter, was the university's vaunted agricultural and mechanical education actually preparing its graduates for modern economic challenges? Did it live up to national or regional standards of technical instruction? Dabney was silent on these matters, and so were most contemporary administrators of southern higher education.[60]

Using quantitative standards to evaluate university progress, Dabney and other educational modernizers implicitly discredited other less tangible, less "scientific" methods for assessing education. The value of education, Dabney wrote in 1901, could be determined by the increase in material abundance: "In fact the relations between education and productivity are so well understood now that you can measure the wealth producing power of a people by the school privileges which they have enjoyed." Efficiency and social utility echoed loudly in Dabney's ode to progress at university. The nineteenth-century preoccupation with character had been replaced by an education that exalted atomistic competition in an expanding market economy.[61]

Dabney might have admitted in his report that enrollments in agricultural education were disproportionately low in relation to the resources expended on it. Responding to an inquiry from a man in Georgia about the merits of joining an agricultural college to a liberal arts institution, the president recited his customary mantra to balanced education. He was also forced to acknowledge just how many students were *actually* enrolled in the agricultural program. Out of a total of 301 students in the academic department in 1898, only 28 declared agriculture and horticulture their major subjects. However, Dabney jumped to defend these statistics. "But notice that in the sciences pertaining to agriculture there were large numbers. For example, Chemistry 70, Botany 24, Zoology 58, Geology 9, Meteorology 9, etc." Dabney asked much of his correspondent to have him believe that students in meteorology and chemistry were latent agriculturalists. In 1898, for example, 23 students enrolled in the agriculture course while 191 students took English, 147 studied mathematics, and 104 studied Latin. The liberal arts proved surprisingly resilient against the juggernaut of technical education. A robust humanities program is even more surprising considering that paid apprenticeships were offered primarily to students in the agricultural and mechanical courses. The majority of students were enrolled in the departments of agriculture and engineering, although the president was forced to admit rather sheepishly that "the number taking engineering far exceeds that taking agriculture."[62]

Dabney's assertion that students chose agriculture and engineering over liberal studies was somewhat misleading. The academic reorganization of 1887–88 had created the College of Agriculture, Mechanic Arts and Sciences. The new college subsumed the literary course and the Latin-science course as well as engineering and the other sciences. Any student of Latin or history necessarily belonged to the College of Agriculture and was required to take "practical" agriculture. This academic arrangement simply reflected Dabney's efforts to bring the university in line with the Morrill Act, which required the colleges to teach science and the classics as well as agriculture.[63]

The president's explanation for the disparity between engineering and agricultural enrollments is equally intriguing. Engineering attracted more students because of the depressed condition of southern agriculture. Although 60 percent of those enrolled in the university came from the rural South, the majority aspired to the professions and business, knowing full well "about the difficulties of farming." Encouraged by their parents, most of the "country boys" sought out the college as a refuge from rural desolation. Dabney argued that the colleges were not to blame for the flight from the cotton fields. The main culprit was the South's economic conditions. In fact, "These colleges and departments of universities are doing more to encourage country boys to stay upon the farm than all the other institutions in the land." Identifying the economic roots of southern poverty, Dabney still insisted that regional advancement required the application of scientific agriculture to the yeoman farm, despite mounting evidence that Tennessee farmers and their sons saw little promise of prosperity on the homestead.[64]

The work of the experiment station and the agriculture department certainly met agricultural needs. Their studies of grasses, forage plants, wheats, cereals, phosphates, and other chemicals used for fertilization benefited southern cultivators who could afford to adopt their recommendations. Given favorable conditions, their discoveries would help maximize agricultural potential in the region. Yet, in examining southern agriculture, New South educators were bound by the assumption that the key to southern advancement was modifying farming techniques, not transforming the region's political economy. If Dabney and his contemporaries subjected the plantation economy to searching criticism, the evidence is not extant. Instead they extolled the virtues of crop diversification and scientific agriculture as the pillars of an agrarian economy that left in place the institutions of sharecropping and the crop lien.[65]

Wedded to the notion that education was the lever of economic progress, the president and other technical enthusiasts promoted the agricultural college as the antidote to rural poverty. A product of his conservative ideology, Dabney's pedagogical agenda also flowed from the logic of the Morrill Acts. The legislation dangled irresistible sums of money in front of impoverished college educators on the condition that they develop agricultural courses. Whereas previous administrators had gladly accepted the money and offered a perfunctory nod to technical instruction, Dabney, Hill, and Alderman took the conditions of the Morrill Acts seriously. And for Dabney, federal funding represented the bulk of income for a university neglected by its state legislature. Still, the president and the board chose to funnel resources into educational programs that reinforced the socioeconomic order and validated its guiding convictions.

In 1887 he and others were confronted with educational alternatives, not a rigid pedagogical framework dictating practical instruction. In choosing to emphasize industrial education in preference to liberal and professional instruction, the Dabney administration strengthened the ties between the university and the declining agrarian order. The emphasis on agriculture also worked at cross purposes to professionalization, one of Dabney's other major objectives. Furthermore, Dabney championed a discipline that was clearly unpopular with most students. As historian James Riley Montgomery points out, "The small number of students registered in a full agricultural curriculum plagued the University administration."[66] Agricultural instruction endured at the University of Tennessee, but it continued to bear the ideological imprint of the New South that Dabney had stamped on it.

Despite his focus on technical education, Dabney strove to improve university admission standards. Elevating standards at Tennessee was complicated by the fact that the school was required by state law to provide tuition-free scholarships to qualified candidates. After passing a competitive exam, scholarship recipients were selected by state senators and legislators. However, the appointments often were determined less by academic merit than by the political interests of Tennessee's legislators.[67] Until 1890, applicants were not required to have completed high school, but only to have passed the entrance examination.

Paralleling efforts to improve standards at other southern universities, Dabney insisted on separating college studies from high school or preparatory studies. A common feature of southern higher education, the preparatory department functioned as a surrogate high school for students insufficiently prepared for university work.[68] In his 1887–88 reorganization plan, Dabney declared that the preparatory department would be abolished. The eventual dismantling of preparatory classes permitted the University of Tennessee to join the Association of Southern Colleges and Preparatory Schools. Established in 1895 by a group of Vanderbilt professors under the leadership of chancellor James Kirkland, the association sought to improve the general caliber of scholarship and standardize entrance requirements at southern colleges. Participating schools were expected to relinquish preparatory departments, institute written examinations, and promulgate clearly defined entrance requirements. In addition to several other specific requirements, accredited institutions could admit only students who had completed fourteen high school units. To qualify for graduation, students of a "standard college" were expected to complete four years of humanities and science courses.[69]

Tennessee's admission to the association is important for two reasons. First, it signified the president's efforts to connect the university to the wider regional movement for educational standardization. The movement for standardization, in turn, grew from the progressive drive for associational reform and sectional uplift. By submitting the university to objective standards of academic performance, Dabney promoted the erosion of the provincial ethos of the antebellum southern college. Second, the simple fact that the school was able to qualify for membership in the association while Hill's University of Georgia and Mitchell's University of South Carolina, for example, could not, highlights Tennessee's relative advancement in the area of admission standards during Dabney's tenure.[70]

At least in terms of admission standards, Dabney endorsed the quality of educational work over the quantity of students in attendance. "In order to do good work in the students," he observed in his review of 1898, "it is necessary that we have good material. For this reason our standard for admission will be advanced as rapidly as the conditions of the preparatory schools admit."[71] And there was the rub. The elevation of university admission standards was inextricably tied to the quality of education at the region's high schools. Improving high school standards would prove a formidable task, considering southern reluctance to finance public education. In harmony with other university modernizers, Dabney admitted that the unilateral tightening of university standards in a region marked by a patchwork of substandard high schools was an exercise in self-delusion.

The standards quandary encouraged reformers to use organic imagery to describe the relationship between common, secondary, and postsecondary schools. Such a relationship presumed a minimal degree of coordination between high school curricula and state college entrance requirements. Reviewing the period 1889 to 1894, the president cited the inability of 126 "sub freshmen" in the school's atrophying preparatory department to advance beyond their first year. He concluded that "the vast majority of these persons were hopelessly backward" and that the university was not "the proper place for them to make up their lost opportunities." The solution was university support for the improvement of public and private preparatory schools. Despite good intentions, though, Dabney was caught in the conundrum that ensnared most other university administrators: To raise admission standards was to sacrifice numbers and court accusations of institutional elitism. This would undermine the school's claims to disinterested state service. Although the state college's "right" to determine its admission standards was "universally admitted," its "duty" to keep admission requirements proximate to the average level for the best public secondary schools, city high schools, and private schools tempered their more ambitious plans.[72]

The president and the Board of Trustees also bolstered admission requirements by adopting a system of accredited high schools as an alternative to a written entrance examination. University officials hoped to encourage the improvement of preparatory schools by underlining university authority over high school curricula. The administration also expected that accreditation would provide an incentive for graduation from high school. More pragmatically, it would provide a steady stream of university candidates.[73]

In 1894 Dabney announced the formation of a permanent committee on accredited schools and admission. The committee included a liaison between the university and the preparatory schools. Reflecting the transitional state of admission requirements, the committee was responsible for examining high schools for accreditation and administering entrance exams. As at Georgia during Hill's administration, accrediting high schools in Tennessee met several obstacles. The most intractable of these, according to Dabney, was the "great want of uniformity in the courses of study in the public schools of the cities and towns, and the still greater diversity among the private schools."[74]

Accredited high schools and the elimination of the preparatory department could not by themselves remedy the educational blight in Tennessee. In 1902 the president admitted that the school had a reached a plateau in entrance standards. "It is believed that the University has advanced as much in standard and increased as much in numbers as will be possible until we have more and better schools." Sparsely scattered throughout the rural South, private schools were the only avenue to the state colleges for most Tennesseans. Public schools were restricted to urban areas. But the high schools were in turn connected to the South's equally inadequate common schools. Until both improved appreciably, the state colleges would remain in stasis. "We are trying here, as in most of the Southern States, to build a great State University upon the foundation of an imperfect system of public schools with almost no high schools."[75] Advocating comprehensive educational reform, Dabney joined other university progressives agitating for the rationalization of state schools.

Although hesitant at first, Dabney's efforts at raising admission standards represented a step in his plan to model Tennessee after the image of the northern research university. Elevating university standards reflected the dual impulses underlying university modernization in the South. Better standards were designed to legitimate the school's claims to academic credibility. By demonstrating that the university was an institution of sober scholarly inquiry, improved standards bolstered the school's ethic of professional social service. Improved standards also reflected the eagerness of some New South college administrators for progressive-style associational cooperation.

Mirroring other state universities, Dabney and his reform-minded colleagues demonstrated their commitment to administrative efficiency by remodeling the school's infrastructure. Modernization dealt a mortal blow not only to the preparatory department but also to the system of student military government in place since 1875. Like many southern colleges, Tennessee organized its students into regimental companies replete with military uniforms, parade square drill, occasional mock battles, and a commandant. Although the paramilitarization of campuses suggests much about the grip of the Lost Cause on southern culture, in practical terms, military discipline was an effective method for controlling adolescents ill prepared for university studies.[76]

The preparatory department was the college's largest, and for the "young and untrained this system was found to be the best one for governing them." The school offered dashing uniforms and a taste of Confederate military glory to young southerners bred on the lore of Beauregard and Lee. But when the department was dismantled, it brought into question the system of military governance itself. "It seems to me," wrote a concerned university supporter, "that we have come to a turning point. We have pushed the university to a point where it has outgrown the . . . barracks system of a military academy and we must either give it room for expansion or congestion will result."[77] As historian Lucius Merriam observed in 1893, "So long as the school was under military control it was used by many parents as a sort of school of correction for incorrigibles."[78] Just as the service-oriented state universities were relinquishing the pedagogical tradition of mental discipline, so too were they abandoning the nineteenth-century tradition of military discipline. And Tennessee was not alone, according to Dabney. "The experience everywhere has been that such a system of government is totally inconsistent with true university life and work."[79] Although military drill was maintained, the regimen was scaled back, and student supervision was handed over to the dean of the college.

Reflecting Victorian imperatives of self-control and propriety, Dabney welcomed the passage of the university from "a system of government by limitations and restrictions to a system of government based wholly upon the appeal to their honor and good sense." Mature and presumably better qualified candidates would be expected to be "diligent in study and prompt and regular in attendance on all prescribed duties." Instead of relying on an intrusive military government to maintain order, the university would inculcate students in the virtues of industriousness and sobriety. Instruction of this sort would equip them for single-minded study and survival in the competitive marketplace. If we are to take the president at his word, the appeal to genteel comportment had a civilizing effect on the atmosphere at Tennessee: "Gratifying evidence of the improvement in spirit is found in the total abolition of all hazing or other rudeness [and] those silly and boisterous disturbances that sometimes characterize large bodies of young men."[80] By academic standards a more respectable institution, Tennessee was also becoming a much more somber place.

It was also losing its character as a club for men only. In May 1893 the faculty met and passed a resolution calling on the Board of Trustees to admit women to the university. According to James Riley Montgomery, the decision was motivated by several factors. Among these were the growing number of coeducational colleges throughout the nation and in Tennessee, the need to offer educational opportunities to the state's predominantly female public school teachers, the fact that the elimination of military government had removed one of the principal obstacles to coeducation, and the expedient recognition that admitting women would increase university attendance.[81] The following year, forty-eight women enrolled as regular and special students. Quickly, they proved their academic proficiency by winning the freshman, sophomore, and junior scholarship awards for 1893–94.[82]

Admitting women had not diminished the academic standards of education at the state university, Dabney assured the trustees. Accepted on the basis of examinations or high school certificates, women were enrolled in the regular courses and were required to fulfill the weekly schedule of fifteen hours of class time. Wanting the benefits of scientific training and higher education, women were permitted no special treatment. The conspicuous exception, of course, were the special classes for women in "domestic science" and physical education. "Everything was thus done to discourage that class of young women who merely wanted to be polished or 'finished' from entering the institution; but everything reasonable was done to encourage women who wanted a thorough, liberal education . . . or education for some profession."[83] The president's decision also won him the approval of James Kirkland, one of the South's leading progressives in higher education. "I am glad," he wrote, "to join hands with you on the woman question. Considering the condition of female education in the South, it seems the duty of male colleagues to open their doors."[84] By 1901 Dabney was able to report that 190 women had attended the university. As among the male students, though, only one in ten, or nineteen in total, had graduated. Those who did graduate invariably became teachers in women's colleges, seminaries, and public schools.[85]

Women may have been admitted on an equal basis to men, but their behavior was judged according to criteria that were far from academic. The greatest concern, considering southern gender conventions, was that women would sacrifice their femininity by studying subjects traditionally restricted to the masculine sphere. According to trustee Edward Sanford, though, university officials had no reason to fear the obliteration of gender categories. Although the decision had been made in "fear and trembling," the admission of "blue eyes and rosy cheeks" to the university had compromised neither the school's academic credibility nor the women's feminine sensibilities. "The report of the professors," Sanford mused, "if they have not been bewitched by the brightness of those eyes, indicate not only that Tennessee yet has daughters as bright and fair as charming Barbara Blount . . . but also diligent, and also ingenious." Apparently, the experiment worked, proving that university education for women would not "detract from their feminine charms, nor deprive them of their graces."[86]

In an effort to assuage nagging doubts about coeducation, Florence Skiffington, dean of the women's department, used the ceremonial opening of the women's dormitory to reaffirm the school's respect for traditional gender roles. While she praised the rigid conservatism of southern gender notions, she placated fears that a college education encouraged women to abandon domesticity by insisting that "recent statistics prove that as large a proportion of college girls marry as non-college girls." Skiffington, like so many of her counterparts agitating for women's inclusion in the world outside the home, was compelled to defend female education in terms that reaffirmed the sanctity of the domestic sphere: "I can not believe that because a girl has been given a deeper insight, and a broader sympathy; has been trained to sound judgement . . . will make any the worse manager of a home for husband and children."[87] Dabney could not have agreed more, quoting in his memoirs Charles McIver's aphorism, "Educate the mothers and you educate the whole population."[88]

Skiffington's remarks resonated with the domestic icons that progressive women invoked throughout the South. As Pamela Dean illustrates in an analysis of the North Carolina Normal and Industrial College for Women, women justified their involvement in social reform by appeals to domestic and religious virtues. Annie Randall, registrar and English instructor at the college, was one of many women educators who espoused the progressive philosophy of regional progress through educational reform. She argued that the mission of college graduates was to convince the taxpayers of North Carolina to finance public schools administered by trained educators. Echoing Florence Skiffington's compromise between tradition and change, Randall suggested that, for the present, "the Southern woman abhors politics . . . [but] where her children's welfare is at stake, she is ready to do battle."[89]

In addition to local taxation and improved schoolhouses, Randall recommended appointing qualified women to school boards that suffered from political partisanship. According to her, education would improve because women would "give the schools the benefit of the counsel and aid of the women, who are their natural guardians." Male reformers also used the domestic idiom to rationalize women's social reform efforts. Charles McIver, president of the Normal School, urged students to become missionaries for education, converting their communities and its legislators to the gospel of financial support for the Normal College, local taxation for schools, and professional education. By explaining women's expanding social roles in familiar maternal and religious terms, reformers alleviated anxieties about growing female independence.[90]

The majority of women who studied at the University of Tennessee during the Progressive Era pursued traditionally female careers. The admission of women was part of a broader development that opened up previously unimagined opportunities for southern white women. However, the women who took advantage of these newly opened doors were expected, according to historian Amy Thompson McCandless, to "conform to traditional images of womanhood promulgated by their benefactors." White women found their entrance into liberal arts colleges much less obstructed than black women did. Both realized quickly "that traditional stereotypes of gender, class, and race permeated the halls of academe and affected their choice of professions." While maternal imagery helped justify women's entry into the university by linking higher education to service in the public schools, it reinforced the boundaries limiting women's professional ambitions.[91]

Another of Dabney's innovations was his term as assistant secretary of agriculture between 1894 and 1898. Rather than leave Tennessee, Dabney combined his university duties with the responsibilities of the federal post. The president brought himself to the attention of Democratic power brokers through his work with the Association of American Agricultural Colleges and Experiment Stations. Like many quasipublic organizations of the Progressive Era, the association worked to consolidate the relationship between service-directed institutions and the state.[92] The association was particularly interested in the distribution of funds from the Hatch Act of 1887, which provided for a national system of agricultural experiment stations. It was also concerned about clarifying the ambiguous legal relationship between the Department of Agriculture and the land grant colleges. The association struggled with the question of whether the money was intended to establish colleges or finance experiment station research. Dabney's position on the issue was clear. Chairing a committee on the Hatch Act issue, he urged that funds be devoted solely to agricultural research, not miscellaneous college expenses. The committee also requested that the stations remain autonomous and under the direction of one administrator. Despite differences over jurisdiction, the association was unified in its effort to forge ties between the Department of Agriculture, the colleges, and the stations.[93]

Faced with a secretary of agriculture opposed to federal supervision of the agricultural colleges, Henry Alvord, special agent for the cooperative exhibit of the experiment stations, asked Dabney to head an association subcommittee to present the case for legal relations between the colleges, the stations, and the government to the president and the secretary.[94] The request put Dabney in an awkward situation: By this time his name had been thrown into the ring for the position of assistant secretary in the Department of Agriculture. Despite their differences, the meeting between secretary J. Sterling Morton and Dabney was amicable. In fact, Dabney so impressed Morton that he asked the university president to consider the position of assistant secretary. By December, Dabney had accepted the job. Enthusiastically, he requested that the Board of Trustees grant him a four-year leave of absence. The board agreed on the conditions that Dabney continue to manage university affairs as much as possible, visit the school four times a year, present annual budget reports to the board, and accept a salary cut for the duration of his term in Washington.[95]

The board's decision was politically unpopular. In 1895, opponents of the decision introduced a bill in the General Assembly to replace the office of trustees with a Board of Regents. A Republican newspaper wrote caustically, "Fire Dabney and fire him at once. We have had enough of him. Let the gang of blood-sucking professors who teach each year at Knoxville be wiped out, and new men put in." Even the governor questioned whether Tennessee law permitted the president of the state university to hold a federal government position during his administration. Several legislators also lodged protests. Although Dabney faithfully fulfilled the terms of the agreement, his leave of absence did little to ingratiate him or the university to the General Assembly.[96]

As assistant secretary, Dabney worked to extend the department's control over the experiment stations. Despite Morton's fear that departmental responsibility for the stations would undermine fiscal restraint, Dabney was able to convince the secretary that only the agricultural department could provide the scientific expertise to manage the experiment stations effectively. Having won Morton's confidence, he was given control of the department's scientific work. According to one historian, Dabney's "generous attitude" toward government support for scientific investigation provided a constructive counterpoint to Morton's preoccupation with budgetary moderation.[97]

Among other things, Dabney's appointment gave him the opportunity to implement a vision of government he had once mapped out for Walter Hines Page. Having made a study of federal agencies engaged in scientific investigation, Dabney concluded that the "remedy for the abuses and evils" lay in reorganizing departments along lines "wholly scientific and entirely removed from political interference."[98] Advocating scientific management, Dabney echoed the cries of myriad Gilded Age reformers for the "purification" of the federal civil service. His work also anticipated the progressive dream of government management by technocratic elites.

Combining the federal post with his duties as president at Tennessee, Dabney advanced the idea that the university was an instrument of state service. In an effort similar to Mitchell's and Hill's later efforts, Dabney tried to coordinate government and university functions by solidifying relations between the Department of Agriculture and the experiment stations. Considering persistent southern antipathy for federal interference in regional matters, Dabney's venture carried added sectional significance. From the perspective of his activity in the American Association of Agricultural Colleges and Experiment Stations, his Washington posting reflected the growing willingness of southern progressives to enlist state support for limited but constructive reform.

His service in the Department of Agriculture also enhanced his reputation as an exponent of practical education. In 1899, the trustees of the University of California seriously considered Dabney for the presidency. Trying to decide whether the university should cast itself as a classical college or a scientific research institution, some board members hit upon Dabney as a candidate representing the scientific emphasis. In a letter to Daniel Coit Gilman, one university supporter expressed his approval of the multitalented Virginian: "I have great respect for his abilities, as displayed in the revivifying of Tennessee University and still more in his masterly work as Assistant Secretary of Agriculture during the last administration when he succeeded in maintaining and greatly strengthening the scientific work of the Department." Dabney's administrative acumen and scientific credentials brought him to the attention of university modernizers outside of the South. His efforts to rehabilitate Tennessee also validated his claim to be a champion of practical education.[99]

His service in Washington fulfilled professional ambitions, but the most salient of his accomplishments was the solidification of state and university relations. This came with a direct appropriation for the school in 1903. The appropriation represented a small return on the president's relentless efforts to extract from the legislature a financial commitment to the university. Dabney lamented in his first report to the Board of Trustees, "Our State has fallen behind her sister States in the last twenty-five years in the work of higher education. It is doing less for higher education to-day than any State of its wealth and population in this country." Disparaging the university's reliance on philanthropic "charity," the president called in vain on the legislature to finance the construction of new buildings and the purchase of needed scientific apparatus.[100]

In 1890 the president renewed the request for state support, this time calling on the legislature to allocate $50,000 for constructing a central academic building to replace the Hill's overcrowded classroom facilities. Although bills providing for a ten-year appropriation of $50,000 were introduced, they failed to win legislative approval. In 1892, Dabney once again chronicled the story of university dependence on land grant funds as a prelude to a request for $50,000. Once again, the request was denied. In his biennial report for 1894 Dabney wasted little energy trying to illustrate the legislature's negligence. Registering the board's request for money to erect a new academic building, he commented perfunctorily, "By neglecting to provide the institution with adequate buildings, the State is greatly retarding its development and injuring its usefulness."[101] What had changed by 1903?

The development of farmers' institutes and the experiment station was an important factor, argues James Riley Montgomery, because it enhanced the school's "reputation with the farming community." Considering the widespread reluctance of Tennessee's farmers to take advantage of the school's "book farming," this explanation is dubious. More convincing is the suggestion that Dabney's support for visits by university representatives to Tennessee's secondary schools helped generate support for the state college. A growing body of loyal alumni also added weight to the university's pleas. Meeting in Memphis, Nashville, and Chattanooga in 1903, Tennessee alumni made plans to submit the university's requests to the General Assembly in 1903. The Memphis meeting, attended by P. P. Claxton and two trustees, produced a university bill for the next session of the legislature. Supported by the trustees and the Alumni Association, the bill called for an appropriation of $20,000 a year for five years to finance building construction. Alumni within the government, including the state superintendent, the Speaker of the House, and James B. Frazier, the state's governor, also lent support for the measure.[102]

The launching of the Summer School of the South in 1902 also contributed to the breakthrough appropriation. Attended by more than 2,000 people, distinguished by the presence of the South's intellectual elite, and supported by respected philanthropic organizations, the school highlighted the extensive needs of southern education. It also gave the university new prestige as a center for educational reform and intellectual ferment. It is also plausible that the summer school put the inadequately funded university under a microscope of regional scrutiny. The attention may have pressured legislators to include the school in the government's yearly appropriation list. If legislators were prompted by publicity to acknowledge the school's needs, they were also convinced that the institution had become, at least nominally, a legitimate department of public service.

Of course, the change in the university's status should not be exaggerated, considering that the original request for $100,000 was pared down to a meager $10,000 for the purchase of farmland for the experiment station. That the legislature had not been swept off its collective feet with affection for the university was proven two years later. Under the leadership of Brown Ayres, the new president, the administration submitted a request for $104,200 to the General Assembly, only to have it slashed to $25,000. Still, the appropriation of 1903 was precedent setting, as Dabney understood, "for the fact that it is the first direct appropriation made to the institution from the treasury of the State."[103] A crucial part of Dabney's legacy in Knoxville was a fragile but more stable relationship between the university and the General Assembly.

Financial tribulation at the hands of a miserly legislature was a common theme in public higher education of the post–Civil War South. It suggests the persistence of a tradition of southern localism that militated against progressive efforts to use the state for social reform. Against progressive attempts to centralize authority, standardize procedure, and use the taxing power of the government to subsidize these changes, southerners protected a low-tax environment and community control over schools. Whereas Dabney viewed his opponents as small-minded partisans, many of his adversaries saw themselves as the defenders of local autonomy and community standards against intrusive bureaucracy. As James Leloudis has observed of North Carolina Baptists who opposed the educational centralization advocated by Charles McIver and others, their vision of "democratic localism" respected "the authority of ordinary people and accepted their desire to establish institutions that served their own needs and aspirations."[104]

Financial hardship also suggests the limitations that regional poverty imposed on university improvement schemes. In 1901, for example, the cumulative income available to the sixty-six institutions of higher education in Virginia, North Carolina, South Carolina, Georgia, Alabama, Mississippi, and Arkansas was $65,843 less than that of Harvard. In that same year, the University of Alabama could claim only $10,000 of its income from the state, and the universities of Kentucky, Mississippi, and Tennessee received no state support at all.[105]

Just as Mitchell's activism alienated Governor Blease, Dabney's support for public education elicited the censure of some legislators and university trustees. As the SEB's propaganda agent, he was responsible for publicizing the South's dismal education system. In hundreds of bulletins and reports churned out for state education crusades, his Bureau of Investigation and Information highlighted the illiteracy and ignorance that supposedly shackled regional rehabilitation.[106] For Dabney, public education was the remedy for southern backwardness and partisanship: "The solid South is a menace to the safety of our country. Behold how completely our politicians have led us into isolation. This country is a hot-bed for every foolishism, financial and political, that comes along. There is no cure for it except public education."[107] The Summer School of the South solidified his reputation as an adversary of educational provincialism. Together with his work for the bureau, it made him a fixture in the constellation of leading educational reformers. However, approval of the SEB and its objectives was by no means universal.

The most strident opposition to the "Ogden movement" was mounted by the *Manufacturer's Record*, a daily newspaper that championed the New South ideology. Along with several other newspapers, the *Record* accused the board of favoring educational equality for blacks and whites. Despite its misrepresentation of the board's racial policy, which by 1903 amounted to abandoning efforts to equalize educational opportunities for southern blacks, the negative press imperiled the board's education campaign.[108] Suspicion that even the board's nominal support for black education threatened the South's racial caste system may explain the opposition of some trustees to Dabney's involvement in the organization. At least this is what William H. Baldwin, member of the board, Hampton supporter, and president of the New York–based Long Island Railway Company, believed. "I have learned," wrote Baldwin to trustee Edward T. Sanford, "that some of the Trustees of the University of Tennessee have been disturbed because Dr. Dabney is undertaking work in connection with the Southern Education Board. I assume that the cause of the criticism is that race prejudice will be excited," which, Baldwin feared, would affect the university adversely. Skirting the race issue, he reminded Sanford that if southerners received the board favorably, it would lead to an enormous infusion of money for the cause of educational reform.[109]

Although Sanford meant to assure Baldwin of the board's endorsement of the education movement, he inadvertently confirmed the trustees' misgivings about Dabney's work: "I think there is some misunderstanding as to the attitude of the Trustees of the University. They are not in any wise opposed to the work of the [Southern Education Association] but on the contrary . . . believe that it will do a splendid work and heartily favor its plans." The problem, Sanford suggested, was that Dabney's program for university modernization had alienated certain political factions in the state.

> The upward path of the University of Tennessee, however, has been very difficult. It has encountered much opposition among politicians especially, and the Board does feel that it is unwise for the University to become officially identified with a movement that is outside of the real function of the University, and especially where *the real purpose of the movement has been misunderstood and antagonism aroused,* which would inevitably be visited to a certain extent upon the University. In short, the Trustees feel that they have troubles enough of their own without assuming others not within the scope of their own Educational Department. [emphasis added]

Sanford's letter is interesting for several reasons. First, it suggests that Dabney encountered resistance from administrators and politicians who were unconvinced by the case for university leadership in social uplift. Second, Sanford confirms that the trustees were anxious about associating the university with an organization whose "real purpose"—promoting an education designed to maintain black subjugation—had been "misunderstood." A proponent and organizer of a reform program potentially disruptive of the social order, Dabney did not seem nearly as safe to the trustees as he had in 1887.

In addition, Sanford's letter highlights the ideological gulf separating Dabney from the trustees. For him, the university was an integral part of a unified system of public education. It made little sense to raise university standards when the majority of the region's schools could not prepare students to meet the college's admission requirements. As he wrote to Charles Vawter, "A State University cannot exist except upon the basis of a system of public schools, certainly not in Tennessee where we have so many church and private colleges." For Dabney, the SEB was not "outside of the real function of the university." Instead, it linked universities and common schools together in a movement to foster public responsibility for education. Presumably, the trustees were concerned that Dabney's association with the SEB would exacerbate animosity toward the university. But Sanford's letter also suggests that the trustees simply disagreed with Dabney's position on the role of the SEB in the movement for educational reform.[110]

If Dabney's program for modernization generated political controversy, his decision to take the post of assistant secretary of agriculture did little to conciliate university opponents. As Sanford clarified in his letter to Baldwin, "Furthermore, we have been subjected in the past to much criticism, though undeserved in my opinion, on account of the fact that the President has been doing double work and serving in other capacities while in the employment of the University, and the political antagonism in the State is such that it would unquestionably do great injury to the University if he should now give any considerable portion of his time to outside work."[111] Dabney was surprised by the tenacious opposition to his reform agenda. In a letter explaining his departure to the University of Cincinnati in 1904, Dabney confessed that "I have gone ahead and done things too fast and too independently. Some of them do not believe in my policy of building up the public schools and the high schools or with regard *to the relations of the University to the people of the South at large*, but I still believe that I am absolutely right" (emphasis added).[112] More than a product of personal enmity, opposition to the president suggested the reluctance of many to embrace the progressive message of regional uplift through public education.

The disparity between his dreams for progressive reform and the persistence of educational penury eventually drove Dabney from Knoxville. He confided to Walter Hines Page that the interminable problem of financing the university was paramount in his decision to leave. "I have despaired," he wrote to Cyrus Northrop, president of the University of Minnesota, "of seeing a great university in the South in my time. We have no state or city that has either the public spirit or the wealth to build it."[113] In yet another letter justifying his decision to leave Tennessee, Dabney cited the need to "wake up the people of Tennessee to their duty to this institution."[114] He was exasperated by having to raise $40,000 to $50,000 a year from external sources to keep the university operating. Admittedly, the money accrued from private sources was not expended exclusively on university matters but was directed to "the upbuilding of the public schools, which are the necessary foundation of every State University."[115] If anything, Dabney's departure illuminated the dogged resilience of southern localism against progressive efforts to rationalize southern society. The progressive campaign to rationalize southern education was inseparable from its efforts to modify the region's political culture. As much as any reform measure, it was this that brought discomfiture to modernizers such as Dabney and Philander P. Claxton.[116]

Writing to George Foster Peabody in 1904, Dabney provided a more acrimonious inventory of his reasons for leaving the University of Tennessee. Expressing sincere gratitude for Peabody's assistance to the summer school and the university, Dabney assured him that the results would vindicate their efforts. "When you have learned more," Dabney wrote sullenly, "about the wretched, almost insurmountable prejudice, narrowness, sectarianism, sectionalism, demagoguism and profound stupidity of the leaders of these people and of the masses of the people themselves, you will agree that the slow methods and conservative measures we had to use were the only possible ones."[117] It is not surprising that Dabney alienated local politicians and trustees. Like Edwin Alderman, Dabney found it difficult to restrain his contempt for those less educated and urbane. Starting from the assumption that the New South version of educational reform was imperative and that those who opposed it were unenlightened, Dabney never understood that many objected to his plans because they threatened local control over schooling and the combination of cultural values and social customs it represented. Also, many were skeptical of the kind of bureaucratic governance that the SEB represented. By conceding authority to appointed experts rather than elected local officials, the educational crusade seemed to undermine community control over its institutions.[118]

Of course, Dabney's opponents would hardly have agreed that his methods were "slow" and "conservative." Considering the SEB's deference to southern racial and social conventions, Dabney's description was accurate. Yet in his support for public education, his relentless drive for university funding, and his launching of the Summer School of the South and the Bureau for Investigation and Research, he challenged the minimalist tradition in education and exposed the deficiencies of Tennessee's schools. His reasons for leaving, then, were twofold. First, he wanted "to be free from this miserable prejudice, narrowness, and this political and (so called) religious machination." Second, he had grown tired of the financial stringency that hamstrung each of his efforts to modernize the university: "I cannot continue to make bricks without straw."[119]

Before taking the position at Tennessee in 1887, Dabney had written his wife expressing his enthusiastic willingness to "spend my whole energy" in the task of revitalizing the university. In striking contrast, Dabney wrote despondently to Peabody in 1904, "I want to be spent for the greatest results," which the conditions in Tennessee prevented. In fact, he confided to Peabody, the South could expect no great university for the next twenty years. "Baltimore had a great chance, but the Johns Hopkins has largely thrown away its opportunity to work an Educational revolution in the South. The University of Virginia is stuck fast in the mire of local politics and sectional prejudice. Vanderbilt is hopelessly sectarian; what can you expect of an institution governed by Methodist bishops! Tulane is our best hope, but is too far off in one corner." No doubt with John Spencer Bassett's iconoclasm and the *South Atlantic Quar-*

terly in mind, Dabney described Durham's Trinity College as "the most Enlightening institution in the South!" Absent was any favorable comment about state universities. Cincinnati, on the other hand, offered a university with abundant financial and moral support. In an attempt to relieve his guilt about abandoning the South, Dabney assured himself that Cincinnati could be made to "exert a profound influence"[120] on the region. Filled with these dreams, Dabney left Tennessee on amicable terms, although he felt that the administration's regret at his departure was less than sincere.[121]

Dabney was far too pessimistic about his administration. Although meager, the appropriation that he secured established a new but tenuous relationship between the university and the state. The appropriation vindicated Dabney's often-recited claim that the university was a legitimate instrument of the state. The first two years after Dabney's departure provided little evidence of any substantial improvement in the college's financial condition. In 1907, however, under the leadership of Brown Ayres and Philander P. Claxton, the university secured a $50,000 appropriation over the next two years. For the first time, state money would be used to defray the school's operating expenses. In 1909 the legislature passed a measure allocating 7 percent of the state's gross annual revenue to support higher education.[122]

University leadership also was instrumental in passing legislation providing financial support for the state's public schools. The result of highly organized educational campaigns launched in 1906, a general education law was passed in 1909 appropriating 25 percent of Tennessee's gross annual revenue for a general education fund. In addition, an act was passed abolishing district school control in favor of a system of county school boards. In 1913, a compulsory attendance law also was passed. Educational progressives had reason to celebrate what Dewey Grantham has described as "impressive gains."[123] These accomplishments reflected the organizational skill of Claxton, Ayres, cooperative board members, and educational enthusiasts in the General Assembly. But they also represented the legacy of Charles Dabney's progressive activism, his conviction that the university had a vital role to play in advancing public education, and his tireless efforts to transform the university into an institution of public service.

An equally important legacy of the Dabney administration was the philosophy of practical education. The board hired him to implement a program of practical pedagogy. By promoting agricultural instruction, the experiment station, the professional schools, and academic specialization, Dabney accomplished this task. Securing Morrill and Hatch funds allowed the president to expand agricultural instruction and experimentation. By the 1930s, agricultural research was still the leading scholarly pursuit at Tennessee.[124] Dabney's pedagogical utilitarianism and his abiding faith in material progress were the logical extension of the New South ideology. Under Dabney's administration, the University of Tennessee embraced practical education not as an abstraction but as the educational philosophy intrinsic to the New South ideology. In doing so, however, it swallowed its banal assumptions about inevitable progress, its seemingly self-evident equation between technical education and social uplift, and its devaluation of traditional education. His administration also reinforced the university's approval of educational institutions that endorsed racial separation and the economic subordination of women.

Professionalizing education in Knoxville, Dabney helped realign university instruction to meet what progressives considered the social needs of the New South. His efforts also fostered the coalescence of the region's new middle class. Along with university presidents in the North, he molded the executive office in the image of the corporate manager. Like efficiency experts throughout America, he sought to impose bureaucratic order by emphasizing standardized procedure and executive control. Mirroring the efforts of university administrators throughout the country, he fervently promoted the ideals of research, academic specialization, and faculty professionalization. Charles Dabney's tenure at the University of Tennessee is not only a chronicle of buildings built and faculty hired. It is also the story of how one university president used his position to teach an antebellum college the lessons of the New South. In turn, that university helped refashion the region.

Dabney and his administration accomplished this by infusing the ideal of public service into the university. Through its support of farmers' institutes and scientific investigation, Dabney believed that the university could help alleviate the region's manifold woes. By encouraging professors to participate in the farmers' institutes and extension lectures, he crystallized the emerging ideal of academic responsibility to society. Agricultural and engineering extension work during the Harcourt Morgan administration in the 1920s as well as university cooperation with the Tennessee Valley Authority during the 1930s illustrated the resilience of Dabney's ideals.[125]

He was also convinced that offering a wider variety of professional courses would supply technical experts for southern industry and commerce. The Summer School of the South would improve the quality of elementary school teaching and serve as a beacon for the southern educational crusade. Attended by thousands, the school became a model for others of its kind. At the same time, it became a powerful source of inspiration for the education campaigns that swept through the South between 1905 and 1913. The controversy surrounding Dabney's association with the SEB suggests that progressives had to accommodate strong traditions of decentralized authority and local control. It also illuminates the cultural and ideological barriers that prevented Dabney from understanding the world that rural southerners inhabited.

Notes

1. Dabney, "Memoir." The letters relating to his daughter's death are found in Dabney's personal papers at the Southern Historical Collection (SHC), Chapel Hill, North Carolina. Unfortunately, I cannot confirm the date of his daughter's death or the particulars of his letters. Like most who have examined Dabney, I focused my analysis on his public life, much to the exclusion of his private life, which is reasonably well documented in the collection at the SHC. The letters provide an invaluable insight into Victorian attitudes toward death and the afterlife. They also offer us a saddening view of a time when pathogens and viruses made life more fragile than we will ever know.

2. Ibid.

3. Montgomery et al., *To Foster Knowledge,* 135. For the popularity among postwar American students of German universities emphasizing original research at the graduate level, see Peter Novick, *That Noble Dream,* 21–23.

4. Dabney, "Memoir," 122–23, 125.

5. Ibid. At the time of the decision to establish a separate college, Dabney had been working in connection with members of the Watauga Club, an agricultural organization, to establish an industrial school in North Carolina that, according to Dabney, "would absorb a very small fund which remained of a land grant . . . the interest which was being used by the University of North Carolina." See untitled personal memoir in folder #71, box 5, Dabney Papers, UNC. Also see "Plan of an Industrial School for North Carolina," folder #73, box 5, Dabney Papers, UNC.

6. Quoted in Dabney, "Memoir," 123.

7. Ibid., 125–26.

8. Ibid., 126–28.

9. Ibid., 188.

10. Dabney to Comfort, July 11, 1887, folder #71, box 5, Dabney Papers, UNC.

11. Ibid.

12. Dabney to Heck, July 11, 1887, University Letter Books, box 1, A.R. 57, Dabney Papers, UTK; O. P. Temple to Dabney, July 13, 1887, in Dabney memoir, folder #71, box 5, Dabney Papers, UNC.

13. Dabney to Mary Brent Dabney, July 24, 1887, folder #72, box 5, Dabney Papers, UNC.

14. Ibid.

15. Ibid.

16. Temple to Dabney, July 18, 1887, in Dabney Papers, UNC; Temple to Dabney, July 29, 1887, folder #72, box 5, Dabney Papers, UNC; Dabney, "Memoir," 199. For a dis-

cussion of the evolution of the managerial university president at a representative northern college, see Leslie, *Gentlemen and Scholars,* chapter 7.

17. Montgomery et al., *To Foster Knowledge,* chapter 7; Montgomery, *The Volunteer State Forges Its University,* chapter 3. Not only Mitchell and Hill, but also James Kirkland, president of Vanderbilt University and Dabney's contemporary, adopted corporate managerialism as a mental framework for their administrations. See Conkin, *Gone with the Ivy,* 97–98.

18. As Frederick Rudolph described the change in the character of university presidents, "The capacity to lead now assumed a tremendous importance in college and university affairs. In contrast with the modern university, the old college was a place where nothing happened and where the president by a kind of indifference or remoteness . . . performed an effortless role in seeing to it that nothing did happen," *The American College and University,* 423; see also the chapter titled "The Organized Institution."

19. Dabney, "Memoir," 204, 205; "President's Report to the Board of Trustees," January 26, 1888, AR 144, folder #40, Dabney Papers, UTK.

20. Dabney to Charles Plumb, September 14, 1887, University Letter Books #2, box 1, AR 57, Dabney Papers, UTK; "President's Report to the Board of Trustees," Dabney Papers, UTK; Dabney met Plumb, a graduate of the Massachusetts Agricultural College, on an inspection tour of northern agricultural institutions. Montgomery, *The Volunteer State Forges Its University,* 43.

21. Merriam, *Higher Education in Tennessee,* 98.

22. Dabney to E. H. Sacramero, March 8, 1888, University Letter Books #2, box 1, AR 57, Dabney Papers, UTK. By the beginning of the twentieth century, agricultural and mechanical colleges were cooperating to promote diversification, the use of farm machinery, and financial management for small farmers. The forces of agricultural progressivism "organized around the A and M colleges, and would become further strengthened with the evolution of the Farm Bureaus and Cooperative Extension Service," in Glotzer, *Higher Education in the American South,* 245.

23. "Report of the President," *University of Tennessee Record* (March 1902): 185, UTK archives.

24. Montgomery et al., *To Foster Knowledge,* 140.

25. "Report of the President," *Report of the Board of Trustees,* 1887–88, 23–25.

26. Ibid., 25–26; Dabney, "Memoir," 219–20.

27. "Report of the President," *Report of the Board of Trustees,* 1887–88, 27, UTK archives; see also Montgomery et al., *To Foster Knowledge,* 141. Accompanying Dabney's departmental rationalization was the establishment of the office of dean of the college. The dean was responsible for monitoring student academic progress, counseling students, and administering admission exams. Although the president still bore an inordinate responsibility for the school's day-to-day operation, the dean, along with the commandant of cadets, alleviated much of the burden.

Academic specialization continued throughout Dabney's administration. In his report for the years 1896 to 1898 the president cited the establishment of a separate department of history and a chair of modern languages, which included French, German, and Spanish. Paralleling the work of Mitchell and Hill, Dabney also made efforts to combine government and university agencies. In exchange for the use of the university's facilities, the Weather Bureau of the U.S. Department of Agriculture offered instruction in meteorology. *Report of the Board of Trustees,* 1899, 14; Montgomery, *The Volunteer State Forges Its University,* 48.

28. Montgomery, *The Volunteer State Forges Its University,* 20–22.

29. Ibid. For the classical and liberal arts positions Dabney turned overwhelmingly to southerners. For instance, Thomas W. Jordan, M.A., from UVA became professor of Latin, English language, and literature. To be sure, there were exceptions to the president's selection of northerners for the scientific and technical positions. For example, Charles E. Wait, Ph.D., formerly of UVA, was appointed professor of general and analytical chemistry at Tennessee. Overall, though, Dabney preferred northerners for key positions such as agriculture and mechanical education.

30. Moore, *Reforming Southern Education,* 57. Dabney's faculty reorganization got him into trouble with the governor, but it won the favor of W. J. McGhee of the Smithsonian Institute. Involved in the University of California's consideration of Dabney for the position of president, McGhee wrote to Daniel Coit Gilman of Johns Hopkins, "Of course the [faculty] reorganization was highly gratifying to the state, and to southern educators generally; indeed, within a year, Dr. Dabney had won the candid support of the entire state, with the exception of a limited number of local people, while in another year everybody was satisfied and delighted with the progress of the institution." McGhee to Gilman, January 2, 1899, folder #86, box 6, Dabney Papers, UNC.

31. "Report of the President," *Report of the Board of Trustees,* 1887–88, 39–46, UTK archives. The principal from which the interest was derived came from the Congressional Land Grant of 1806.

32. Ibid.

33. Ibid., 51–59.

34. Ibid., 59.

35. Ibid., 61–63.

36. *Report of the Board of Trustees,* December 20, 1890, 8–16, UTK archives.

37. Ibid.

38. Alan I. Marcus, *Agricultural Science and the Quest for Legitimacy,* 38–39.

39. "Report of the Board of Trustees," *University of Tennessee Record* (January 1899): 16, UTK archives.

40. Montgomery, *The Volunteer State Forges Its University,* 76; see also "Report of the President," *University of Tennessee Record* (January 1900): 288, UTK archives.

41. "Report of the President," *Report of the Board of Trustees,* December 20, 1890, 25, UTK archives.

42. Ibid., 26–27; "Report of the President," *Report of the Board of Trustees,* 1894, 32–33, UTK archives.

43. "Report of the President," *University of Tennessee Record* (February 1903): 92; see also "Biennial Report of the Board of Trustees," *University of Tennessee Record* (February 1903): 72–73, UTK archives; Montgomery, *The Volunteer State Forges Its University,* 52–53.

44. "Report of the President," *University of Tennessee Record* (March 1904): 15–17.

45. "Report of the President," *Report of the Board of Trustees,* February 1903, 92, UTK archives.

46. "Report of the President," *University of Tennessee Record* (March 1904): 8–14, UTK archives.

47. Ibid., 8–14.

48. In fact, the GEB sustained the Summer School of the South in its first few years with an annual grant of $10,000 covering the sessions 1903 to 1905. Philander P. Claxton to Wallace Buttrick, February 12, 1908, GEB folder, box 57, Peabody Papers, LOC.

49. Grantham, *Southern Progressivism,* 270. Montgomery supports the argument that the summer school advertised both the University of Tennessee and the movement for southern educational reform. See Montgomery, "The Summer School of the South," 361–81.

50. "Report of the President," *University of Tennessee Record* (February 1903): 89–91, UTK archives.

51. Ibid. However, the translation of progressive theory into practice often failed. As William Link demonstrates, local resistance to school consolidation, increased taxation, and rural school supervisors often scuttled the efforts of progressives to create a centralized education system. Link, *The Paradox of Southern Progressivism,* 278–283.

52. "Report of the Board of Trustees," February 1901, 12, UTK archives. The president attributed the department's growth to the marvels of the new building. From seven in 1890 the department's enrollment climbed to eighty-five by 1899.

53. "Report of the President," *Report of the Board of Trustees,* 1887–1888, 62–63.

54. "Report of the President," *Report of the Board of Trustees,* 1890, 40–41; ibid., 1892, 28–29; ibid., 1894, 34–35, UTK archives.

55. "Report of the President," *Report of the Board of Trustees,* 1894, 34–35.

56. Dabney, "The Organization of Scientific and Technical Education," address before the Association of Southern Colleges and Preparatory Schools, Columbia, S.C., November 1, 1899, in *University of Tennessee Record* (January 1900). It should be noted that Dabney's address was for the consumption of representatives of both public and private southern institutions, many of whom did not share the president's enthusiasm for technical instruction. In large part, the address was an attempt to justify scientific training at southern universities.

57. Merriam, *Higher Education in Tennessee,* 97.

58. Morton to Dabney, April 5, 1899, folder #86, box 6, Dabney Papers, UNC.

59. "Report of the Board of Trustees," January 1898, 12–13. These included the academic, agricultural, mechanical, medical, and law departments. Dabney's penchant for quantitative measurements of progress was evident in this last yardstick of progress: With the exception of the law department, the others represented not so much the addition of academic disciplines but the rationalization of existing curricula.

60. "Report of the Board of Trustees," January 1898, 12–13.

61. Ibid. For a chronicle of Dabney's building accomplishments, see Neal O'Steen, "The University of Tennessee," 266–68; quote is from Dabney, "As Is Education So Is Production," 3. For a discussion of the transition from a pedagogy emphasizing moral authority, personal relations, and respectability to one that placed a premium on personal initiative and enterprise in the marketplace, see Leloudis, *Schooling the New South,* chapter 1.

62. Dabney to J. B. Bell, September 29, 1899, box 2, XIII C, "Agricultural College," University Papers, 1867–1901, UTK archives.

63. Dabney, "Technical Education in the South," unpublished address, folder #32, box 26, Dabney Papers, UNC; Montgomery, *The Volunteer State Forges Its University,* 43.

64. Dabney to Bell, September 29, 1899, box 2, XIII C, "Agricultural College," University Papers, 1867–1901, UTK archives.

65. The exponents of diversification and scientific farming could prove that soil conservation, livestock production, and the cultivation of feed and food crops would supplement the incomes of struggling farmers. What they ignored were the structural factors militating against crop diversification. Historian Gilbert Fite examines why southern farmers, most of whom were sharecroppers and tenants, resisted the injunctions to diversify: "Habit and tradition were strong, many landowners insisted that their sharecroppers and tenants grow cotton, farmers were suspicious of 'book farming,' and management abilities were low among the relatively illiterate farmers. The soils and climate of the South made it difficult to change crop and livestock patterns. . . . The absence of markets for some commodities was also a deterrent to diversification of commercial crops. Finally, the lack of capital and long-term credit at reasonable costs precluded farmers' reorganizing their operations into more profitable enterprises." Most farms were simply too small and the methods of production too rudimentary to adopt scientific farming. As Fite points out, southern farmers desperately needed commercial surpluses to acquire the revenue necessary for a decent standard of living. Capital was also needed if farmers were to apply the modernizers' innovations. "The critical problem of how to help southern farmers to become successful commercial operators was largely ignored by the diversifiers," in *Cotton Fields No More,* 81–90. See also Glotzer, *Higher Education in the American South,* 244.

66. Montgomery, *The Volunteer State Forges Its University,* 44.

67. *Report of the Board of Trustees,* December 20, 1894, 27, UTK archives.

68. The elimination of the preparatory department actually was a gradual process that culminated in the dismantling of the final subfreshman class in mathematics in 1894. The exceptions were classes offering instruction in Latin and Greek, which were

not offered by the public schools. "Report of the President," *Report of the Board of Trustees,* December 20, 1894, 23. Dewey Grantham summarizes the educational blight in this way: "Outside of the larger cities, there was really no system of public education worthy of the name, and the numerous private institutions were for the most part little better." In addition to state constitutional prohibitions against levying taxes for schools, the "maintenance of publicly supported high schools was almost totally absent from state law, and in some commonwealths no annual appropriations were made for higher education," in *Southern Progressivism,* 246. For an equally dismal appraisal of high schools before the education crusade, see Harlan, *Separate and Unequal,* 28.

69. Grantham, *Southern Progressivism,* 272.

70. Dabney, "Review of the Year," *University of Tennessee Record* 1 (February 1898): 13, UTK archives.

71. Ibid.

72. "Report of the President," *Report of the Board of Trustees,* December 20, 1894, UTK archives.

73. "Report of the President," *Report of the Board of Trustees,* December 20, 1890, UTK archives; Montgomery, *The Volunteer State Forges Its University,* 29.

74. "Report of the President," *Report of the Board of Trustees,* December 20, 1894, UTK archives.

75. "Report of the President," *University of Tennessee Record* (March 1902): 177–78, UTK archives.

76. Interestingly, it was the Morrill Land Grant Act of 1862 that revived southern military education after the Civil War. The Morrill Act required land grant schools to insert military tactics in the curriculum but it did not require them to become military schools on the scale of places such as The Citadel. But like most other southern land grant institutions, the University of Tennessee did adopt the accoutrements of a full-blown military school. Northern schools, by contrast, tended to adopt a minimalistic approach to military instruction. The southern preference for an expansive application of military government was rooted in the Lost Cause. See Andrew, "Soldiers, Christians, and Patriots," 677–710.

77. T. M. Landau to Dabney, 1889, folder #74, box 5, Dabney Papers, UNC. See also John U. Led to Dabney, January 23, 1889, ibid.

78. Merriam, *Higher Education in Tennessee,* 101.

79. "Report of the President," *Report of the Board of Trustees,* December 20, 1890, 39–40, UTK archives.

80. Ibid. By no means was the liberal capitalist ethic of self-control dominant throughout the South. As historian Ted Ownby points out, "The lessons of economic morality—sobriety, thrift, and self-denial—that accompanied the development of a commercially minded Northern middle class in the nineteenth century were slow to gain acceptance in the rural South." The cultural dynamic central to the postbellum South was the conflict between evangelical maxims and the masculine attitudes inherent in Southern honor. In Ownby, *Subduing Satan,* 11–12. The university strengthened

the traditional evangelical ethos by reinforcing its compatibility with the behavioral demands of industrial capitalism in the New South.

81. Montgomery, *The Volunteer State Forges Its University,* 34; "Report of the President," *Report of the Board of Trustees,* December 20, 1894, 28–30, UTK archives.

82. Montgomery et al., *To Foster Knowledge,* 148.

83. "Report of the President," *Report of the Board of Trustees,* December 20, 1894, 28–30, UTK archives.

84. Kirkland to Dabney, July 16, 1893, folder #76, box 5, Dabney Papers, UNC.

85. "Report of the President," *University of Tennessee Record* (January 1901): 24–25, UTK archives. In his memoirs, Dabney made it clear that this was the principal reason for admitting women to the university. See subheading "Women in the University of Tennessee," 240–41. Dabney, "Memoir."

86. E. J. Sanford quoted in Montgomery et al., *To Foster Knowledge,* 150.

87. Florence Skiffington, "The Broader Education for Women," *University of Tennessee Record* 6 (1901): 358–61.

88. Dabney, "Memoir," 240.

89. Dean, "Learning to Be New Women," 291–95; quotes on p. 295.

90. Ibid., 294–95.

91. McCandless, "Progressivism and the Higher Education of Southern Women," 302, 323. For a discussion of the conflict between a curriculum emphasizing womanly virtues and the new elective curriculum, designed to meet women's professional aspirations, at private women's colleges in the South, see McDonald, "To Educate Neither Belles Nor Bluestockings," 59–70.

92. Established in 1887, the association might be seen as a manifestation of the organizational voluntarism stimulated by the war. As Morton Keller argues, "Large numbers of Americans then, ranging from secessionist southerners to nationalist northern intellectuals, from civic-minded business and professional men to workingmen, farmers and entrepreneurs, were spurred by the war to create new forms of voluntary association." The experience of wartime mobilization taught them the possibilities of organization but left them frustrated with a "polity that did not readily satisfy their demands," in *Affairs of State,* 12.

93. Moore, *Reforming Southern Education,* 63.

94. Alvord to Dabney, May 6, 1893, folder #76, box 5, Dabney Papers, UNC.

95. Moore, *Reforming Southern Education,* 67.

96. Montgomery, *The Volunteer State Forges Its University,* 73–74, including quote.

97. True, *A History of Agricultural Experimentation and Research,* 183. His new responsibilities included coordinating the experiment stations with the department and supervising the Office of Irrigation Inquiry. Benefiting from his experience at the North Carolina experiment station, he created a dairy division, a division of agrostology (concerned with revitalizing land after cultivation through the use of new plants), and a bureau of agricultural soils under the jurisdiction of the Department of Agriculture.

98. Dabney to Page, March 6, 1894, folder #79, box 5, Dabney Papers, UNC. In an-

other letter to Page, Dabney expressed his desire to coordinate all scientific agencies with the Department of Agriculture. Reflecting late nineteenth-century positivism, Dabney celebrated technocratic managerialism: "A great national department of Economic Science is the dream of the scientific men of Washington. We have all the elements of it now. . . . Only one thing more is needed—a permanent scientific director, to form the keystone in a perfectly formed and united arch of scientific agencies supporting the industries of the people." Dabney to Page, February 21, 1896, folder #81, box 5, Dabney Papers, UNC.

99. W. J. McGhee to Daniel Coit Gilman, January 4, 1899, folder #86, box 6, Dabney Papers, UNC. Dabney was also sought for the presidency of Johns Hopkins. See Dabney to Samuel Garner, March 1901, and "Southern Man Needed for the Presidency of J.H.U: Why not Charles Dabney?" ibid.

100. "Report of the President," *Report of the Board of Trustees,* 1887–88, 61–62.

101. Ibid., December 20, 1894, 34; see also ibid., 61–62; ibid., December 20, 1890, 42; ibid., December 20, 1892, 14, UTK archives.

102. Montgomery, *The Volunteer State Forges Its University,* 77–81.

103. "Report of the President," *University of Tennessee Record* (March 1904): 1, UTK archives.

104. Leloudis, *Schooling the South,* 115.

105. Woodward, *Origins of the New South,* 436.

106. Ibid., 403; Dabney, "Memoir," 279–81.

107. Dabney to General John Eaton, February 25, 1901, folder #96, box 6, Dabney Papers, UNC.

108. Harlan, *Separate and Unequal,* 97–98; Anderson, *The Education of Blacks in the South,* 94–96.

109. Baldwin to Sanford, January 13, 1902, folder #97, box 6, Dabney Papers, UNC.

110. Sanford to Baldwin, January 22, 1902, folder #97, box 6, Dabney Papers, UNC; Dabney to Vawter, August 26, 1904, box 7, Dabney Papers, UNC.

111. Sanford to Baldwin, ibid.

112. Dabney to Vawter, ibid.

113. Dabney to Northrop, January 22, 1904, file 104, box 7, Dabney Papers, UNC.

114. Dabney to R. Webb, February 8, 1904, file 105, box 7, Dabney Papers, UNC.

115. Ibid.

116. Historian William Link describes Charles Dabney, Walter Hines Page, Samuel Mitchell, and Charles McIver as "intersectionalists" who advocated a comprehensive change to the rural way of life. "In contrast to social reformers elsewhere in early twentieth century America, they identified underdevelopment, rather than excessive industrialization, as a fundamental cause of their region's social problems," in Link, *A Hard Country and a Lonely Place,* 84–88.

117. Dabney to Peabody, January 8, 1904, box 57, Peabody Papers, LOC.

118. For a discussion of the elitism of early reformers in the North Carolina graded school movement, see Leloudis, *Schooling the New South,* 85–88.

119. Ibid.

120. Dabney to Peabody, General Education Board file, box 57, Peabody Papers, LOC.

121. Montgomery et al., *To Foster Knowledge,* 155.

122. Ibid., 163–65.

123. Grantham, *Southern Progressivism,* 252–53.

124. Montgomery et al., *To Foster Knowledge,* 183.

125. For a discussion of the university's continuing commitment to public service and its relationship to the Tennessee Valley Authority, see Montgomery et al., *To Foster Knowledge,* chapter 8.

5

A University for the State: Chancellor Walter Barnard Hill and the University of Georgia, 1899–1906

A proponent of education for social advancement, Walter Hill cast his vision of the university in the idiom of the New South creed. In his efforts to revise and expand university curricula, reorganize systems of administration, improve admission standards, attract financial support, screen faculty appointments, and construct alliances with regional organizations, he followed the dominant currents of progressive educational reform.[1] No less than William R. Harper of Chicago or Andrew D. White of Cornell, Walter B. Hill was, in Thorstein Veblen's words, a "captain of erudition" who embraced the values of efficiency and rationality.[2]

At a time when most southerners were skeptical of any kind of public education, Hill portrayed the university as an instrument of social service. The university should be a force for revitalizing southern society. Although popular among northern progressive educators, the service ideal of university education assumed special meaning in the New South.[3] State governments bent on remedying the alleged fiscal excess of Reconstruction opposed anything but nominal financial support for higher education. Hill and others compensated by trying to generate mass support for educational reform. At the same time, they promoted the image of the university as an extension of the State. To accomplish these goals, the chancellor and forward-looking board members solicited financial assistance from wealthy northern philanthropists.

In these ways, Hill helped construct the foundation for what would become a modern university. In the process, he contributed to the formation of a nascent bureaucratic state in the South of the early twentieth century. Mediating between tradition and progress, he infused the southern progressive vision of orderly change into his program for university reform. In this way, his work anticipated the South's confrontation with modernity.[4] In his attempt to refashion southern values of defensive rural autonomy and individualism, Hill became an architect of what one historian has described as the "Social Efficiency State."[5] At the same time, his program to professionalize academic learning encouraged the formation of the South's new middle class.

Born in Talbotton, Georgia in 1851, Walter Barnard Hill was soft-spoken and amicable. His personal attributes gave little indication of his potential for strong executive leadership. After attending the University at Athens from 1868 to 1871, he graduated with a bachelor's degree and a year of training in the law. On leaving Athens, he began practicing law at his father's firm in Macon. When the elder Hill became a superior court judge in 1873, Walter Hill formed a partnership with N. E. Harris, a college friend, which lasted until Hill's election as chancellor in 1899.[6]

Before Hill made it his mission to professionalize the college presidency, he busied himself with professionalizing the practice of law. An accomplished and erudite lawyer, he gained a reputation for his thorough court preparation and his scholarly analysis of arcane legal matters. Hill contributed to the formation of the Georgia Bar Association in 1884. He was also a member of the American Bar Association. He put considerable time and energy into revising the Georgia Code of Law. His judicious attention to technical detail would serve him well at the University of Georgia (UGA).[7]

Representing prominent railroad companies before the United States Courts and the Supreme Court, he acquired a national reputation for his litigation skills. In 1887, he was elected president of the Georgia Bar Association. Three years later, he testified before congressional subcommittees on judicial reform. That same year, he was invited to give an address in New York City at the centennial celebration of the founding of the Federal Judiciary. The program included such prominent figures as justice John Marshall Harlan, senator William Evarts, and chief justice Edward M. Paxson.[8] Clearly, Hill benefited from the associational network that developed out of the late nineteenth-century drive toward professionalization.

Legal matters did not absorb all of Hill's attention. While living in Macon he was an active member of the Methodist Episcopal Church and a devoted prohibitionist. His vigorous activism reflected something of the social control impulse underlying much of southern progressivism.[9] Hill believed that the proscription of alcohol consumption was not simply a southern issue but a cause worthy of a well-organized national movement. Opposition to the liquor traffic generated friction with several of the party's prominent members. His prohibitionism may have alienated some powerful Democrats, but it garnered him the respect of leaders in the temperance movement. One of these prohibitionists was Rebecca Latimer Felton, the influential political activist and reformer. Indefatigable, Hill also served as a trustee for Vanderbilt University;

as one of three white trustees for Paine College, a school for blacks in Augusta; and as a member of the law department at Mercer University.[10]

Hill's election to the chancellorship of the state university in 1899 marked an important departure for higher education in Georgia. It symbolized the university's embrace of technical, professional education as a legitimate pursuit for public higher education. Although by no means complete, this shift away from the tradition of classical education toward scientific training reflected the pedagogical utilitarianism at the core of progressivism. New South progressives such as Hill hoped that educational reform would provide the catalyst for southern regeneration. The university would be the incubator for the leadership and ideas that would drive the reform movement.

Against the opposition of conservatives, who hoped to maintain the school's tradition of selecting a minister to head the college, a group of Georgia trustees sought a nonclerical administrator for the position. The plan was to find a candidate more suited to the demands of a modern university. Since 1878, the college had been guided by strong defenders of the classical tradition. But the classics had come under withering criticism from proponents of the New South creed. Central to the New South ideology was the conviction that industrialization and agricultural diversification would alleviate southern poverty. Men such as Henry Grady, editor of the *Atlanta Constitution* and leading champion of the New South, vigorously promoted technical education as a key component of economic progress. Under the administration of P. H. Mell, however, the university failed to cultivate a technological college. A reflection of the state's lack of confidence in the university's commitment to practical education was its decision in 1887 to locate the new Georgia Institute of Technology in Atlanta. According to historian Thomas G. Dyer, the loss of the technical institute seriously hampered the university's efforts to provide practical education.[11]

The university administration matched its lack of enthusiasm for technical education by its virtual indifference to the Agricultural College. Chancellor Boggs, who served from 1889 to 1899, together with Henry C. White, president of the State Agricultural College from 1890 to 1907, did little to address the grievances of Georgia farmers dismayed by the university's cursory efforts at agricultural extension and demonstration work. The administration's unwillingness to remedy the lamentable state of agricultural instruction also antagonized supporters of denominational colleges. Representatives of the private colleges accused the state university of extravagance and argued that it diverted money from Georgia's more pressing educational needs. Fortunately, Hill's credentials as a prohibitionist and an active Methodist appeased the denominational critics while his professional qualifications satisfied the state press and the public.[12] With Hill's election, the board acquiesced to the demand for a more utilitarian education.

The image of the corporate manager shaped the chancellor's conception of administration. Defining his relationship to the school's administrative system, Hill, along with other southern progressive educators, turned to the example of university presidents at the nation's leading institutions. In his annual report to the Board of Trustees for 1900, he highlighted the trend among northern universities toward corporate management techniques. He undergirded his own position by pointing to the growing number of laypeople in key executive positions at larger northern schools. Quoting from an article on the changing character of university administration, Hill reinforced the ideas of efficiency, administrative rationality, and executive autonomy. He also extolled the virtue of technical expertise in academic management. Admitting the pitfalls of comparisons between business and university management, he felt obligated to "call attention to the general movement now going on in the world of education, which tends to the concentration of authority and responsibility in corporate management."[13] Applauding his managerialism, one journalist wrote, "The leading university of the present day must have at its head a business man—a man of large purpose, of comprehensive grasp, and a far seeing mentality."[14]

More than an attempt to buttress the chancellor's autonomy against trustee intrusion, Hill's claim to managerial latitude reflected the growing complexity of higher education in the early twentieth century. As professional interests distanced board members from school operations, college presidents assumed a larger role in determining university policy. The chancellor also spoke the language of business efficiency in which board members were increasingly conversant. Determined to promote bureaucratic efficiency, Hill also was intent on enhancing the professional status of his office. The academic revolution of the late nineteenth century found its vanguard in the efficiency-minded university presidents who sought to streamline administration and shore up executive authority.[15]

Although impressed by Hill, Georgia trustees did not meekly acquiesce to his administrative agenda. As late as 1905, he could still complain that the board conducted "the election of professors and promotion of tutors as part of their individual patronage." The board often neglected to consult faculty members when legislating on matters that required their expertise. An indication of the board's unilateral style of governance was its refusal to include the chancellor at regular board sessions. Although Hill often appeared before the board to present reports, the policy of excluding the chancellor from board meetings remained unchanged until 1905. Pointing to the University of Wisconsin as an example of modern administration, Hill worked to reduce trustee autocracy and rationalize relations between the board, the chancellor, and the faculty.[16]

When Hill arranged for a group of board members to visit the University of Wisconsin, he hoped that they would learn from their northern counterparts that their primary responsibility was to formulate university policy, not exercise executive control. Appealing to the ethic of professionalism, Hill addressed the members not as trustees but as lawyers. The chancellor attacked the board's longtime practice of making administrative changes based on limited information gathered from annual campus visits: "Suppose that a committee of competent lawyers from New York—men whose ability and whose superiority in a certain sense would be readily acknowledged—should come down upon you in your office for one week, turn you out, and undertake during that period to try your cases in the court house, to advise your clients and to run your office business without any previous knowledge of these matters and without even calling you into consultation—what havoc would be wrought!"[17]

Continuing his analogy, the chancellor contrasted the chaos created by meddling lawyers with the efficiency generated by professional experts working "in an advisory capacity." Hill's argument for a rational division of labor between the board and faculty rested on the assumption that the latter "lived in an academic atmosphere, somewhat removed from touch with actual life." The faculty should accept the leadership of the more hard-headed trustees. But on technical questions of curriculum and departmental development, the board should defer to its expert faculty. Certainly, this was not the voice of the antebellum college president extolling the university as a sanctuary for "mental discipline." When making decisions relating to the faculty's domain, he proposed that the board should not act until it had canvassed "the opinions and views of the faculty on those facts." Although the board apparently received his disquisition as "a strange new gospel," it signaled its conversion by passing a resolution stating that in the future the chancellor would be invited to attend all sessions of the Board of Trustees.[18] The board's decision gave added legitimacy to Hill's scheme of bureaucratic administration. It also suggested the chancellor's growing influence in university administration.

The chancellor's efforts to professionalize the hiring process were reflected in his faculty appointments. When the chair of philosophy and education was vacated in 1903, Hill recruited T. J. Woofter, a University of Chicago Ph.D. then working at the State Normal and Industrial School, for the position.[19] When the school established the position of university state agent, which also carried with it a faculty appointment, the chancellor saw to it that J. S. Stewart, president of the North Georgia Agricultural College at Dahlonega, was hired. Stewart's work in the accrediting of high schools led Charles Dabney to describe him as a pioneer in improving secondary education in the South. Similarly, the completion of a new library building in 1904 spurred the faculty to suggest hiring a director trained in library science. The chancellor accepted the faculty's suggestion, canvassing both northern and southern institutions for suitable candidates.[20] Although the chancellor worked to professionalize the faculty, he stopped short of allowing it to compromise his larger plans. He may have favored increased faculty salaries, but he balked at pressing the issue in 1904 when he feared it might jeopardize the university's newly acquired financial stability.[21]

In the attempt to redefine the relationship between the board and the university, Chancellor Hill supported legislation requiring the trustees to visit the school before commencement. In July of 1904 the Board of Visitors, composed of university trustees and charged with investigating university operations, suggested that the trustees visit the university while the school's "actual work was in progress." This, the Board of Visitors believed, would help the trustees appreciate the school's genuine needs. The trustees subsequently passed a resolution authorizing its Board of Visitors to examine the university during the school term as well as at commencement. To ensure the bill's passage, Hill wrote to senator W. H. Davis, who had taken charge of the legislation, explaining its importance.[22]

Throughout his administration, Hill solicited the support of influential legislators for university development. Whether the issue was agricultural education, the summer school, or appropriations for campus extension, Hill struggled to forge closer ties between the university and the state. In an address titled "The Twentieth Century University," he summarized his progressive educational philosophy. The university, he announced, "In collaboration with State boards, bureaus, and commissions . . . should look after social and economic conditions."[23]

University involvement in the state's material and social welfare would be the distinguishing characteristic of the twentieth-century university. The chancellor argued that the modern university "will connect its activities more closely with the business and life of the people." Departments of sociology and political economy could be used much like the federal government's agricultural experiment stations. In accumulating and disseminating information, these departments would allow policymakers to "adjust wisely their system of taxation, to solve municipal problems, and to improve the conditions of their penal institutions, reformatories, asylums, almshouses, tenement houses, and so forth." Municipal governments beleaguered by anarchic systems of taxation would benefit from the expertise of economics departments whose professors could apply systems of "scientific taxation." University students trained in sociology could act as field agents reporting on the conditions of reformatories. Their publications, along with statements of "fundamental principles," might lead to "radical reforms in the treatment of criminal and defective classes." Departments of chemistry, sanitary engineering, and medicine would contribute to the welfare of the state by investigating public health. Scientific research into pure food, drugs, water, efficient sewers, and effective building ventilation would "diminish sensibly the rate of sickness and death." Although the university should never abandon its classical curriculum, Hill made it clear that the principal functions of the twentieth-century university were "to investigate, to teach, to publish."[24]

Redefining the structure of the UGA was essential to Hill's plan for university outreach. At the core of the chancellor's concept of the "collective university" were the progressive tenets of administrative rationality and efficiency. The origins of the collective university were in the school's charter, but competition and distance between the branch colleges had prevented its realization. A board committee first recommended renewing the collective university idea, but Hill revitalized it and injected into it his evolving vision of progressive education.[25]

A unified organization would convince university critics of the accomplishments of higher education, he argued. Instead of educational fragmentation, a collectivized university system would generate a sense of common purpose. Coordinating university curricula would prevent inefficient duplication. Moreover, cooperation would benefit the university at Athens and the branch colleges by eliminating the antagonisms that jeopardized funding from a notoriously tight-pursed legislature. Finally, Hill believed that college unity would help equalize the distribution of donations from private sources.[26]

The formation of a voluntary University of Georgia Auxiliary exemplified the progressive impulse for coordination. The auxiliary functioned as a semipublic organization linking citizens and alumni to the university. It also promoted the collective university. However, its primary purpose was to provide a channel for financial contributions from private citizens. By mobilizing alumni and benefactors through a bureaucratic organization, the administration achieved a measure of control over donations and an instrument for planning university development. The chancellor hoped that the auxiliary would mobilize new sources of revenue and inject life into the moribund collective university.[27]

Modeling his vision of the collective university after the administrative plan outlined in his first annual report, Hill promoted a system of loosely affiliated colleges under the guiding hand of a central board of trustees. A modern university needed a board that would formulate policy initiatives while leaving the president functionally autonomous. The collective university would resemble a modern corporation: Like subsidiaries of a major company, each college would have its own faculty and "local commissions" to direct affairs specific to the school, "but under the control of one Board of Trustees—this ultimate control insuring the unity and congruity of the system."[28]

To facilitate coordination between schools, Hill recommended in October 1900 the creation of a council of executives from each institution.[29] The council would meet annually to discuss the interests of the collective university. Following the chancellor's advice, the board created the University Council in 1901. The new council consisted of representatives from the North Georgia Agricultural College at Dahlonega, the Georgia School of Technology in Atlanta, the Georgia Normal and Industrial College at Milledgeville, the Georgia State Industrial College for Colored Youths near Savannah, and the State Normal School in Atlanta.[30]

To promote the collective university, a committee of the Board on Branch Colleges received approval to include each college's catalogue in the university's annual catalogue. To attract support for coordination, the board decided to finance the distribution of 10,000 copies of the new catalogue. The board also directed the chancellor to make annual visits to each branch college. In addition, Chancellor Hill used commencement week to emphasize intercollegiate cooperation by inviting white, male student representatives as well as the presidents from the several colleges to participate in the exercises. With the hearty approval of the board, this practice was continued throughout Hill's administration.[31]

One notable exception to representation on the new council was the Medical College at Augusta. Although the board considered the Medical College an essential feature of the university, its representatives admitted that it had long been considered a separate institution. During Hill's administration the trustees from both institutions sought to improve relations between them. After meetings in November 1903 and May 1904, the university's Board of Trustees agreed to harmonize the curriculum by offering science courses that would prepare students for medical courses at the college in Augusta. Functioning as an intermediary between the board and the Medical College, Chancellor Hill worked to coordinate courses and eliminate duplication.[32]

The chancellor considered coordination an important step in professionalizing medical training in the state. Hill admired Harvard, Columbia, and Johns Hopkins for requiring that medical school applicants have a bachelor of arts or bachelor of science degree. As he observed regretfully, the South was "not prepared to take so advanced a step." Even so, he believed that its medical schools should at least insist that candidates have the equivalent of a high school education. Medical training would improve when candidates received part of a general university education before enrolling at the Medical College in Augusta.[33]

Hill promoted the idea of the collective university with aggressive advertising. Mirroring progressive strategies in the public schools campaign, Hill used the media and a university-sponsored agent to generate interest in educational reform. He also called for an advertising fund to publicize course offerings and extension lectures. In part, fear of competition from denominational schools explained Hill's agitation for the fund. He warned the board that Mercer University and Emory College had already jumped on the promotional bandwagon, hiring agents and advertising in state newspapers. Although attendance had risen for 1900, Hill predicted that the gains would prove ephemeral if the board failed to adopt their competitors' methods. To buttress his position, he pointed to the rewards reaped from a partial advertising campaign launched in Florida the previous year. Astutely, Hill argued that the university's tenuous relationship with the state legislature might be stabilized by an investment in boosterism. "The University would not only get the benefit of the advertising," he wrote, "but its patronage of the newspapers would give to it the support of the press, which would be valuable in its influence on the General Assembly and in other directions."[34] Nevertheless, the board did not create the fund until 1902 and then appropriated little money for it.[35]

Publication of the University *Bulletin*, it was hoped, would counterbalance the board's half-hearted endorsement of the advertising fund. The *Bulletin* would foster a "closer attachment to the old mother" among alumni and publicize evidence of educational progress. Like other progressives, Hill supported the bulletin in the belief that disseminating knowledge could act as a catalyst to social change, the *Bulletin*'s primary mission.[36] Using the media to build popular support for the university was insufficient, however, if not complemented by aggressive field work.

Hill first brought the idea of hiring a university publicist to the board's attention in 1899. The university agent would conduct statewide education revivals that would stimulate university enrollment and solidify alumni support. When the proposal was rejected, he submitted a joint resolution from the branch colleges calling for a state agent to promote the collective university.[37] Persuaded by New York philanthropist George Foster Peabody's offer to pay one half of the agent's salary and expenses for two years, the board authorized the position in 1903. On the recommendation of Hill and A. L. Hull, a member of the board, the trustees accepted J. S. Stewart for the job.[38] The university publicist was also expected to function as a high school accrediting agent and as professor of secondary education at UGA.[39]

Establishing a position that combined a faculty appointment with external, professional work set a precedent for the fusion of state and academic functions. Financed at first by philanthropy, the agent would eventually operate at state expense. Before the appointment of a state agent, the chancellor himself operated as the university's chief publicist. Attending countless high school commencements, giving addresses before educational reform organizations, and allocating money to advertise the addition of new departments, Hill made university promotion a priority in his administration.[40]

A logical extension of Hill's collective university was his effort to coordinate state education. The Georgia Constitution of 1877 did not provide financial support for high schools, and unlike many others in the South, the university did not have a preparatory department. These two factors combined to keep college attendance down in Georgia. In addition, high school curricula lacked uniformity in course offerings, quality of instruction, or length of school terms. In an address to the Southern Educational Association at Columbia in 1901, the chancellor intimated the impending changes in admission policy. "All public schools instituted or to be supported by funds or public moneys in this state, shall be considered as parts or members of the university, and shall be under the foregoing directions and regulations."[41] To improve high school standards, he endorsed the idea of developing a list of accredited schools. Most of the responsibility for this initiative went to state agent J. S. Stewart.[42]

Consistent with progressive techniques of "scientific" social analysis, Stewart engaged in extensive field research of Georgia's secondary schools.[43] Meeting local officials and prompting community leaders to construct new schools using local resources, he established the framework for a coordinated system of education. His conciliatory approach apparently won over school authorities throughout the state. Stewart believed that the remedy for the state's shoddy high schools was a system of accreditation then in use by several northern states. Eventually, the board adopted requirements that each high school have at least two teachers, one of whom might be its principal; that each candidate complete thirteen units (a unit was measured as 180 days of class in a particular subject); and that all high school teachers conduct no more than ten recitations a day, each consisting of no more than thirty minutes.[44]

Stewart justified his plan as a strategy for improving cooperation between educational institutions. "The accredited system," he wrote, "exalts the secondary school and its principal. It gives it a state and interstate standing for efficiency and enables communities to build up academies of recognized standing. . . . The accrediting system increases the efficiency of the school [and] improves the scholarship of those entering college."[45] Some school administrators and principals expressed firm support for Stewart's plan: "I am highly pleased," wrote the principal of a school in Darien, Georgia to Chancellor Hill, "with your plan and trust that it will be the means of securing better training in all the schools of the state that pretend to do high school work."[46] Stewart's efforts made Georgia the first state in the South to introduce a system for accrediting high schools. In 1904, 7 public four-year high schools and 4 private four-year high schools had gained accredited status. By 1919, the university had accredited 142 four-year public high schools and 24 private schools.[47]

The importance of Stewart's work for rationalizing state education was not lost on Chancellor Hill. Stewart's extensive traveling and lecturing avoided "antagonizing any form of education" while it effectively "emphasized the unity of the University organization." High school accrediting would standardize secondary education. Thomas Reed, editor of the Athens *Daily Banner* and author of an unpublished history of the university, observed that eliminating the rigorous entrance examination would help close the gap between high school and college by attracting students previously incapable of meeting the requirements. Charles Dabney conceded that the revised entrance requirements were low. Even so, according to Hill the change in admission standards brought the school in conformity with the guidelines of the Southern Association of Preparatory Schools and Colleges. In 1905, 215 students graduated from accredited high schools. (Dabney does not provide a total number of graduates from high schools for that year.) By 1920, 3,391 students of a total enrollment of 22,353 graduated from accredited schools.[48]

Changes in university entrance requirements mirrored those adopted by the State College of Agriculture between 1900 and 1905. The board's efforts to "strengthen and make effective the courses of instruction" in the College of Agriculture amounted to eviscerating the classical component of the degree requirement.[49] The school's considerable growth after 1900 reflected the absence of the tough classical examinations administered in Franklin College, the university's liberal arts school. Although the university's state high schools achieved greater uniformity in academic standards, its overall entrance requirements declined during Hill's period.

Despite the premature claims of improved standards, Stewart and Hill constructed the edifice of a bureaucratic system of high school evaluation. The adoption of standardized procedures for filtering candidates signaled the movement toward a coordinated system of education. The General Education Board (GEB) seemed to agree. In 1905 it took over the responsibility for paying half the salary of the university's state agent from George Foster Peabody. The GEB was so impressed with Stewart's accomplishments that it extended the same offer to ten other southern states. On a regional scale, Hill's administration was instrumental in grafting progressive reform measures onto the framework of southern education.[50]

The chancellor's commitment to improving the educational system went beyond issues obviously connected to the university. Following the prompting of the Southern Education Board (SEB), Hill sponsored a meeting of county superintendents in September 1902. Attended by Charles D. McIver, the South's most distinguished educational progressive, the meeting addressed in statistical detail the conditions and needs of education in Georgia. To a considerable extent, it provided the impetus for the state's campaigns for secondary education. In the summer of 1903 Hill aligned himself with the movement for local taxation for public schools, a plan that was first unveiled at the April 1902 meeting of the Conference for Education in the South at Athens.[51]

The immediate obstacle to local taxation for school improvement was the state constitution of 1877. Not only did it make no provision for public secondary education, but it effectively prohibited local taxation by requiring that two successive grand juries recommend the measure before a referendum could be held on the issue. To pass the measure, the constitution required a two-thirds majority. In an effort to overcome the constitutional roadblock, teachers supported a bill permitting the state to vote on an amendment that would eliminate the grand jury requirement and allow local taxation by counties or districts. Anticipating its passage, governor Joseph M. Terrell called a meeting of education leaders. Hill attended, as did McIver, who represented the SEB. To mobilize public support for the measure, the governor appointed a committee with Hill as chair, state superintendent of education W. B. Merritt as secretary, and Warren Candler, president of Emory University, and Hoke Smith as executive officers.[52]

The bill passed and the committee, with funding from the SEB, began to churn out articles and pamphlets advocating adoption of the McMichael amendment. The committee supported the newspaper campaign with rallies featuring addresses by reformers and politicians. It also published a handbook for speakers that included extracts from the speeches of educational luminaries such as J. L. M. Curry and Charles McIver. Resourcefully, the committee used county court sessions to advertise the local tax position. The publicity campaign countered the assertion that the amendment threatened local control. As Hill pointed out, the amendment only gave communities the option of adopting local taxation in support of public schools. To further the cause, Hill and Merritt formed the Georgia Education Conference. In addition to bringing reformers together during the summer school session, the conference produced the *Summer School News,* which espoused local taxation and education reform. Confidently, Hill attributed the defeat of an amendment separating school taxes along racial lines to the Georgia Education Conference. Altogether, Hill's and the committees' efforts paid off. Despite concerted opposition, the McMichael amendment was ratified by a slight majority in October 1905.[53]

The Georgia Educational Conference also mobilized women in a school improvement campaign. The conference took its lead from the 1902 meeting of the Conference for Education in the South, which endorsed the formation of school improvement clubs. At its meeting in July 1904, the conference called on women to form school improvement societies. Conference leaders justified women's involvement in the campaign by invoking "the strong devotion of the women of the state to the welfare of the children." Like most contemporary advocates for expanding women's activism, conference leaders praised the "fine qualities and powers of womanhood which make them so indispensable to the churches of the land." Gifted with religious sensibilities and the nurturing habits of motherhood, women had a unique role to play in school improvement.[54]

To turn the resolution into reality, Chancellor Hill turned to Nellie F. Phinizy to organize women into school improvement societies. Hill suggested that an organization centered in Athens could supervise the county societies and disseminate literature on their behalf. Hill proposed that women be appointed as district agents to cooperate with county superintendents and give addresses on the club's work at local schools. The chancellor suggested enlisting suffragist Rebecca Latimer Felton as an itinerant agent. Although Phinizy declined the chancellor's offer of the presidency, the organization went ahead. At a meeting in August 1904, Hill's wife, Sallie, was elected president of the School Improvement Club. Women were also elected to the offices of vice president, secretary, and treasurer. With a contribution from the SEB, school improvement leaflets were printed and distributed throughout the state. In support of the movement, its members sustained a large correspondence.[55]

The Georgia school improvement initiative was part of a regionwide campaign launched in North Carolina in 1902. Supported by the SEB, the movement forged a network of school improvement organizations that absorbed women's clubs and teachers throughout the region. According to Mary Cooke Branch Munford, president of the Richmond Education Association and leader of the school improvement effort in Virginia, the movement was developed and coordinated almost entirely by women. By 1909, a woman had been appointed as field organizer in each of the southern states. Extending their domestic credentials to education, the organizations focused on improving school buildings inside and out. They collected money to buy flowers, donated new furniture, planted trees, cleaned and upgraded school interiors, built fences, and provided heating and clean water supplies for the schools. More than schoolhouse maintenance, volunteers actively promoted local taxation, farm demonstration, and public health in the curriculum.[56]

While promoting school reform, improvement societies also afforded women a greater measure of independence. As historian James Leloudis has demonstrated, members of the North Carolina Women's Association for the Betterment of Public Schools replicated the political autonomy denied them in the electoral process by permitting only women the right to vote for officials. Members were expected to participate in local improvement campaigns and to vote in the annual elections; men could join as dues-paying "associate members." School improvement clubs gave women an opportunity to assume leadership roles from which they were excluded in other fields. As executives, delegates to annual conventions, and field agents, women achieved professional fulfillment and social autonomy. As public speakers in the school campaign, they gained new confidence in their abilities and overcame their inhibitions about engaging in activity that was traditionally considered within the male domain.[57]

The School Improvement Leagues afforded women new opportunities for social leadership, but at their core they functioned as vehicles of progressivism. Paralleling the educational revival, improvement leagues were meant to generate community pride in their schools and a commitment to the new vision of education. Schools would not simply mirror the cultural values of the community. Instead, under the leadership of professional educators, they would "interpret the life of its own neighborhood to the young citizens." Echoing male progressives, Munford suggested that the improvement clubs were contributing to the emergence of the schoolhouse as "the natural centre of social organization."[58]

No less than the universities and the organizations that underwrote the education campaign, the School Improvement Leagues forged close ties with government agencies. As Munford observed, league field organizers carried out their work "in close sympathy with and under the prestige of the state department of education." Commenting on the work of the improvement clubs, Philander P. Claxton of the SEB anticipated that they would eventually become an integral part of each state's department of education. Exponents of progressive uplift and rationality, the School Improvement Leagues also functioned as agencies of state construction.[59]

For the Hill administration, coordinating education and promoting high school improvement were important, but neither reduced the university's financial burdens. To rejuvenate the university, Hill had to convince the legislature to abandon its tradition of sporadic appropriations in favor of a more rational system of financial support.

Stabilizing the university's political position depended on improving agricultural education. Agricultural enthusiasts in the legislature regularly castigated the school's lackluster offerings. However, they did little to underwrite their pleas for the department's development. Federal funds, they argued, were sufficient to provide for the needs of the agricultural department. In fact, in the university's first hundred years, the state had appropriated less than $82,000 for the university's needs, amounting to an average of less than $1,000 a year.[60]

In his first year of office, Hill decided to make a direct request for an appropriation to develop agricultural instruction and the summer school. An invitation to the Georgia State Fair held in Atlanta in October gave him a forum to promote agricultural education and to ask for state support. The chancellor pressed his objective before a joint session of the General Assembly in November. Announcing that the university farm needed $10,000 a year to operate, he asked for an annual appropriation of $14,500. He suggested that the remaining sum be allocated to a summer school. Despite Hill's efforts, the legislature rejected an appropriation that year.[61] The next year, Hill went to the General Assembly with a request for building funds, but with an undisclosed plan to use some of the money to upgrade agricultural education. In the attempt to strengthen the connection of the university to the state, Hill invited several members of the General Assembly to visit the campus. At the same time, he carried on extensive correspondence with numerous representatives. The chancellor's assertive lobbying resulted in annual appropriations of $22,500 for 1901 and 1902.[62]

Certainly, by northern standards, $45,000 over two years was not an overwhelming sum for a state university.[63] However, Hill's accomplishment is impressive when compared to the financial status of the university the year he was elected. In 1899 the university's income was $71,020.93. Of this amount, the federal government contributed $41,000, of which $24,000 was appropriated under the second Morrill act. Of the remaining sum, the state of Georgia contributed a mere $8,000 as payment of interest on a university loan to the General Assembly in 1815. By the beginning of Hill's administration, the state had given just $81,400 to the university; at the end of Hill's term, it had acquired $151,000, almost twice as much as its total appropriations between 1801 and 1899.[64] As Hill made poignantly clear in the Centennial edition of the *Bulletin,* "Mrs. Hearst spent more money in a single transaction for the plans of the buildings which she gave to the University of California than Georgia has given to this university . . . in all this hundred years."[65] With the addition of the university to the General Appropriation Act, a precedent was set for annual allocations to the university.[66]

Although the appropriation fell short of what Hill had requested, it signified the legislature's recognition of the university as a legitimate extension of the state. The chancellor suggested the nature of the change when he applauded not only the gift but "the spirit with which it was given—the appropriation having been voted unanimously by the House and Senate Committees on Appropriations, and passing both House and Senate with practical unanimity."[67] Hill shed his diplomatic tone in a letter to Philander P. Claxton of the University of Tennessee: "The plain truth is that for a great many years the State absolutely did nothing for the University. . . . During a long period, therefore, Georgia could only be quoted as a horrible example to be shunned." The tradition of neglect, he admitted, ended with the appropriation of a maintenance fund.[68]

The change in the university's financial status reflected the school's transition from college to professional institution. Instead of a troublesome constitutional obligation sustained by sporadic gestures of Victorian charity, the university entered into a network of state institutions whose claim to financial support was premised on its ability to provide public service. Of course, this transition was hardly completed by 1905. Resistance to sizable university appropriations continued to plague the institution. But powerful voices of progressive educational reform received a hearing in 1901. The chancellor and forward-looking board members had won support for their claim that the university had a legitimate social function.

In the centennial edition of the *Bulletin,* Hill admonished legislators to view the annual appropriation as a springboard for "the beginning of a new policy of the State towards this institution." He hoped that the centennial celebrations would provide a "lever to move public opinion and to lift the University to the high position she ought to occupy." Exhorting supporters to finance an alumni hall, he said it could serve as an "example which will infect the public and magnetize the Legislature into a wise and responsive generosity." An aggressive campaigner, Hill used the pages of the *Bulletin* and the centennial exercises held during commencement week to consolidate the administrative transformation wrought by the General Assembly.[69]

Appropriations from the General Assembly represented only a portion of the university's revenue during Hill's tenure. His chancellorship also inaugurated a new relationship with powerful philanthropists. Northern philanthropy—and influence—became a crucial factor in realigning the school along progressive lines. The university benefited primarily from its association with George Foster Peabody. A native of the state, he earned a fortune in New York as a successful investment banker. A member of the SEB, he first became interested in the university in 1901 when, invited by Oscar Straus, another native Georgian and wealthy New York entrepreneur, he attended the school's commencement exercises. While in Athens, Peabody was the guest of Harry Hodgson, alumnus, local business leader, and vigorous university promoter. Impressed by the commencement and persuaded by Hodgson, Peabody arranged to bring Robert Ogden, prominent national educational reformer and president of the SEB to the 1902 Southern Education Conference in Athens.[70]

A combination of Hill's personal charm and the presence of educators such as Charles McIver persuaded Peabody to donate $50,000 for a new library. This was the second of Peabody's gifts to the collective university. Earlier that year he had contributed $13,000 for the construction and equipment of a practice school for the State Normal School. In 1904, he helped the university auxiliary acquire 1,000 acres to develop the State College of Agriculture. Along with numerous donations, Peabody contributed roughly $250,000 to the institution, or two and a half times as much as the Georgia legislature gave during the nineteenth century.[71] In addition to his charity he worked to cultivate the interest of influential organizations, such as the GEB, and wealthy northern philanthropists in the university's development.

The change in the university's relationship with the legislature provided an impetus for adding new and improving existing departments. The enhancement of the Law School vividly expressed the chancellor's commitment to professionalization. Hill and others believed that the trained lawyer would play an important role in stimulating economic growth and advancing progressive reform. Attentive to academic currents outside the South, Hill justified the improvement of law school standards as a response to national professional standards: "The Association of Medical Colleges of America, organized some years ago, has been greatly instrumental in raising the standard of medical education. It is hoped that the Association of American Law Schools will ultimately bring all the law schools of America up to its requirements."[72]

But the law school at UGA fell miserably below national standards. Staffed by only one full-time professor, the school depended on the generosity of local lawyers, who gave periodic lectures for inadequate pay. The one-year law curriculum was an anomaly by national standards, which prescribed a two-year course. The skeletal law library fell far short of the statutory knowledge most states expected of their law graduates. And, unlike the agricultural department and Franklin college, the law school had no dean. In his report to the trustees in 1900, Hill endorsed the recommendation of law professor Sylvanus Morris and trustee Howell Cobb that the law course be extended to two years. Regretfully he admitted that "conditions are not yet quite ripe for the proposal of this important change."[73] At the same time he recommended that Morris be appointed Dean of the Law School. Finally, Hill took immediate steps to improve the quality of the deficient law library by contributing his own 500-volume collection for student use.

The chancellor had not achieved a decisive victory for modernizing the law school. The board appointed Morris as dean, but they maintained the law school's subordinate status by denying him full membership in the university faculty. Also, the board declined responsibility for paying the full salaries of the law professors.[74] Clearly, in 1902 the board was not united behind professionalization. Its policies still reflected the sensibilities of the nineteenth-century classical college. Though mostly lawyers themselves, the board had not completely absorbed the creed of academic specialization. In many ways, Hill fashioned himself an instructor for the trustees in the school of progressive education. Throughout his term, the board functioned alternately as an agent of bureaucratic change and a bulwark of tradition.

Moving cautiously, the board requested that a faculty committee prepare a proposal for a two-year law course. Along with Morris and Cobb, Hill presented a schedule for a two-year course to the board in November 1900.[75] The trustees declined to make any changes without extensive study. In conjunction with a committee appointed by the board, recommendations were formulated and approved in April 1901. Hill understood that imposing more stringent admission requirements carried a price. "Experience elsewhere has shown that a large reduction of the number of students is the immediate result of raising of standard by lengthening the course, but that this temporary loss is more than offset after several years by the ultimate gain." However, the decision to introduce the two-year program did meet with the enthusiastic approval of the Georgia Bar Association, the state's newly vigilant guardian of professional legal standards.[76]

Coordinating the chancellor's office with the law school was another strategy Hill used to enhance the status of legal instruction. He objected to the purely nominal relationship between the law school and the chancellor. To remedy it he offered to teach law courses on the condition that the board relieve him of the chancellor's traditional responsibility for teaching metaphysics. With the trustees' consent, Hill enriched the program by teaching courses in federal law, the history of law, and legal ethics. The chancellor's mission to professionalize the law school continued throughout his administration. After the board's trip to Wisconsin in 1905, he recommended raising the school's standards to make a high school diploma the minimum requirement for admission. Ever concerned with the law school's dismal literary resources, he lobbied for the addition of a new library. However, the plans for the library fell victim to the familiar financial constraints shackling university development.[77]

Although partial to the interests of the law school, Hill pursued a broad program of professionalization. The New South's commitment to commercial development was abundantly evident in his agenda for professionalization. Inspired by leading northern universities, he announced in 1903 his plan to recommend establishing a School of Commerce. Planning to offer insurance courses through the School of Commerce, he contacted the vice-president of Equitable Life, a major northern insurance company, for information and recommendations for courses of study.[78] In his 1904 report he called on the board to make a commerce department a priority. The chancellor pointed to the federal government's new commerce department as an example for universities concerned about the "wider sphere of public opinion." In his ongoing effort to adjust the university to the economic interests of the New South, Hill justified his recommendation by an appeal to the State Agent's report of "a genuine and strong demand for the creation of such a department."[79]

A department of commerce would also meet the demands of southern business for practical education. In his 1905 report, the chancellor validated his proposal by invoking Atlanta entrepreneur J. J. Spalding's endorsement of business education before the Georgia Bankers' Association. In the same report, Hill once again reminded the board of the "favorable impression" made by the University of Wisconsin's School of Commerce during a recent visit to Madison.[80] In March 1905 he was still hopeful that a "strong movement to create a department of commerce" would propel his plans forward, but the school failed to materialize during his administration.[81]

The chancellor also worked toward creating schools of dentistry and pharmacy. To lend professional credibility to the School of Dentistry proposal, Hill invited the State Society of Dentists to the university in June 1904. In his plans for expansion, he instructed the engineering consultant to include a building for the Dental College. Along with the School of Commerce, however, the Dental College never got beyond the planning stages during Hill's tenure. The chancellor had more success with his 1903 proposal for a College of Pharmacy. He pointed out that the required courses in biology, chemistry, and physiology were already offered by existing departments. The board approved Hill's recommendation, but a fire destroyed the building that was to house the new department in January 1904. The school finally opened in the fall of that year, with six students enrolled in the program.[82]

Following the example of the University of Wisconsin, the chancellor included a School of Architecture in his 1905 report on university development. Hill hoped that Georgia would be the first southern university to have such a department. Although these plans foundered for lack of financial support, Hill was able to add a School of Forestry through the beneficence of George Foster Peabody. The New York philanthropist made the offer through Hill, who presented it to the board in 1905. Peabody offered to pay $625 quarterly for the salary of a professor of forestry and $500 for equipment. The board accepted and, in 1906, hired a professor for the position.[83]

As part of a comprehensive program of modernization, Hill also championed academic specialization. In keeping with the late nineteenth-century enthusiasm for the social sciences, he encouraged the improvement of economics, history, and political science. The chancellor and the faculty looked toward making the disciplines of history, economics, political science, and sociology independent. His fondness for the social sciences was prompted at least in part by personal experience. "I had the same experience that you describe in political economy" he wrote to W. H. Heck, assistant agent of the GEB. "I emerged from a college course on the subject without a real knowledge of it and without realizing it was a vital topic. I am in full sympathy with your views as to the importance of teaching the social sciences."[84] In keeping with the university's movement toward a utilitarian education, the chair of the School of History suggested that the discipline of sociology would include both "the scientific study of society, and the narrower . . . criminology, pauperism, prison reform, charity organization, etc."[85]

Progressive thinking also reshaped pedagogical training. Responding to Hill's request for recommendations on departmental improvements, T. J. Woofter, professor of education, proposed the subdivision of his school into fields of philosophy, psychology, and education. If research never became a driving force at the school during Hill's period, Woofter suggested that many southern professors held it up as an ideal. Realizing that, even within specialized departments, "certain introductory courses" would never permit "originality," Woofter believed that "as we ascend the scale, research becomes more and more important. In fact, research is the breath of mental life, whereas mere authority is only the dry bones." Echoing the progressive creed of university activism, Woofter highlighted the social benefits of research: "The University must furnish the constructive thinkers and leaders. No greater opportunity for genuine service is now open to the university."[86]

Crucial to reformers was the university's role in educational reform, the linchpin of the southern progressive movement. Progressives were convinced that developing southern education was the essential prerequisite of regional advancement. Productivity and social reform required an educated populace. Two initiatives that illustrated this conviction were the School of Education and the Summer School for Teachers. Although the chancellor inherited these programs, he laid the groundwork for the former and successfully launched the latter.[87]

In his annual report of 1900 Hill presented the recommendation of David Barrow, Dean of Franklin College, for the development of high school level pedagogy to the trustees. He was careful to assure the board that an education department would not duplicate the work of the State Normal School. Pedagogical training was also necessary to accomplish the objectives of the accrediting system. "The interests of the University depend," he wrote, "to a large extent, upon the number of teachers it sends out and upon the success of their work. Teachers who leave the University without this training are at a serious disadvantage compared with the graduates of other institutions." Pedagogical instruction could be combined with courses in psychology, he suggested.[88]

In 1903 the board took advantage of the General Assembly's renewal of an annual appropriation for university maintenance to create a department of philosophy and education. Because of the chancellor's increasing involvement in nearly every aspect of the school's administration, the board finally relieved him of the duty of teaching philosophy and ethics. The decision further confirmed the university's gradual abandonment of the antebellum humanist tradition. The chancellor was first and foremost an administrator, not an educator. The university also now had a long-overdue department of education, however understaffed.[89]

Hill continued his efforts to promote educational training at Georgia, especially after he learned that the Peabody Fund intended to establish a college for teachers in the South. The chancellor persuaded the board to make an offer for the school, but in January 1905 the Peabody trustees decided to allocate $1,000,000 to fund a College of Education in Nashville. The trustees then announced that the remainder of the fund would be used to establish education departments at institutions throughout the region. Hill tried to channel the amount assigned for Georgia to the university. Despite his efforts, the fund was not distributed during his administration.[90] Plans for the school were deferred, but Hill succeeded in making the professionalization of teacher training a central feature of the university's blueprint for development. Coordinating education depended as much on cultivating professional educators as it did on standardizing entrance requirements.

As with many other programs on his administrative agenda, Hill inherited the development of a summer school for teachers. During William Boggs's administration, the university offered the use of the Old Rock College—what would become the State Normal School—for a summer school as a gesture of support for improving elementary education in Georgia. A summer school for teachers was offered between 1891 and 1893, but the efforts of the Georgia Teachers' Association to revive the idea in 1898 failed to materialize when the General Assembly refused to provide funding. Nevertheless, the faculty went ahead and planned a list of courses for the summer school.[91]

At a meeting in 1899 the chancellor and the board discussed the course offerings and devised a strategy to secure financial support for the school. State educators had been unrelenting in their efforts to pressure the university into providing a summer session. As one public school superintendent put it in a letter to Hill, "With very little expense our state university can open its doors in summer sessions and become the center of work for the mature teachers of Georgia."[92] Before a joint session of the General Assembly that year, Hill requested an annual appropriation of $4,500 for the summer school. Fiscal stringency frustrated the movement for the summer session. Undaunted, Hill recommended in 1900 that the board continue its efforts to secure the necessary appropriation.[93]

A familiar theme in the history of the UGA—dependence on external financial support—played out once again in the saga of the summer school. In 1903, the GEB offered $3,000 for a summer session. The "citizens of Athens" matched the GEB donation, and, with an additional $1,000 from the trustees, the summer school was launched.[94] Hill applauded it as an opportunity to foster educational cooperation by "bringing the University into more intimate relation with the teachers and the whole system of education in Georgia."[95] Staffed by faculty from the university and the State Normal School, the school attracted

674 students, 500 of whom were teachers enrolled in courses upgrading their skills in common school pedagogy. Hill hoped that a greater number of teachers would be drawn the next year to the regular university courses. In any case, he concluded that the school was a success.[96]

However, the momentum building from the successful summer session was halted when the GEB decided not to renew its contribution the next year. In an attempt to explain the board's decision, executive secretary Wallace Buttrick cited the lack of a comprehensive study of summer schools in the South that could act as propaganda for soliciting financial support from northern businesspeople.[97] Hill's interpretation was more perspicacious. The board's donation was an effort to publicize the need for supplementary teacher instruction and the state's responsibility to support it. The board expected some evidence of a commitment by the General Assembly before any further donations were made.[98]

The suspension of funding threatened to close the summer school permanently. The project was kept afloat by money from yet another northern source, the Peabody Educational Fund. The university's application for Peabody funding was given additional assistance by Hoke Smith, Peabody trustee, state senator, and friend of the university.[99] In February 1904, the Peabody Fund extended the life of the summer school with a $1,500 grant. A $1,000 appropriation from the Board of Trustees, a subscription of $2,000 from the city of Athens, and $1,600 from previous registration fees placed the summer session in a secure financial position for 1904.[100]

The chancellor believed that the success of the first session illustrated the need for a summer school. It also demonstrated, as did the accrediting system and the work of the state agent, that the university had a larger function to perform in "the educational work of the State." It became a concrete expression of his progressive plan for the university: to make it an institution for state service. But Hill challenged the General Assembly to provide support for the summer session or accept responsibility for its failure.[101]

The Board of Directors of the summer school agreed that the school could not be sustained by sporadic charity. In planning yet another assault on the stingy Georgia legislature, the board requested that Thomas J. Shackleford, trustee and legislative representative, initiate the drive to secure a $5,000 appropriation. But Hill and Shackleford thought that agitation should come not from the university but from the Georgia Teachers' Association. The chancellor reasoned that although the summer school performed a vital function for the college, it was not technically a department of the university. Explaining to state representative A. W. Evans why he had declined to go before the General Assembly, Hill stressed that if he were to represent the bill, he would emphasize that it was not a university measure per se but a response to the demands of teachers who wanted a college education. In fact, Hill conceded, an appearance before the Appropriations Committee probably would require him to admit that the college derived only an indirect benefit from the summer session.[102]

Hill's comments underscore his ongoing struggle to expand the university's social influence. Hill and the board hoped to finance a project at state expense that had a tenuous connection to the university's traditional academic agenda. They justified it by the belief that the summer session was vital to the improvement of public education. Rather than a top-down initiative, the summer school was a response to the demand of rural teachers for additional instruction and professional recognition. Hill explained to Evans that the need was not for university courses, but for normal school instruction. Many of these students could not afford a year of normal school courses, let alone a three-year program: "There are some really pathetic incidents illustrative of [teachers'] efforts to perfect themselves," Hill confided to Evans. "There are several ladies here who have reached middle life and one has brought with her a little girl, who makes a picturesque figure hanging on to her mother's apron string in the classes."[103] Instead of standing idle during the summer, the university would apply its resources to educational uplift. Progressives hoped that summer schools would mitigate the isolation of rural teachers and solidify the university's claim to state service.

Though a proponent of the summer school, Hill was also concerned about its impact on the college's own financial position. As Hill wrote candidly to his wife, "It [the summer school] is not specifically university work. It does some good indirectly to the University and is a good thing for teachers who come—especially in its general, broadening influence, but is not a cause to die for!"[104] To put some distance between the movement for the summer school and the university's needs, Thomas Shackleford, trustee and legislative representative, decided not to introduce the bill. Instead, it was entrusted to A. W. Evans, another legislator favorable to the university. In addition, Hill tried to minimize conflict between the university's and the Summer School Committee's requests by ensuring that the General Assembly would not consider both on the same day.[105]

Far from abandoning the Summer School movement, Hill worked to advertise it. Collaborating with members of the Summer School Committee, the chancellor produced a circular that implored teachers and superintendents to persuade their representatives to support the appropriation. He also met with members of the committee to "map out a line of proceeding" for the summer school hearings. Furthermore, the chancellor cogently explained the school's justification for state support in an article for the *Summer School News.* At the suggestion of A. W. Evans, Hill had the article distributed to each member of the House and Senate. Evans succeeded in getting the summer school included in the General Appropriations Bill, thus avoiding delay and the need to make annual requests. The bill was passed in August 1904. In their annual report, the Board of Trustees strongly recommended that future provision be made for the school.[106]

Like progressives trying to channel reform efforts through regional associations (exemplified by the Southern Educational Conference), the chancellor promoted the idea of a summer school network for the exchange of teachers and lecturers. To generate interest in the idea, he wrote to the administrators of several summer schools throughout the South. In his efforts to secure respected teachers for the lecture circuit, he wrote to the eminent psychologist G. Stanley Hall of Clark University. When Hill was mistakenly informed that the University of Tennessee's Summer School of the South was going to offer free tuition, he wrote to Philander P. Claxton to verify the report. The chancellor's concern with the program at Tennessee reflected his interest in regional coordination, but it probably also suggested the competitive streak that often underlay the rhetoric of fraternal cooperation.[107]

In a move comparable to progressive efforts to regulate corporations and public health, the administration used the summer session as a vehicle for standardizing elementary school instruction. The summer school helped improve the quality of common school education in the state. In addition, it made college training accessible to hundreds of Georgia teachers unable to attend the university's regular session. The school also lent credibility to the idea that teachers should meet certain minimum professional standards. In working to mold public support for the summer school, Hill and others exploited the promotional tactics of the southern progressive movement.

The movement for a summer school also was part of the broader process of southern modernization. Like the university auxiliary, the summer school and the Georgia Teachers' Association contributed to the gradual erosion of southern localism. In its place arose an institutional-based idea of community that fostered values inimical to southern individualism. By lending support to the Georgia Teachers' Association, the university helped to validate the functionally defined organizations that blossomed during the Progressive Era. The summer school, the Georgia Teachers' Association, and the university auxiliary were examples of how the university accelerated the formation of the South's new middle class. Accompanying them were professional schools and training in the social sciences, which solidified a class of managerial technicians, lawyers, administrators, professional teachers, and corporate bureaucrats differentiated by occupation. The university supported associations that broke down rural isolation and inculcated the values of a new urban ethos. Educational progressivism contributed to a process of class stratification central to the emergence of the modern South.[108]

The demand for a summer school for teachers was pressing, but the need to address the problems of agricultural education was urgent. The relationship of the agricultural college to the university was one of the thorniest problems of Hill's administration. Its solution reflected at once the growing appeal of progressive ideas of administration and the New South milieu that informed much of the thinking about agricultural education.

The principal issue facing Hill and the board was whether the university had fulfilled its obligations under the terms of the Morrill acts to provide adequate instruction in agricultural science. Passed by Congress in 1862, the Morrill Act granted public lands to states for the express purpose of creating agricultural and mechanical colleges. Under the second Morrill Act of 1890, land grant colleges were to receive $15,000 per year. That amount would be increased annually by $1,000 until the total reached $25,000. Georgia took advantage of the federal government's offer in 1872 when it established the State College of Agriculture in connection with the university. As noted before, Morrill funds soon came to be the largest percentage of the university's income. Like those of other universities, however, Georgia's college developed into little "more than a pretentious trade school" when the administration began siphoning federal funds to support everything but agricultural training.[109]

The university's parsimony toward the state college is not surprising considering the state legislature's fiscal intransigence. Lacking buildings, deficient in storage space, dependent on nutrient-depleted soils, and led by a president whose interests were in chemistry rather than agriculture, the "Rock college farm" was in a desolate state in the 1890s. Critics alleged that a symptom of the college's failure was its low enrollment: Winter attendance for 1896 stood at six. Frustrated with the universities' neglect of agriculture, the agrarian-dominated General Assembly sponsored several bills during the 1890s to remove the State Agricultural and Mechanical College from Athens to Griffin, where the state's experiment station was located.[110]

The college's president, H. C. White, did little to improve agricultural instruction. In fact, in 1897 he suggested that agriculture could not be taught. The college could provide instruction in chemistry and botany, but it was the responsibility of the student to weld these elements together into a science of farming. White's views antagonized James B. Hunnicut, the school's professor of agriculture. Active in the Farmer's Institute movement, which originated in Alabama and was established in Georgia in 1889, Hunnicut argued that demonstration exhibits were eminently more effective in promoting scientific farming than the academic instruction offered at the college. He criticized the university's disinterest in the practical concerns of state farmers. He also castigated the board's decision to remove land from the Rock college farm for use by the State Normal School. Not surprisingly, his comments did not endear him to the college's administration. Acrimonious exchanges between the president and the professor continued until 1898, when Chancellor Boggs and President White succeeded in forcing Hunnicut's resignation. Purchasing the well-respected *Southern Cultivator,* he became a powerful adversary of the state college and a firebrand for improved agricultural instruction.[111]

Early in his administration Hill made a commitment to improve agricultural instruction at the university. Historian Gerald Ray Mathis has suggested that Hill, though preferential to liberal arts instruction, supported the upgrading of agricultural instruction out of a "sense of fairness" and a recognition of its "utilitarian" value. There is evidence that Hill was deeply committed to advancing agricultural education, however. In a letter to Peabody in 1902, Hill wrote, "I find that the educational interest which gets closest to me is the Agricultural. I realize its relation to the general welfare of the people." If anything, his interest in agriculture was consistent with his larger program for advancing practical, service-directed education. The chancellor may have had an affinity for the liberal arts. Even so, his plan to relinquish the metaphysics assignment in favor of teaching law suggests a preference for professional instruction.[112] His vigilant support for professional training certainly outweighed any interest he expressed in the liberal arts curriculum.

In his first annual report, Hill recommended acquiring equipment and faculty to accommodate the expanded agricultural curriculum that Hugh N. Starnes, the college's new president, had designed. The chancellor endorsed Starnes's request to outfit the university farm with dairy equipment. Hill also asked that the General Assembly finance new buildings for the department. The trustees complied with most of Hill's requests, assisted by the legislative appropriation of 1900–1901. The board allocated $5,000 for equipment, hiring an instructor in dairying and animal husbandry, and renovating the old Philosophical Hall for use by the school. The appropriation represented a formidable challenge to the Griffin representatives.[113]

The chancellor's views on agriculture combined New South hopes for agrarian revival with the language of progressive uplift. Scientific farming would regenerate the agricultural economy and stem the tide of rural southerners moving into the cities. In 1902 Hill recommended distributing nature study leaflets among common school children as a means of awakening "a genuine love of country life." To adjust the agricultural program to the needs of state farmers, he suggested creating a one- or two-year course for those unable to afford a full four years. He also asked that entrance requirements be lowered for those applying to the shorter program. In support of his recommendations, Hill once again drew the board's attention to the examples of agricultural colleges at leading northern universities such as Cornell, Wisconsin, and Ohio. For many of Hill's plans, Wisconsin, a center of progressive educational and political thought, provided the model. Anticipating the trip to Madison that had been planned for board members and key legislators in 1904, Hill wrote to W. A. Henry, dean of the university, requesting a meeting between the state school superintendent or commissioner of agriculture and a delegation of Georgia's representatives. Convinced that the "matter of agricultural education in the common schools and the high schools" had been "solved" in Wisconsin, Hill was hopeful that its architects would share their expertise with the Georgia group.[114]

Above all, improving agricultural instruction required state funding. The Morrill grants were intended only to provide a foundation for more generous state appropriations. For all of their strident criticism of the State College of Agriculture, the legislature, with the exception of $15,000 for equipment and the funds from the appropriation of 1901, had "never given one cent" for its maintenance. This stood in stark contrast to the generosity of other states toward their land grant colleges. South Carolina, for example, gave $60,000 to its agricultural institute in one year. Hill made no attempt to defend the quality of agricultural instruction at the college, but he reinforced the notion of social service to pry support from the state's legislature. As Hill wrote to J. Pope Brown, one of the legislators agitating for the removal of the college to Griffin, "I do not, by any means, claim that it is all that it ought to be, but unfortunately it never can be what it ought to be until patriotic Georgians give to its support and assist the earnest efforts [of] the trustees and the faculty to build up the department."[115]

In addition to upgrading the state college, Hill also lent university support to the Farmers' Institute. Under the direction of H. C. White, president of the college, the institutes fell into disuse. When the state gave control over them to the president and the chancellor, Hill took the opportunity to inject life into the program. In 1904, Hill invited C. Harvie Jordan, president of the Farmers' National Congress and newly appointed director of the Georgia institutes, to give occasional addresses to the students on agricultural issues and the organization. Jordan enthusiastically complied, giving addresses and inviting legislators interested in agricultural education to lecture at the university. In addition to district farmer's institutes, Jordan planned an annual Farmers' Institute rally for the summer of 1905. Although the rally was never held, Jordan's plans enjoyed the chancellor's solid support.[116]

In 1902, Hill helped defeat yet another effort to have the agricultural college removed to Griffin. At a meeting of the State Agricultural Society, representative William L. Peek submitted a resolution calling for removal. Hill, in attendance, mounted a cogent defense of the college by clarifying one of the principal misconceptions about the Morrill grants. The colleges were not established for the singular purpose of teaching agriculture, he argued. Instead, they were designed to give those involved in "industrial pursuits" an opportunity to learn the practical sciences related to agriculture and the mechanical arts unavailable at most traditional colleges. Emphatically, Hill declared that "it was never intended to force the boys of farmers going into these institutions so to study that they should all come out farmers." Apparently, Hill's peroration was largely responsible for the defeat of the resolution.[117]

Yet Hill's efforts on behalf of agricultural education were hardly enough to stifle the criticisms of men such as James Hunnicut of the *Southern Cultivator.* Excoriating university handling of the land grant funds and state neglect of agricultural education, Hunnicut declared that the state college was "not even the form or shadow of a mechanical college, and only the shadow of an agricultural college." Agricultural education had succeeded in southern states that provided separate colleges for its instruction, he asserted. The chancellor held up South Carolina's Clemson College as an example of effective agricultural education.[118]

Hill began to respond vigorously to these attacks in 1904. He challenged the contention that separating the state college from the university would significantly raise enrollment in agricultural courses. In a letter to the Office of the Experiment Stations in Washington, he wrote that the comparatively large enrollment in South Carolina's and Virginia's land grant colleges was attributable not to an overwhelming interest in agricultural education in those states but to the technological courses offered at their institutions. Unlike Georgia, where the School of Technology was separate from the agricultural college, technical and agricultural instruction was combined in these states. Engineering and mechanical training attracted "three-fourths or four-fifths of the number" to these schools, not agriculture.[119]

Writing to Henry McDaniel, former governor of Georgia and chair of the

Board of Trustees, Hill clarified his diagnosis of agricultural education. In the university's inability to attract agricultural students, Georgia was no anomaly. He observed that no state had succeeded in recruiting a significant number of students into their specialized agricultural schools. "This is due principally to the apathy of the farmers [and] disbelief in agricultural education, he wrote. Hill leveled a telling critique at the agricultural militants, arguing that "in Georgia the case has been aggravated by the fact that dissatisfied parties for thirty years have dinned into the ears of the farmers that the School of Agriculture is a failure." The chancellor strongly urged that the university take a more aggressive position. News of yet another bill calling for removal added an incentive to resolve the interminable controversy. Having received favorable reports from the State Department of Agriculture and the State Agricultural Society and having defeated recent efforts at removal, the university was in a position to make a direct assault on prevailing attitudes about the college. He asked, why not find a way to "take the wind out of the sails of the agitators?"[120] In its present condition, he wrote to Clark Howell, the university was "at the mercy of every agitator" who hoped to gain political favor among farmers by exploiting the agricultural college question.[121] Taking the offensive might put the university safely out of the reach of political opportunists.

The chancellor boldly suggested that if public opinion demanded it, the school would turn over the federal fund to a separate institution on the condition that the state compensate the university for the loss. The onus would then be on the state to finance the construction of new college buildings.[122] As an alternative to this drastic measure, Hill suggested consolidating the experiment station, then located in Griffin, with the state college in Athens. Only in its separation of the two institutions was Georgia an anomaly; everywhere else, the experiment station and state college were combined.[123] More than a method for silencing opposition, Hill's recommendation was an extension of his program of progressive rationalization. With the removal of the experiment station to Athens, the agricultural research would be united with the theoretical instruction provided by the state college.

The capstone of Hill's plan to "take the wind out of the sails of the agitators" was the movement for an authentic agricultural college.[124] To generate support for the proposed college, Peabody suggested to Hill in March 1904 that a group of legislators and board members make a trip to the University of Wisconsin, the national leader in progressive education. State and university cooperation in social reform distinguished Wisconsin as a university committed to the social service ethic. Hill and Peabody hoped that Wisconsin's accomplishments would awaken the Georgia legislators to the possibilities of more liberal university appropriations. Peabody also offered to finance the trip. With an invitation from Charles Van Hise, president of the University of Wisconsin, Hill persuaded key legislative representatives, including Martin Calvin, chair of the Committee on Agriculture, to join the mission to Madison. Perhaps more than any other single event, the trip to Wisconsin symbolized Hill's missionary progressivism. Progressive educational reform required the conversion of public opinion and Georgia's political leadership to the creed of state-funded, service-directed higher education.[125]

The trip was a tremendous success. It crystallized support for an agricultural college by convincing legislators of the social benefits of university outreach. On the return trip to Athens the members of the party developed policy proposals, formulated plans of legislative action, and appointed committees to present the plans to the Board of Trustees. One of the resolutions drafted by the participants captured the mood of social service evoked by the trip: "That in the upbuilding of the University of Wisconsin we see what the consecrated labor of able men endorsed by the liberality of their state legislation can effect in making an institution of research and learning which directly benefits every citizen of the state."[126] Brimming with enthusiasm, the once skeptical Hamilton McWhorter, university trustee, proclaimed to Peabody his hope that the hastily drafted plans would place the university on a level of "state support which it has never enjoyed." If their plans were to materialize, "the trip to Wisconsin will have accomplished more towards the growth of the university than any effort within its history of a century." The members of the Wisconsin party agreed that the priority would be developing the School of Agriculture.[127]

While Hill and the Committee on Development collected proposals from the faculty for university improvement, Peabody urged the chancellor to agitate for a substantial allocation to the agricultural department. If the New York philanthropist did not exert direct control over university policy, he nevertheless wielded considerable influence. "It seems to me," he wrote to Hill, "that there can never be a right growth if the Faculty and the Trustees in making their recommendations are at all governed by their thought of what may be the immediate response of the people through the Legislature." With this in mind, he strongly urged the chancellor to ask for an unprecedented $100,000 for building an agricultural hall. At the same time, Peabody set the campus extension movement in motion. To accommodate a new agricultural hall and other building plans, Peabody urged the chancellor to "secure options" on at least 100 acres of property contiguous to the campus. In May 1905 he offered up to $25,000 for the venture if the total cost were as much as $100,000. Hill hoped that acquiring additional land would educate the General Assembly in its responsibilities for university improvement and provide a springboard for its mammoth appropriation request.[128]

Persuaded by Peabody's suggestion, Hill drafted cost estimates based on information collected from universities with agricultural colleges. He also requested financial data from these schools as ammunition in his attack on the legislature's penury toward the State Agricultural College. The chancellor hoped to exploit the charitable atmosphere generated by the Wisconsin trip by highlighting the liberality of states such as Texas toward their agricultural colleges. Writing to David F. Houston of the College Station in Texas, Hill boasted that the trustees had "come back full of enthusiasm for progress and the first emphasis of it will be in the improvement of the agricultural department here." Hill's report on development, published in January 1905, featured the letters of several respondents, including David Houston and P. H. Mell of Clemson College, South Carolina.[129]

The movement for agricultural improvement received timely support from one of its former critics, representative J. J. Conner. An opponent of the development of agricultural education before the trip to Wisconsin, Conner wrote a series of articles in 1905 advocating the expansion of the agricultural college. Hill responded enthusiastically to Conner's support but cautioned him not to overemphasize the state college's weaknesses in his efforts to generate a legislative response. Conner assured the chancellor that he had made a careful distinction between the state's neglect and the university's prudent supervision of the state college. The "helplessness of the University management on account of a lack of funds to properly equip the ag'l college," he wrote, would be held "as a reserve force" against any future legislative opposition. Sensitive to a political climate hostile to taxation, Conner advised the board not to pursue a plan to finance agricultural expansion on the basis of a direct mill tax. Apparently, he convinced the board to abandon the mill tax proposal and request instead a university appropriation. The chancellor and the board subsequently enlisted him to introduce a bill calling for a $100,000 appropriation to the State College of Agriculture.[130]

In early 1905 the chancellor's plan to integrate the experiment station with the university was renewed. Like the plan to develop the agricultural department, the proposal for integration was revitalized by the trip to Wisconsin. Campus extension would facilitate the construction of an experiment station and an agricultural hall. Writing to James Smith, previous benefactor of the university, Harry Hodgson echoed Hill's argument that a combined experiment station and agricultural college would rationalize Georgia's educational facilities. "The chief lesson we learned in Wisconsin last November was that the greatest success for agricultural education could only come through the consolidation of the experiment farm now at Griffin with the University here at Athens . . . so as to give [agricultural students] a broad and liberal education."[131]

The quest for relocation was aided by the deplorable condition of the Griffin experiment station. It was surrounded by factories, its farm produce scavenged by trespassing locals, and the level of agricultural research conducted at Griffin in 1905 was of dubious quality. Ultimately, however, Hill's plans for the experiment station were defeated by Griffin's legislative representatives. Their opposition is hardly surprising. The removal of the station would have meant a substantial loss of state revenue for the county. The chancellor's assurances that the university would compensate for the loss by trying to secure an agricultural high school for Griffin proved less than consoling. In this case, local interests prevailed over progressive coordination and efficiency.[132]

When finally introduced in June 1905, Conner's bill met with fierce opposition from the Griffin forces. In July, Conner wrote to Hill asking that Shackleford and Hodgson come to the State Capitol to lend assistance until the bill was reported out of the Appropriations Committee. Conner and Hodgson also encouraged the chancellor to present the case for the appropriation before a joint session of the General Assembly. Conner warned that if the bill failed, the university could expect a renewed campaign against its management of the Morrill funds. To appease the school's adversaries, Hill recommended to the governor that the agricultural college be administered by a board of trustees representative of Georgia's farmers. The board would have control over school matters, including the election of a president and the hiring of faculty. Furthermore, the trustees of the agricultural college would be subordinate to the university board only in matters affecting the collective university. Eventually, the proposal became an amendment to the Conner bill.[133]

Hill's concession may have persuaded the committee to approve the bill, but the margin of victory was slight. Representatives normally favorable to agricultural education but concerned about fiscal excess joined the Griffin defenders in opposing the bill. Troubled by the bill's dimming hopes for passage in the 1905 session, Representative Conner, with Hill's sullen acquiescence, decided to postpone a final vote until the next session. Meanwhile, Hill once again went before the General Assembly to oppose a bill sponsored by Representative Flynt of Spaulding County calling for removal of the state college from Athens. The bill was defeated in August.[134]

The chancellor's considerable expenditure of energy over the last session left him exhausted. In a sadly ironic letter to his longtime friend N. E. Harris, Hill wrote, "What is the matter with college presidents? Pollock dead, Chappell dying in Mexico; Hall quite ill and half a dozen other of my limited acquaintances all knocked out, including my venerable self." In an effort to regain his health, Hill and his family took a month-long vacation to Europe. The chancellor returned refreshed but not restored; in December of that year the fifty-four-year-old Hill died of pneumonia.[135]

The Conner bill survived, however. The Georgia State College of Agriculture and Mechanic Arts was established in 1906 by an appropriation of $100,000. The legislation also provided that the college be governed by its own Board of Trustees, subject to the chancellor of the university. Hill's legacy went beyond the agricultural college, however. Under the administration of David C. Barrow, Hill's successor, departments and schools "became real administrative units." Barrow fulfilled his predecessor's plans for an expanded curriculum by developing the social and behavioral sciences, law, forestry, business, pharmacy, and education. While the curriculum became more complex, a professionally conscious faculty improved the quality of instruction and supported the addition of new departments. The impulse for public service, professionalization, and efficiency continued to govern university development.[136]

The professionalization Hill sponsored is important for understanding not only the emergence of the new college professor but also the consolidation of the South's new middle class. The professionalization of law, dentistry, education, and business made the university a critical agent in forming a class tied to the new commercial order. As historian Edward Ayers explains, "While those institutions of higher learning [colleges, universities, and technical schools] contained only about 26,000 students at the turn of the century, the students included those who were to exercise the most power in the emerging South."[137]

During Hill's tenure, the university became a conduit for the South's new professions. National pressures drove the administration to expand the university's law course from one to two years. It was the state university and not the independent practitioner that Georgia's professional law association looked to for a supply of trained lawyers. Increasingly, the emerging educational bureaucracy was also administered by university-trained professionals. J. S. Stewart's dual position at Georgia is but one example. Schools of education as well as summer schools produced a swelling cadre of university-trained school administrators, superintendents, teachers, and inspectors. Medical schools at southern universities produced the region's physicians, and professions such as journalism, architecture, accounting, and engineering searched for qualified candidates among university graduates. As historian Dewey

Grantham explains, the urban industrial order required the services of professional lawyers, doctors, engineers, educators, and journalists. The twentieth century witnessed "the marked increase in the opportunities for their members and the professional organizations and the standards they established." Along with efficiency experts in public administration, public health, social work, and clerical work, these professionals formed the burgeoning middle class in the South.[138]

Despite these changes, the region's political economy continued to reflect the influence of decentralized authority and an agrarian economy. But in the urban, industrializing South of places such as Atlanta and Nashville, where "a distinct southern urban business class . . . rapidly formed a coherent social class", the university-trained professional was increasingly prominent. Convinced of their capacity for leadership by virtue of their training, middle-class southerners assumed influential positions in the movements to align southern education, business, law, public health, and social practices according to progressive tenets. Along with business elites, the new middle class "created an ideological framework that enabled them to join their agenda for economic development to broad social reforms and to present their interests as those of the South at large."[139] To many southerners recently drawn into a market economy, though, the efforts of southern progressives to administer the urban industrial order often took on the appearance of paternalistic control.

The influence of the southern progressive movement on the university went beyond accumulating new departments. Under Hill's leadership the university became an agent of the state committed to the doctrine of social service. Public service was not simply a secularized evangelism but a philosophy of education closely tied to a program of state construction. Social service became the adhesive connecting the university to the state. Through associations and the fusion of government offices with academic posts, the chancellor brought the university's resources to bear on social and economic issues. The Bureau of Business Research, the Institute of Natural Resources, and the Cooperative Extension Service grew out of the seeds of the social service ideal that Hill sowed as chancellor.

The Hill administration made the UGA a repository for progressive ideas, a southern example of progressive higher education, and a centerpiece of a state-supported bureaucratic matrix. But if the dream of forging bonds between the university and the government satisfied progressive dreams, it did not transform the South. Debt peonage, economic dependency, racial discrimination, and anti-intellectualism persisted. Fundamental social change in the region would await federal intervention on a scale never imagined by progressives.

Notes

1. Professionalization became one of the major functions of the new bureaucratic university. Historian Burton Bledstein argues that the university "by and large . . . came into existence to serve and promote professional authority in society." Universities legitimated professions striving for exclusivity, standardization of qualifications, and economic control. In Bledstein, *The Culture of Professionalism,* 123–32.

2. Veblen quoted in Rudolph, *The American College and University,* 418.

3. Ibid., 356.

4. Singal, *The War Within,* 6–10.

5. Link, *The Paradox of Southern Progressivism,* chapter 7. The theme of progressive bureaucratic control versus localism and individualism is central to Link's analysis and helps illuminate the work of Hill and of the other educational leaders of the period.

6. "Walter Barnard Hill," *Georgia Alumni Record* (November 1933): 9, Vertical File, Hargrett Rare Book and Manuscript Library/University of Georgia Libraries; Mathis, "Hill, Walter Barnard," 452.

7. "Walter Barnard Hill," *Georgia Alumni Record,* 10. This brief account of Hill's life and administration was based primarily on an address given by Hill's law associate, N. E. Harris, at memorial exercises in 1906. The following quote can safely be considered Harris's own reflection on Hill's legal acumen: "The revised code was published in 1873 and was known as the Erwin, Lester and Hill's Code. Dr. Hill did the work of annotating this code. . . . The result was one of the best and most complete specimens of code annotation to be found in the history of Georgia's code expansion."

8. Mathis, *Walter Barnard Hill, Chancellor,* 453.

9. Grantham, in *Southern Progressivism,* uses three categories to illuminate southern progressivism. Social control and regulation distinguished southern campaigns for disfranchisement, black proscription, antimonopolism, prison reform, and prohibition. See p. xix.

10. Hill to A. O. Bacon, July 10, 1899, box 1, Hill Collection, UGA; Felton to Hill, July 14, 1899, folder #14:2, box 14, Hill Family Papers, UGA; Mathis, *Walter Barnard Hill, Chancellor,* 61; Mathis, "Hill, Walter Barnard," 453.

11. Dyer, *The University of Georgia,* 139.

12. Mathis, "Walter B. Hill, a New Chancellor," 81–82.

13. "Chancellor's Annual Report to Board of Trustees, June 14, 1900," *Bulletin of the University of Georgia* 1 (October 1900): 12–13 (hereafter abbreviated as "Chancellor's Report").

14. "Wonderful Work Developing Greater University of GA. Done By Chancellor W. B. Hill," unidentified newspaper clipping, July 1905, folder #3, box 18, Hill Family Papers, UGA.

15. On the question of the search for authority among both college administrators and faculty and its relationship to professionalization, see Haber, *The Quest for Author-*

ity and Honor in the American Professions, 285–85; Veysey, *The Emergence of the American University,* 350–51. As at other institutions of higher education, the trustees at the UGA came from a distinctly professional background. Of the ten members appointed during Hill's tenure, eight were lawyers. Among the members from previous administrations were former governor Henry D. McDaniel; senator A. O. Bacon; former speaker of the House Howell Cobb; Nat E. Harris, Hill's law partner; P. W. Meldrim, president of the Georgia State Industrial College for Colored Youths; and Clark Howell, editor of the Atlanta *Constitution.* Although it is arguable whether politicians belonged to the "new" professions, the absence of clergymen is noteworthy. Thomas Reed, "History of the University of Georgia," unpublished manuscript, Hargrett Rare Book and Manuscript Library/University of Georgia Libraries, vol. 7, p. 2086.

16. Hill to George Foster Peabody, June 28, 1905, box 6, Hill Collection, UGA.

17. Ibid., 4.

18. Ibid., 5–6.

19. T. J. Woofter to Hill, July 31, 1899, folder #14:13, box 14, Hill Family Papers, UGA; Hill to Board of Trustees, April 11, 1903, box 2, Trustees' Correspondence, UGA.

20. Hill to D. B. Hall, July 2, 1904, box 2, Hill Collection, UGA; for Hill's exhaustive search for a professional librarian, see his correspondence for June 25, 1904, box 2, Hill Collection, UGA. Among other institutions, Hill wrote to Princeton, Yale, Chicago, Harvard, Columbia, and the Pratt Institute Library. The chancellor and the board also tried to attract Louis R. Wilson, the distinguished librarian of the University of North Carolina at Chapel Hill, to consider the job at Georgia. See Hill to Wilson, June 11, 1904, box 2, Hill Collection, UGA. On acquiring a director trained in library science, see "Chancellor's Report," June 14, 1900, *Bulletin,* 10.

21. Brooks, *The University of Georgia under Sixteen Administrations,* 132; Hill to N. E. Harris, May 14, 1904, box 2, Hill Collection, UGA.

22. Hill to W. H. Davis, July 14, 1904, box 2, Hill Collection, UGA.

23. Hill, "The Twentieth Century University," unpublished speech, no date, box 7, vol. 1, Hill Collection, UGA.

24. Ibid.

25. Mathis, *Walter Barnard Hill, Chancellor,* 118.

26. Hill, "What Is the University?" 3, 6, 9–10.

27. Ibid.

28. Ibid., 6.

29. "Chancellor's Report," June 14, 1900, 7.

30. "Chancellor's Report," *Bulletin* 3 (July 1902): 2. In a letter to the secretary of the Faculty of Medicine, Hill clarified his idea of the university council. Against the secretary's suggestion that the council meet with a committee of the medical college to discuss forging closer ties with the university, Hill recommended that the committee negotiate with the Board of Trustees. He explained that the council "is composed only of the Presidents of the several colleges or schools composing the university, using that word in the collective sense. It meets only for conference and merely takes up the sub-

jects of common interest, such as the joint catalogue, etc." He made it clear that the council functioned in an advisory rather than legislative capacity. Hill to Thomas Wright, February 6, 1904, box 1, Hill Collection, UGA.

31. "Report of Committee on Branch Colleges," June 1900, Bulletin (October 1900): 28; "Chancellor's Report," *Bulletin* 2 (May 1901): 5; "Report of Committee on Branch Colleges," *Bulletin* (October 1900): 29; "Chancellor's Report," *Bulletin* 3 (July 1902): 3–4; Reed, "History of the University of Georgia," 1886.

32. "Report of Committee on Medical College to the Board of Trustees," July 1904, folder "July 4–6," box 2, Hill Collection, UGA; Hill to DeSaussure Ford, January 27, 1905, box 4, Hill Collection, UGA; Mathis, *Walter Barnard Hill, Chancellor,* 237.

33. Hill to August Kohn, January 26, 1905, box 4, Hill Collection, UGA.

34. Hill to the Board of Trustees, October 30, 1900, box 1, Hill Collection, UGA.

35. Mathis, *Walter Barnard Hill, Chancellor,* 109.

36. "Chancellor's Report," *Bulletin* (May 1901): 18. A good example of Hill's progressive faith in the power of awakening public opinion is his work on behalf of an amendment to allow local school taxation. At the 1904 meeting of the Conference for Education in the South at Birmingham, Hill gave an address on the campaign in Georgia: "If its adoption had been the only question, there would have been no apparent necessity for any agitation or campaign, but it was felt desirable to interest the people in the subject actively . . . and more especially to prepare the minds of the people by a preliminary campaign on the amendment." In *Discussions of Our School Problems,* 4.

37. Mathis, *Walter Barnard Hill, Chancellor,* 256; Reed, "History of the University of Georgia," 2000.

38. Hill and A. L. Hull to Board of Trustees, April 11, 1903, box 2, Trustees' Correspondence, UGA.

39. Dabney, *Universal Education in the South,* 411. Although he was engaged primarily in evaluating high school education throughout the state, J. S. Stewart, the first state agent, was also entrusted with drumming up funds for plans to expand the State Normal School. Stewart tried to avoid antagonizing southerners concerned about protecting community control: "His work has been most beneficial in arousing interest in the University of Georgia . . . but he has thus far feared to make any effort for subscriptions among the masses of the people, as we believe the time is not ripe for this." Hill to L. G. Myers, August 24, 1904, box 3, Hill Collection, UGA.

40. Report of the Board of Visitors, 1902–3, folder "Reports—1903," file 1, box 2, Trustees' Correspondence, UGA; also see Hill to L. G. Myers, August 24, 1904, box 3, Hill Collection, UGA; Hill to Augustus Longstreet Hull, August 10, 1903, box 1, Hill Collection, UGA; Hill to Moses Cuyton, June 22, 1905, UGA; Hill to A. S. Hough, June 22, 1905, UGA; Hill to Business Manager of *Pensacola Morning Paper,* June 22, 1905, box 5, Hill Collection, UGA.

41. Hill, "Relation of the Universities and Colleges to the Public Schools," 273–74.

42. Dabney, *Universal Education in the South,* 410–11.

43. For examples of Hill's work in accumulating data about common and second-

ary education, see Hill to Mr. Robeson, January 22, 1904, and Hill to W. B. Merritt, January 22, 1904, box 1, Hill Collection, UGA.

44. Hill to J. W. Crabtree, February 6, 1904, box 1, Hill Collection, UGA.

45. Joseph S. Stewart, "The Accredited High School," 3.

46. W. D. Reid to Hill, April 17, 1904, box 1, Hill Collection, UGA.

47. Dabney, *Universal Education in the South,* 411–13.

48. "Chancellor's Report," May, 31, 1904, *Bulletin* 4 (July 1904): 10–11; "Students are admitted to the University either on satisfactory examination in the required subjects, or on the certificate of the Principal of an Accredited High School." In "Admission to the University," *Bulletin* 6 (April 1906): 17; Dabney, *Universal Education in the South,* 411; Hill, "Report of Committee on Development of University to Board of Trustees," January 1905, 10.

49. Henry McDaniel, *Annual Report of the Board of Trustees,* October 7, 1901, 5, folder "1900–1901," Hargrett Rare Book and Manuscript Library/University of Georgia Libraries (hereafter abbreviated as *Trustees' Report*).

50. *Trustees' Report,* October 1905, 10–11, folder "1904–1905"; "Minutes of the Board of Trustees," June 20, 1905, 694, Hargrett Rare Book and Manuscript Library/University of Georgia Libraries (hereafter abbreviated as "Trustees' Minutes"); Hill to Wallace Buttrick, April 21, 1905, box 5, Hill Collection, UGA.

51. Mathis, *Walter Barnard Hill, Chancellor,* 248.

52. Hill, untitled address, in *Proceedings of the Conference for Education in the South,* 118.

53. Ibid.; Hill, "Report for the State of Georgia" to the Southern Education Board, March 6, 1905, box 17, Hill Collection, UGA; and Hill to McIver, December 24, 1903; McIver to Hill, December 19, 1903; Hill to W. B. Merritt, September 27, 1904; Merritt to Hill, September 28, 1904, Hargrett Rare Book and Manuscript Library/University of Georgia Libraries.

54. Hill to Nellie F. Phinizy, July 30, 1904, box 3, Hill Collection, UGA; see also "Georgia Educational Conference," n.d., 1904, box 4, Hill Collection, UGA.

55. Hill to Phinizy, July 30, 1904, box 3, Hill Collection, UGA; "Report of the State of Georgia" to the Southern Education Board, March 6, 1905, box 17, Hill Collection, UGA.

56. Claxton, "Educational Ideals," 422–23; Munford, "Woman's Part in the Educational Progress of the South," 638–45; Link, *The Paradox of Southern Progressivism,* 138–39.

57. Leloudis, *Schooling the New South,* 155–61.

58. Munford, "Woman's Part in the Educational Progress of the South," 644–45.

59. Ibid.; Claxton, "Educational Ideals," 422–23.

60. "Chancellor's Report," *Bulletin* 1 (January 1901): 4.

61. Mathis, *Walter Barnard Hill, Chancellor,* 155–56.

62. Dyer, *The University of Georgia,* 156.

63. Hill illustrated the university's deplorable financial condition by contrasting Georgia's record with other comparable southern states. By 1901, Virginia had acquired

a $4,000,000 endowment, and North Carolina had received state contributions amounting to $2,750,000. As Hill put it, "It is not gratifying to State pride" to consider Georgia's parsimonious $81,400 appropriation since the institution's founding in 1801. In "Chancellor's Report," January 1901, 12.

64. Brooks, *The University of Georgia under Sixteen Administrations,* 115. The Trustees elected to allocate $35,000 of the appropriation to a new dormitory, named Candler Hall, and a refectory, named Denmark Hall. See *Trustees' Report 1900–1901,* Hargrett Rare Book and Manuscript Library/University of Georgia Libraries.

65. "Chancellor's Report," January 1901, 4.

66. Reed, "The University of Georgia," 617. For an account of the university's financial situation after the Civil War and leading up to 1890, see Wallenstein, *From Slave South to New South,* 160–69.

67. "Chancellor's Report," January 1901, 12.

68. Hill to Philander P. Claxton, February 2, 1904, box 2, Hill Collection, UGA.

69. Ibid., 22.

70. Ware, *George Foster Peabody,* 107–13.

71. Ibid., 107–13; Brooks, *The University of Georgia under Sixteen Administrations,* 125–27. Not all southerners were as sanguine as Hill about soliciting educational philanthropy. Commenting on the meeting of the Conference at Athens in 1902, one concerned reformer wrote, "I revolt at the thought of the crowd of Southern mendicants pressing themselves upon him [Wallace Buttrick of the GEB]. To me the Athens meeting was sublime in its sentiments, but I can not forget my sensations of horror . . . at the sordid public references or still more patently self-seeking private inquiries of those whose sole interest in the movement . . . was 'How can I get hold of some money.' They were oblivious to the higher things." John J. McMahan to G. S. Dickerman, November 6, 1902, subseries 1.1, box 6, SEB Papers, UNC.

72. "Chancellor's Report," July 1902, 16.

73. "Chancellor's Report," June 14, 1900, 11; Mathis, *Walter Barnard Hill, Chancellor,* 201–2; see also Hill to Board of Trustees, October 30, 1900, box 1, Hill Collection, UGA.

74. Mathis, *Walter Barnard Hill, Chancellor,* 204.

75. "Trustees' Minutes," November 8, 1900, 571, Hargrett Rare Book and Manuscript Library/University of Georgia Libraries.

76. "Chancellor's Report," May 1901, 19. Although the board balked at fully integrating the law school into the university, it subscribed to Hill's argument for improving standards: "The standard of professional education in all of the professions has been steadily advanced in all of the leading institutions throughout the country, and the action of the Board in respect to the Law Department was a recognition of the just demand that Georgia should not fall behind in the line of progress." *Trustees' Report 1901–1902,* 10.

77. Hill to Howell Cobb, July 21, 1899, folder #12, box 14, Hill Family Papers, UGA; Mathis, *Walter Barnard Hill, Chancellor,* 203; "Report of Committee on Development of University to Board of Trustees," *Bulletin* 5 (January 1905): 25; Hill to P. W. Meldrim,

January 21, 1905, box 4, Hill Collection, UGA; Meldrim to Hill, January 24, 1905, box 4, Hill Collection, UGA.

78. Hill to G. E. Tarbell, January 26, 1904, box 2, Hill Collection, UGA; Tarbell to Hill, February 3, 1904, box 4, Hill Collection, UGA.

79. "Chancellor's Report," May 31, 1904, 19.

80. Hill, "Report of Committee on Development of University to Board of Trustees," *Bulletin* 5 (January 1905): 10–11.

81. Hill to Robert E. Park, March 16, 1905, box 4, Hill Collection, UGA.

82. Hill to D. W. Harrison, May 11, 1905, box 5, Hill Collection, UGA; Hill to A. H. Patterson, June 24, 1904, box 2, Hill Collection, UGA; Hill to Charles Leavitt, November 22, 1905, box 5, Hill Collection, UGA; Leavitt, *A Great Chancellor's Vision: The University of Georgia—A Practicable Development Outlined by Walter Barnard Hill, L.L.D.* unpublished manuscript, 1905, 27; "Chancellor's Report," July 1903, 10–11; "Trustees' Minutes," June 15, 1903, 631; "Chancellor's Report," May 31, 1904, 22; *Trustees' Report, 1904–05,* 5.

83. Peabody to Hill, 1905, box 4, Peabody Papers, LOC; Hill to Charles M. Strahan, February 2, 1905, box 4, Hill Collection, UGA; Hill to Peabody, March 28, 1905, box 5, Hill Collection, UGA; "Trustees' Minutes," November 15, 1895, 703–5. The chancellor hoped that moving the office of the state geologist to the university would rationalize educational resources. Transplanting the departments of entomology, geology, and health to Athens would accomplish the same: "Duplication of expense and effort," wrote Hill, "can be saved by consolidation in these respects," in "Report of the Committee on Development," *Bulletin* 5 (January 1905): 26.

84. Hill to W. H. Heck, January 21, 1905, box 4, Hill Collection, UGA.

85. Hill to H. W. Quaintance, February 22, 1905, box 5, Hill Collection, UGA; Hill, "Report of Committee on Development of University to Board of Trustees," *Bulletin* (January 1905): 17–18.

86. T. J. Woofter to Hill, December 14, 1904, box 4, Hill Collection, UGA.

87. Mathis, *Walter Barnard Hill, Chancellor,* 200–201.

88. "Chancellor's Report," June 14, 1900, 5.

89. "Chancellor's Report," *Bulletin* 3 (July 1903): 1; "Trustees' Minutes," January 17, 1903, 619.

90. "Chancellor's Report," July 1903, 10; *Trustees' Report 1902–1903,* 8–9; Wallace Buttrick to Hill, December 23, 1905, box 7, Hill Collection, UGA; Mathis, *Walter Barnard Hill, Chancellor,* 212–13.

91. Reed, "History of the University of Georgia," 1884; Mathis, *Walter Barnard Hill, Chancellor,* 213–14.

92. J. C. Woodward to Hill, July 18, 1899, folder #14:7, box 14, Hill Family Papers, UGA.

93. Mathis, *Walter Barnard Hill, Chancellor,* 214–15; "Chancellor's Report," June 14, 1900, 6–7.

94. Hill to A. W. Evans, July 15, 1904, box 3, Hill Collection, UGA.

95. "Chancellor's Report," July 1903, 2.

96. "Report of the Committee on the University Summer School," unpublished report, 1904, box 4, miscellaneous, Hill Collection, UGA.

97. Buttrick to Hill, December 23, 1903, box 1, Hill Collection, UGA.

98. Hill to Evans, July 15, 1904, box 1, Hill Collection, UGA.

99. As Hill wrote, "I thank you in behalf of all concerned for the assistance you have procured for the Summer School, without which I do not believe the school would have been possible this year, as the G.E.B. failed us completely." Hill to Smith, February 13, 1904, box 1, Hill Collection, UGA.

100. "Report of the Committee on the University Summer School," 1904, box 1, Hill Collection, UGA.

101. "Chancellor's Report," May 31, 1904, 24.

102. Hill to Thomas J. Shackleford, June 25, 1904, box 2; Hill to T. W. Reed, July 1, 1904, box 2; Hill to A. W. Evans, July 15, 1904, box 3; all letters in Hill Collection, UGA.

103. Hill to A. W. Evans, July 15, 1904, box 3, Hill Collection, UGA.

104. Hill to "De," July 10, 1904, folder #1, box 17, Hill Family Papers, UGA.

105. Hill to Clark Howell, July 2, 1904, box 2; Hill to Evans, July 6, 1904, box 2; Evans to Hill, July 7, 1904, box 2; all letters in Hill Collection, UGA.

106. Hill to J. C. Woodward, July 18, 1904, box 3; Hill to Professor William Slaton, July 2, 1904, box 2; A. W. Evans to Hill, July 29, 1904, box 3; Hill to Evans, July 30, 1904, box 3; all letters in Hill Collection, UGA; see also *Trustees' Report, 1904–05,* 6.

107. Hill to R. B. Fulton, February 20, 1905, box 5; Hill to G. Stanley Hall, February 21, 1905, box 5; Hill to Philander P. Claxton, February 27, 1904, box 1; Philander P. Claxton to Hill, February 29, 1904, box 1; all letters in Hill Collection, UGA.

108. Grantham, *Southern Progressivism,* 5–9.

109. Veysey, *The Emergence of the American University,* 15; Veysey's observation applies not to the UGA but to the land grant colleges in general; Dyer, *The University of Georgia,* 120, 148; Karina, *The University of Georgia College of Agriculture,* 79–87.

110. Karina, *The University of Georgia College of Agriculture,* 88–94.

111. Ibid.

112. Mathis, *Walter Barnard Hill, Chancellor,* 187; Hill to Peabody, August 20, 1902, box 57, Peabody Papers, LOC.

113. "Chancellor's Report," June 14, 1900, 4–5; *Trustees' Report, 1900–1901,* 6–7.

114. Hill to Henry, November 5, 1904, box 4, Hill Collection, UGA; see also Gaston, *The New South Creed,* 30, 64–68; "Chancellor's Report," July 1902, 11–13; Hill took the lead from the faculty. They recommended a course that would function as a "protracted Farmers' Institute." The short course would diminish "the temptation to desert the farm . . . since the entire training they would receive would bear directly and exclusively on improved methods of agriculture and it is highly probable that by far the greater portion of those attending would return to put into practical operation the knowledge they may have acquired." In "Suggestions for the Establishment of a 'Localized Farmers' Institute' at the University," unidentified newspaper clipping, 1899, folder #10, box 14, Hill Family Papers, UGA.

115. "Chancellor's Report," July 1902, 13–14; Hill to Brown, December 12, 1903, box 1, Hill Collection, UGA.

116. Jordan to Hill, January 19, 1904, box 1; Hill to Jordan, January 25, 1904, box 1; Jordan to Hill, February 15, 1904, box 1; Hill to Jordan, February 18, 1904, box 1; Jordan to Hill, April 9, 1905, box 5; Hill to Jordan, April 25, 1905, box 5; all letters in Hill Collection, UGA; "Chancellor's Report," May 31, 1904, 16–17; Karina, *The University of Georgia College of Agriculture*, 97, 98.

117. Unidentified newspaper clipping, July 1902, folder #3 (July 24–31), box 18, Hill Family Papers, UGA.

118. Quoted in Dyer, *The University of Georgia*, 159; Hill to H. C. White, July 18, 1904, box 2, Hill Collection, UGA. When James B. Hunnicut died, his son took over the paper and began publishing virulent attacks on college president H. C. White. Hill planned to meet with Hunnicut in June 1905 to discuss his concerns, but the chancellor's increasingly weakened health prevented it. Hill did not dismiss White, but Hunnicut's attacks undoubtedly galvanized the pro–state college forces in favor of a sizable appropriation from the legislature. G. F. Hunnicut to Hill, May 29, 1905, box 5; Hunnicut to Hill, June 12, 1905, box 6; both letters in Hill Collection, UGA.

119. Hill to D. J. Crosby, May 24, 1904, box 2, Hill Collection, UGA. Hill continued to investigate the problem of agricultural education. He wrote to Herman Babson, professor at the Massachusetts Agricultural College, to ask about the benefit of separating agricultural instruction from other subjects. He also wanted to know the percentage of agricultural students who actually returned to the farm after graduation. Hill to Babson, July 5, 1904, box 2, Hill Collection, UGA. He then wrote to Georgia legislator L. G. Hardman, alerting him to Babson's 1901 article in *The Outlook* that seemed to confirm Hill's belief that the majority of northern agricultural students were as disinclined as southern students to assume farm work after graduation. Hill to Hardman, July 14, 1904, box 2, Hill Collection, UGA. For the role of agricultural colleges' diversified curricula in the development of agribusiness, see Kirkendall, "The Agricultural Colleges," 17–18.

120. Hill to McDaniel, May 24, 1904, box 2, Hill Collection, UGA.

121. Hill to Clark Howell, May 24, 1904, box 2, Hill Collection, UGA.

122. Ibid.

123. Hill to E. H. Calloway, May 24, 1904, box 2, Hill Collection, UGA.

124. Three days after Hill wrote to McDaniel, Calloway, and Howell, he wrote to James Smith, benefactor of the Normal School, in search of a gift for agricultural education that might "start the liberality of the General Assembly in that direction." Hill continued, unsuccessfully, to ply Smith for funds throughout the remainder of his administration. See Hill to Smith, May 27, 1904, box 2, Hill Collection, UGA.

125. Mathis, *Pilgrimage to Madison*, 2–4; Peabody to Charles Van Hise, October 3, 1904, box 3, Hill Collection, UGA; Dyer, *The University of Georgia*, 161.

126. Hill to Van Hise, November 28, 1904, in Mathis, *Pilgrimage to Madison*, 82.

127. McWhorter to Peabody, December 6, 1904, box 4, Hill Collection, UGA.

128. Peabody to Hill, December 2, 1904, box 4; Peabody to Hill, December 14, 1904, box 4; Peabody to Hill, May 5, 1905, box 5; Hill to Norman Dodge, May 18, 1905, box 5; all letters in Hill Collection, UGA.

129. Quote from Hill to Houston, December 6, 1904, box 4, Hill Collection, UGA; also see Hill to P. H. Mell, December 1, 1904, box 4, Hill Collection, UGA. George T. Winston of the West Raleigh, North Carolina College of Agriculture and Mechanic Arts, for instance, reported that the last legislature (1904) appropriated $50,000 for an agricultural building, along with $20,000 for equipment and $12,500 for barns and greenhouses. Winston wrote that $82,500 represented only "the beginning of our agricultural plant, to which we hope to add materially hereafter." In "Report on Committee of Development of University to Board of Trustees," 3–10. By 1901 the State Agricultural College had received from the state a paltry $15,000 and, by 1904, only an additional $5,000.

130. Conner to Hill, March 31, 1905, box 5; see also Hill to Conner, March 30, 1905, box 5; Hill to Conner, April 3, 1905, box 5; Hill to Conner, June 27, 1905, box 6; all letters in Hill Collection, UGA.

131. Hodgson to Smith, May 8, 1905, box 5, Hill Collection, UGA.

132. Hill to Calloway, May 24, 1904, box 2, Hill Collection, UGA; Mathis, *Walter Barnard Hill, Chancellor,* 338–40.

133. Conner to Hill, July 11, 1905, box 6; Conner to Hill, August 1, box 6; Hodgson to Hill, July 7, 1905, box 6; Hill to J. M. Terrell, June 30, 1905, box 6; all letters in Hill Collection, UGA.

134. Mathis, *Walter Barnard Hill, Chancellor,* 341–46.

135. Hill to M. V. Calvin, August 11, 1905, box 6, Hill Collection, UGA; Dyer, *The University of Georgia,* 162; Hill to N. E. Harris, August 11, 1905, box 6, Hill Collection, UGA.

136. Dyer, *The University of Georgia,* 164, 173.

137. Ayers, *The Promise of the New South,* 420. Statistical evidence from the period is meager, but a university report from 1904 suggested that 70 percent of the students enrolled in the bachelor of science degree program chose a "scientific or business calling," and 63 percent chose "a professional life" after graduation. The statistics may be misleading because it is unclear whether the figures represent tabulations from 1904 or 1866. Even the table that offers figures on the professions chosen by university alumni since 1866 reflects a decided preference for practical career opportunities. Of 3,624 graduates, 1,870 of whom are unaccounted for, by far the most—627—chose careers in "business," which included merchants, bankers, druggists, and insurance company employees. "Tables Showing Data Required by the Resolution of the General Assembly, Approved August 13, 1904," in "Report of the Board of Trustees," 1904–1905, Hill Collection, UGA.

138. Grantham, *Southern Progressivism,* 7–8.

139. Doyle, *New Men, New South, New Cities,* 314–15.

6

A Missionary University: Samuel Chiles Mitchell and the University of South Carolina, 1909–13

Southern progressivism resonated through the administrations of Walter Barnard Hill and Samuel Mitchell. But unlike Hill, who devoted most of his time to improving bureaucratic efficiency and professionalization, and Charles Dabney, who linked the utilitarian doctrine to agricultural education, Samuel Mitchell worked relentlessly to expand the university's influence throughout the state.

Their differences suggest the complexity of educational progressivism. They also suggest that, like Alderman and Dabney, Hill and Mitchell were men with unique personalities, not disembodied abstractions. Whereas Hill's political acumen shielded him from strong opposition in Georgia, Mitchell's missionary agenda led him into a quagmire of political scandal and localist hostility. Of course, Hill was fortunate enough not to confront gubernatorial animosity.

Mitchell's troubles began when the governor accused the timid president of diverting a Peabody grant for the education of white women to finance the instruction of black men. Although the controversy eroded the school's precarious standing, Mitchell pursued an ambitious program of university modernization. Regional revitalization was the responsibility of trained and intelligent leaders, he believed. Mitchell planned to make the university respond to education's "latent potency [to] create industries, uplift the masses, adjust racial differences, and regain political prestige."[1] Combining New South economic axioms and a utilitarian pedagogy, he formulated an aggressive plan for university intervention in society.

Born in Coffeeville, Mississippi in 1864, Mitchell lived in Texas for several years before attending Georgetown College in Kentucky. The destruction of his father's cotton factoring firm during the Civil War plunged the Mitchell family into poverty. Only with the financial support of the owner of a bookstore for whom Mitchell worked in Galveston could he attend the Baptist college of Georgetown.

At Georgetown, Mitchell developed an interest in history under the influence of Arthur Yager, a Ph.D. from Johns Hopkins and former student of Herbert Baxter Adams. Mitchell absorbed Yager's enthusiasm for "scientific" history and his New South version of the Civil War and Reconstruction. According to biographer John Carroll Presley, Mitchell also repudiated sectionalism and classical education as vestiges of a moribund Old South.[2] Although a student of Latin and Greek, he came to believe that classical education was, in the words of historian Daniel W. Hollis, "an opiate that caused the Old South to divert attention from its social and economic shortcomings." The study of history was a didactic exercise that offered young southerners a guide to practical change.[3]

In 1895 he began a doctorate in history at the University of Chicago on "The Change from Colony to Commonwealth in Virginia." Even before he graduated in 1899, he had begun teaching at the University of Richmond in 1895. Politically and socially active during his time at Richmond, Mitchell participated in campaigns to improve rural schools, public health, and roads. He also opposed lynching and supported prohibition. While at the University of Richmond he cultivated a close relationship with the reform governor Andrew J. Montague. He was also an active participant in the annual Conference for Education in the South. Although a Baptist, Mitchell subscribed to Darwinism, the Higher Criticism, and the major tenets of the Social Gospel. Elected to the presidency of South Carolina in 1908, Mitchell delayed taking the position in Columbia because of a previous commitment to teach at Brown University for a year. At Brown, he developed an association with the eminent sociologist and positivist theoretician Lester Frank Ward.[4]

Underpinning Mitchell's progressivism was the New South ideology. He joined the chorus of New South advocates who anticipated the time when the South would share in the American promise of abundance and prosperity. Part of the solution was sectional reconciliation. Mitchell extolled the virtues of education for harmonizing northern and southern interests: "Education is the most effectual means of unifying our people. It at once breaks down social caste in the South and assimilates us in habit and sentiment with all other sections of our common country. The school releases the South from isolation and makes for a national spirit."[5] Echoing the New South ideology, Mitchell wrote in an article for the *South Atlantic Quarterly* that the South's three major problems were "Economic Development, National Integration, and Racial Adjustment." Education was the key to resolving these thorny questions. The college, in particular, should advance economic recovery by fostering nationalism in the region.[6]

Mitchell's vision of the university reflected his New South convictions. In the platitude-laden idiom of late Victorian America, he asserted that the college's primary mission was to "vitalize reason." The university would advance industrialization through courses in industrial chemistry, electricity, mining, and engineering. Higher education would help dissolve partisan politics, the bane of the New South, in the acids of the "historical spirit." In addition, modern techniques of sociological analysis would be applied to race relations. Speaking in the language of progressivism, Mitchell argued that the college would contribute to social efficiency by promoting universal education. It had already stimulated the elevation of educational standards through the work of its graduates in rural common schools. The university "spirit," he announced, had "been a powerful factor in molding public opinion in the interest of popular enlightenment."[7]

The foundation of his educational progressivism was the conviction that the university had a duty to society and the state. Like Walter Hill, he rejected college insularity and the idea that the university should cater to the interests of the "cultured classes" or the college trustees. "Unless the life of a college is vitally related to all of the instinctive needs of society and the deep impulses of the average man, it has been weighed in the balance and found wanting. . . . The success of every college is gauged solely by its services to mankind at large." The university's primary mission was not to transmit liberal culture or mental discipline but to promote service-oriented education. The college was distinguished by "men chock full of inspiration and the spirit of social service" rather than by ornate buildings and novel courses.[8] University service in the twentieth century would be rendered by efficiency experts applying specialized knowledge to a wide range of social problems. No longer a dubious financial obligation, the progressive university would function as an extension of the modern state.[9]

The university that Mitchell encountered on his arrival in Columbia in 1909 bore little resemblance to his ideal of the modern university. The years after the Civil War found the University of South Carolina (USC) financially insolvent and at the caprices of Redeemer era politics.[10] The school was reorganized five times between the end of the war and the beginning of Mitchell's administration. In 1885, Benjamin Tillman included USC in his politically motivated attack on South Carolina's privileged classes. The university was a haven for "provincialism, stagnation, and self-idolatry" that had contributed little or nothing to the rebuilding of the Palmetto State. Tillman's solution was to create separate institutions of higher education to serve predominantly agrarian South Carolina. One of these new institutions was Clemson Agricultural College. Financed by a fertilizer tax designed for the college's exclusive support, Clemson quickly became a privileged institution. The university was demoted to a liberal arts college, losing its graduate school, normal school, and pharmacy school along with its agricultural and mechanical departments.[11]

In 1906 the South Carolina College was once again classified as a university, but the legacy of the Tillman attack persisted. In 1909 Clemson and the Winthrop Normal and Industrial College for Women received $145,833 and $132,685, respectively; by comparison, the university received $84,775. Clemson's enrollment for that year stood at 648, whereas the college at Columbia attracted only 298 students. Financially disadvantaged and unpopular, USC held out little promise at the beginning of the twentieth century.[12]

Mitchell hoped to revitalize the university with the message of university service to the state. In a 1912 college bulletin, he announced that the modern university's priorities were to teach, research, energize public schools, disseminate knowledge throughout society, stimulate public discussion, and "relate the life of the State to the larger movements in the modern world." Mitchell made no distinction between "the State" and the responsibilities of the modern research university. The university was the centerpiece of a public system of education that he hoped would become an additional branch of government. Sensitive to the university's political vulnerability, he insisted that the main task at South Carolina was "to win sympathy, restore confidence, [and] to relate the University to the progressive forces within the State, especially the farms and mills." Echoing Chancellor Hill, Mitchell insisted that the state university was responsible for creating unity among South Carolina's schools, coordinating their resources in the interest of rational progress. South Carolina's educational system was responsible for addressing practical issues in a progressive manner. Reform of the jury system, "reverence for law," the rights of children, good roads, "national spirit," and business "integrity" were no less the province of educational professionals than reading and writing.[13]

The notion of corporate management influenced Mitchell's administrative style as it influenced Chancellor Hill's. Mitchell applauded the new breed of university leaders, who "must be endowed with the same sort of executive ability that is required of the president of a great corporation." Scholarly qualifications were not enough; the modern college president needed administrative and managerial acumen. A "general capable of inspiring and handling all the multitudinous forces at his command," the new college president would impose the academic equivalent of Taylor's scientific management on a "great educational plant."[14] Distinguishing himself from the fossilized pedagogy of mental discipline, Mitchell also rejected the image of the retiring, bookish president in favor of the interventionist executive. True to his word, he subordinated his teaching duties to his work as a propagandist for educational progressivism.

To advance his utilitarian agenda, Mitchell mobilized popular support. In the style of progressive evangelization, he undertook an exhaustive campaign of meetings and lectures to promote university improvement, enrollment, and public consciousness about higher education.[15] He demonstrated his commitment to a progressive agenda by underlining the connection between educational revival and the movement for improved roads, public health, sanitation, libraries, and agriculture. However, his crusade was "less a work of education than of statesmanship; or rather the primary aim is economic, social and political progress by means of education." The president also encouraged the formation of alumni chapters throughout the state. An alumni network would improve the university's public image, promote attendance, and augment the school's political influence.[16] The university would not only adapt to the larger movements in the world but also assume a strategic position as a state instrument in the movement for southern progress.

Combined with his education program was a heavy dose of progressive paternalism. Visiting the mill villages scattered throughout the South Carolina piedmont, he hoped to eradicate "denominational intolerance" and replace it with a more "practical" religion. Like many middle-class professionals, Mitchell was troubled by a fiercely independent mill population unwilling to yield to the discipline of the new industrial order. Part of his response was to bridge the gap between workers, blacks, and elites by fostering social cohesion and cooperation. Compulsory school attendance would solve the problem of child labor by inculcating the social habits needed for "political sanity and progress." In addition to his own work, he lent university support to the task of social uplift in the mill villages. Students and faculty taught Sunday school and night school and participated in lectures given at the mills' YMCA. The university hoped to acculturate the mill hands by inviting them to attend the school's many popular lectures, concerts, and extension courses. The administration also encouraged students to take an active role in mill village reform. Little wonder, then, that several of Columbia's leading mill magnates welcomed the president's education campaign.[17]

Extension courses were part of Mitchell's effort to project the university's influence throughout South Carolina and connect it to the activist state: "The University of South Carolina desires to do its share as a part of the public school system of the State, in advancing the interest of its schools and in furthering the intellectual growth of its people."[18] The extension movement sponsored night classes in English, French, and economics by December 1909. Three courses of public lectures were offered during the 1908 session, including such addresses as "The Economic Importance of Good Roads," "How the University Can Help Columbia," and "The Mill Population of South Carolina." The president hoped to generate support for the extension courses by accommodating local businesspeople. He also called for higher professional standards among the city's teachers. When professor of English H. C. Davis proposed a correspondence course designed for teachers, Mitchell approved it in the belief that it would strengthen the cause of education in South Carolina.[19]

Many of the faculty responded to Mitchell's philosophy by participating in state and regional reform organizations. In the annual report of the board to the legislature, Mitchell singled out Leonard T. Baker, professor of pedagogy and future president of the university, for special praise. The redoubtable Baker had represented the university at the Southern Educational Association of Preparatory Schools and Colleges and the State Teachers' Association. He also found time to make countless addresses to county teachers' associations.[20] The president and several of the faculty also offered their expertise to private industry and public agencies. When the Columbia Chamber of Commerce requested expert assistance for its Committee on Navigation of the Congaree River, Mitchell suggested M. Goode Homes, professor of civil engineering. The president believed that making the Congaree navigable was the linchpin in developing Columbia as "a great distributing point."[21] He went so far as to suggest that Professor Homes "can aid greatly many communities without cost in building country roads" if county boards of commissioners requested his assistance. The president's confidence in Homes's expertise was not unfounded; he had already served as a consultant on road improvement in Fairfield County.[22] For the president, the university's assistance to the Chamber of Commerce exemplified the application of knowledge to social service, the central tenet of educational progressivism.

Several of the professors' lectures appeared in bulletin form and were circulated throughout the state. The president justified the added expense on the basis that their "primary duty has been to popularize the University and to interpret anew its spirit of service to all the people." In 1911, the school issued a special bulletin announcing extension lectures in communities throughout South Carolina. The special bulletin, like Mitchell's promotional lectures, was designed to focus public attention on the university's involvement in social revitalization. Agricultural education also drew the president's attention. In 1910 he wrote to David R. Coker, scion of an influential family and trustee of the university, to request a manuscript on his agricultural experiments for publication. Coker obliged, suggesting topics for bulletins including "Plant

Breeding for Farm Crops" and "Some Forage Crops and Their Value to the South." The more enthusiastic practitioners of social service contributed articles to state newspapers on a range of social issues including road building, rural schools, and high school development. Reporting to the Board of Trustees in June 1911, Mitchell endorsed the professors' "rare initiative in seeking to serve the people of the State in many causes, such as good roads, public health, [and] more efficient schools."[23]

Mitchell was not the only state university president in the Carolinas interested in university outreach. His efforts to connect the university to social reform were mirrored by Edward Kidder Graham, president of the University of North Carolina from 1914 to 1918. Benefiting from financial support that Mitchell never enjoyed, Graham, professor of English at Chapel Hill before his term as president, set out to expand the university's influence in state affairs. According to one contemporary, Kidder intended to "release the educational principles and scholarly ideals of the university [into] channels of service and utility to the great masses of the people."[24] He initiated university assistance to state campaigns for good roads, public health, sociology, rural improvement, urban planning, and related social problems. More successful than Chancellor Hill in establishing a School of Commerce and Business Administration, he appointed a professor of economics to head the new department.[25]

Creating an extension bureau, Graham went beyond Mitchell by institutionalizing university service. The principle was the same, though. The bureau sponsored correspondence courses, extension lectures, road studies, social surveys, and public health seminars. President Graham gave further evidence that the progressive zeitgeist had reached Chapel Hill by establishing academic positions in rural social economics and rural education. Courses in business administration, university support for statewide economic studies, and publication of the university *Extension Bulletin* resulted from Graham's prodigious efforts. If anything, North Carolina's efforts enjoyed a more conspicuous legacy: The founding of the Institute for Research in Social Science in 1924 and the Institute of Government in 1931 projected Graham's social consciousness into the modern South.[26]

Endowed with more modest resources, Mitchell still managed to cultivate USC's extension efforts. By 1910 the program had been expanded to include courses in Sunday school pedagogy and Victorian poetry. Along more expressly progressive lines, Mitchell initiated a course in public health to be taught by physicians from the State Board of Health. By offering health courses for public servants, the university forged an associational network that connected the state's education facilities to the Rockefeller Sanitary Commission and the State

Board of Health.[27] Advocating a course in bacteriology, the president underlined the progressive emphasis on coordinating public education with public health: "It is an integral part of a modern college. At this time it will enable the University to identify itself with the gratifying activities as to public health and sanitation in South Carolina."[28] To defray the cost, Mitchell sought assistance from the Rockefeller commission. Secretary Wickliffe Rose endorsed the university's "advanced position in this matter of public health" and guaranteed the salary of at least one professor. He also assured Mitchell that the matter of the second professor's salary would be brought before the commission's executive committee. Conscious of the university's financial stringency, the president implored the sanitary commission to allocate at least $500 annually to support a second professor.[29]

His efforts to integrate state agencies with academic functions mirrored the work of fellow progressives Hill and Dabney. They hoped to connect the university to an interventionist state realigned by bureaucratic efficiency and social responsibility.[30] The courses would combine university and state resources and produce technical experts capable of undertaking progressive reform: "This strengthens the University, and will raise up a body of men who will carry out in their several communities the health and sanitary reforms so much needed." Predicated on progressive utilitarianism, the extension lecture series exemplified the president's program to "extend the sphere of usefulness of the University so as to embrace all the interests of the State."[31]

The lecture series met with faculty cooperation and strong public support.[32] Herbert G. Officer, a former student of the university then studying at Columbia, wrote to Mitchell expressing his approval of the extension program. "They are of great value in awakening in the rural communities a desire to know more about what is going on around them and to try and better their communities." The president's larger mission of bringing the university to the state was clear to Officer: "The people are already beginning to look to the university for guidance in their forward movement and to trust more implicitly its leadership." If Mitchell's gospel of social service had yet to convert the legislature, it had apparently won popular support. Even among legislators, Mitchell's educational progressivism had made inroads. A committee appointed in 1911 to investigate education applauded university outreach and social service.[33]

As important as public approval was to university modernization, political support was invaluable. As state governor and chair of the university Board of Trustees, Martin Ansel endorsed Mitchell's infusion of progressivism into the university. The governor supported the president's major initiatives, including promotion of the YMCA on campus, the course on public health, the university extension program, the lecture series, and the university bulletin. Increasing enrollment was evidence of university growth during Ansel's term. In 1907, his first year as governor, student enrollment stood at 285. By 1910, his last year, it had climbed to 407. The change in the university's financial status also suggested Ansel's favorable disposition toward the school. In 1906, the university's total income was $52,229; in four years it had skyrocketed to $112,256. Partly a reflection of Mitchell's aptitude in marketing the university, the school's improvement was also a function of Ansel's determination to maintain a hospitable atmosphere for education reform.[34]

Mitchell also sought to expose the university to broader currents of progressive thought by inviting leading southern reformers and intellectuals to give lectures on campus. "I am a strong believer in education by personality and this course of lectures by public men is already having its effect upon the life of the University," he wrote. Among others, Mitchell secured Clarence Poe, editor of *The Progressive Farmer,* Walter Hines Page, famous southern progressive and critic, Dr Charles Stiles, crusader against hookworm, and Lewis Parker, university alumnus and president of seventeen cotton mills, to give lectures at the university.[35]

The president's lecture series also featured Edwin Alderman of the University of Virginia, who gave an address titled "The University and Democracy," and chancellor James Kirkland of Vanderbilt University, who discussed "Education for Efficiency." The lectures of these prominent reformers illustrate Mitchell's attention to progressive voices outside of South Carolina. A close-knit network of southern progressives exchanged ideas, reinforced each other's commitment to reform, and legitimized the movement for university engagement in social issues. Out of this brain trust, Mitchell hoped to create a cabinet of social engineers for each southern state. Acting on this conviction, Mitchell and other faculty members regularly turned to professional experts for assistance. In search of a lecturer on good roads, for example, he wrote to and received a favorable response from the Office of Public Records in the Department of Agriculture.[36]

The touchstone of progressive reform was the improvement of southern education, and Mitchell promoted it no less than Dabney and the others.[37] In response to a request for topic suggestions for an upcoming meeting of the State Teachers' Association, Mitchell echoed the major concerns of southern progressive educators.[38]

In harmony with the progressive ideology, Mitchell called on the conference to examine ways to make school supervision more efficient. Superintendents should be better paid and should meet certain professional standards. They should also specialize in enforcing school regulations and improving classroom instruction. In addition, Mitchell proposed that local taxation and popular support for a "good neighborhood school" were critical to educational advancement. He advocated school consolidation, the development of standardized four-year high schools, and coordination of the state's elementary schools, colleges, and universities. To improve the quality of schoolhouses, Mitchell joined other progressives in calling for local school improvement leagues. The capstone of his agenda was expanding the education department. Improved pedagogical training would produce expert educators capable of administering modern schools. Taken together, the president's suggestions provided a template for progressive reform.[39]

The president's plan to improve pedagogical instruction was given a boost from external sources. In 1909 the Peabody Education Board and the Southern Education Board (SEB) gave a grant to the university to establish the dual position of professor of elementary education and state supervisor of rural schools. It was hoped that an inspector of rural schools would help break down rural isolation and promote social cohesion: "The growth of community life in the country is the most significant thing occurring in this State at the present time, and it behooves us to reinforce every agency working to that end."[40] Wickliffe Rose of the SEB negotiated with J. E. Swearingen, State Superintendent of Education and university trustee, on the conditions of the offer. Swearingen was careful to ensure that the rural school supervisor would be under the authority of the State Department of Education. Concerned that the position might be jeopardized by "uncongenial men in the Governor's chair," he depoliticized the appointment by requiring the two agencies to make the offer through the university's board. Swearingen, together with Mitchell, suggested W. K. Tate of Charleston for the job. Asserting its prerogatives, the Peabody board reserved the right to nominate a candidate for the position.[41]

The condition attached to the Peabody offer raised the ire of some trustees concerned about university autonomy. Trustee J. Q. Davis approved the offer in principle but insisted that the trustees should discuss "the propriety of accepting the contribution from the Peabody people with a provision that we shall be trammelled in selecting the inspector." For Davis and other university administrators confronted with the double-edged sword of philanthropic donations, the issue was one of control. "Should the University send out a representative and not be free to select him?" Davis was also concerned that the board's offer would upset faculty harmony because the rural school supervisor would be paid $1,000 more than full professors. Though supportive of Tate's nomination, Davis insisted that it be made clear that "he owes his commission to the board free from outside dictation."[42] Like the General Education Board (GEB), the Peabody and the SEB operated according to what historian William Link describes as a "rationalized policy" that made funding grants contingent on the adoption of more businesslike administrative practices.[43] Davis may have been in sympathy with these goals, but he voiced the obvious concern that financial support from external sources often came at the price of university independence.

Like J. S. Stewart's work as secondary school inspector at Georgia, Tate's position combined government and academic responsibilities. Following the precedent set by the GEB, Tate was affiliated to both the university and the State Board of Education.[44] Mitchell wrote to Tate expressing his hope that he would become nothing less than "an Educational Engineer." Soon after Tate's appointment, he began to teach a course at the university in rural school pedagogy. In progressive fashion, Mitchell envisioned extensive coordination between the new rural school supervisor, the professor of secondary education and high school inspector, the state sanitarium, the school improvement associations, and the various public health agencies and departments. The connection he made was not unusual: Progressives routinely combined education and public health reform.[45] To southern progressives, both were part of a seamless web of social problems afflicting the South. For Mitchell, state and university collaboration reflected the "spirit of cooperation" inherent in the effort to promote the "enrichment of rural life" in South Carolina.[46]

State and university cooperation made enormous strides by 1911. Through the work of W. H. Hand, professor of secondary education and high school inspector, and W. K. Tate, the university established links with the State Board of Education. The university forged similar connections to the State Board of Health and the State Department of Labor, Commerce, and Manufacture. E. J. Watson, commissioner of the Department of Labor, established a state exhibit in Leconte College that featured manufacturing techniques and South Carolina's resources. The president also offered rooms in the science building for the State Department of Agriculture's chemical laboratories, which Commissioner Watson gratefully accepted. The State Board of Health occupied rooms in the same building. The university also reached out to the federal government by offering a series of lectures in conjunction with the U.S. Department of Agriculture. Plans were formulated in 1911 to make the course a permanent addition to the curriculum. Premised on New South assumptions about balanced agriculture and rural revitalization, the course was designed to "keep the whole student body sympathetic with country life" and cognizant of the "progress" in agriculture throughout the state.[47]

Cooperation between state agencies and the state university was crucial to the progressive vision of social efficiency. Addressing a conference of state supervisors of rural schools in Nashville in 1912, Mitchell declared, "Seeking to integrate your efforts with the permanent institutions of society and with the taxing power of the whole people, you have come into cooperation with the State University." The president offered the State Board of Health's work on the USC campus, the state high school inspector, the director of farm demonstration work, and the weekly addresses by the U.S. Department of Agriculture's director of farm management as examples of progressive cooperation. He also applauded the agencies' field workers for channeling information to faculty and students. The primary benefit of cooperation between state agencies was public service. The work of state agencies on campus was "helping to make the institution a means of real service to the whole people by forming a bond between the universities and the communities which its seeks to serve."[48]

No less than efforts to regulate railroads and improve public health care, state and university cooperation became a pillar in the edifice of the bureaucratic state: "Back of all our efforts there is beginning to emerge the structural motive to base society on science, to rationalize human living, to lift to the highest efficiency . . . the health of the family and community."[49] Connecting university reform efforts to existing government departments, Mitchell and other progressives validated the idea that the college was a vital appendage of the state. Simultaneously, the university lent prestige to politically vulnerable government bureaucracies. Both cooperated in the effort to replace southern localism with social efficiency.

While Mitchell advanced university and government cooperation, he also enlisted social organizations in the campaign for university social service. Prominent among these was the Young Men's Christian Association (YMCA). The theme of social service took hold of the imaginations of many YMCA campus chapters in the early twentieth-century South.[50] Stemming from the evangelical reform tradition, the YMCA provided fertile ground for southern progressivism. Middle-class southerners harmonized an increasingly secularized Christianity with the program of regional progress. "More and more we are going to get our religious and social leadership from state supported colleges. This is due in part to the intense activity of the Y.M.C.A." On southern campuses, the YMCA functioned as an associational agency within a developing bureaucratic state. Ostensibly a private organization, the nondenominational YMCA received state funding to pay the salary of its full-time secretary, along with ancillary expenses.[51]

Planning to make the YMCA a permanent feature of the university, Mitchell sought out suitable accommodations and a full-time secretary. Funds for a YMCA had already been collected by supporters and held by Dr. J. William Flinn, whose home on campus became a center of student activity. Board member August Kohn first suggested the idea of establishing the YMCA on campus, which the president warmly endorsed. With funds from the university budget and student contributions, Flinn Hall was constructed. The alumni selected W. P. Mills, the YMCA's first secretary. A graduate of the university and a Rhodes scholar, Mills became "an exhilarating factor in the life of the student body."[52] To keep Mills at Flinn Hall, Mitchell persuaded the board to pay $1,000 a year. Under Mill's direction, Flinn Hall provided a cafe, a guest room for university visitors, and study groups for examining "special problems" such as race relations.

The YMCA galvanized student support for the progressive movement at the university. Mitchell proclaimed that it "transformed the social and moral conditions of the campus. No other fact in the recent life of the University is to be compared with Flinn Hall in the reach and power of its influence for good. The students have sprung to it with enthusiasm that is altogether inspiring."[53] Reflecting the progressive affinity for the Social Gospel, Mitchell praised the YMCA's translation of religion into a "practical matter of life." In opposition to narrow denominationalism, Mitchell promoted the YMCA as an agent of social unification. Southern localism would disintegrate as the YMCA and other agencies remolded the region in the image of progressive efficiency. Not unlike the combined university and government agencies, the YMCA would promote regional cooperation and reform. In addition, it would legitimize social reform in the eyes of conservative Protestants.[54]

University support for the YMCA reflects the larger processes transforming southern higher education in the twentieth century. If a "distinctly college-centered liberal Christian education" persisted as the defining characteristic of both private and public universities in the New South, it was a Christianity modified by assumptions about the need for a "practical" religion. Religion, for many progressives, was valued more for the efficacy of its moral "impulses" than for its doctrinal content.[55] State college presidents endorsed the YMCA program, with its blend of Christian revivalism and moral reform, because it accorded with their gospel of social service. The church was obligated to address the "problems of rational living such as Economy, Equality, Public Health, and a more sensitive civil conscience." Mitchell argued that southern universities were established to train men for the ministry, but the drive for southern modernization made it necessary to train men to undertake the demanding and important work of the YMCA. With YMCAs emerging in colleges, the mill towns, and "all the enterprising towns of the South," Mitchell believed that state universities were uniquely qualified to train candidates for an "inter-denominational field." No hint of Christian piety was evident in the president's celebration of what the YMCA did for "the helpfulness of the body, the quickening of the mind, social fellowship, and in a word, the reinforcement of life."[56]

Rather than a stimulant to evangelical revivalism, the Sunday school was a "strategic factor" for education, which itself was simply a "process of character formation."[57] In writing of W. P. Mills, the president privileged a career in social reform over the work of the ordained ministry: "I believe that in directing the training of Y.M.C.A. workers, he will have a far greater field of usefulness even than in the Presbyterian ministry."[58] Mitchell's support for the YMCA was decidedly utilitarian. By channeling the reform energies pulsating through the campus chapters of the YMCA into the progressive movement, Mitchell and university leaders incorporated the organization into the university's social service mission.

To promote the fusion of religion and educational progressivism, Mitchell proposed that the university offer a bachelor of arts course for aspiring YMCA workers. Training in YMCA techniques would be added to courses in history, language, philosophy, science, and sociology. Trained graduates would then serve as secretaries, physical directors, and settlement workers in the organization. In December 1910 the trustees approved the degree, which eventually came to include courses in economics, psychology of adolescence, psychology of religion, public health, and comparative religion.[59]

An organization dedicated to social service in the South could hardly expect to avoid the issue of race. In 1910, W. D. Weatherford, a member of the YMCA's International Committee, published a book titled *Negro Life in the South* for use by student discussion groups. The YMCA regional secretary requested that Mitchell consider forming a student group to discuss the race issue, using Weatherford's book as a text. Although concerned about the possible ramifications of such a "delicate undertaking," the president authorized the group, reasoning that "the instincts of students are sound."[60]

Two years later, the general secretary of the YMCA's international committee asked Mitchell to assess Weatherford's work and the YMCA's sociological undertaking. The president responded glowingly, asserting that Weatherford "knows the negro problem at first hand, and is tugging away at in a truly constructive and statesmanlike way." He praised the book for bringing racial issues before the students in what, for the time, seemed an enlightened manner. "A large class has for two years studied his book under the guidance of a strong member of the faculty, and many of the students have gone out in the spirit of genuine helpfulness to visit the homes of the colored people." The "practical value" of the class was evident from a conference held between a group of university students, Mills, Mitchell, and Channing Tobias, a black YMCA volunteer and organizer of the conference. The participants discussed the crime of lynching in a "frank and practical" manner and the corrosive effects it had on the law, "which alone can protect the homes of the South." In the YMCA, Mitchell proclaimed, the South had found "one of the finest agencies" for the rational management of race relations. Whether or not the president's effusive rhetoric accurately reflects his views of the YMCA's capacity for defusing racial antagonism is difficult to determine. Consistent with his progressive sensibilities, though, he approved of its comparatively rational examination of race relations.[61]

The integration of the YMCA into the university network is important for several reasons. First, it demonstrates the harmony between early twentieth-century southern liberal Protestantism and the regional progressive movement. Progressive visions of a rehabilitated South coincided comfortably with a liberal Protestantism committed to moral and social uplift. United by the idea of southern progress, the combination of liberal Protestantism and progressivism was a powerful force that led the South toward a more humane social order. Second, it reflects the university's effort to expand the definition of the state and its responsibilities. Supported by public funds and linked to the state university, the YMCA's work on southern campuses exemplified the campaign to use semiprivate organizations in the program for social efficiency and improvement.

Third, the YMCA bachelor's degree illustrates the efforts of educational modernizers such as Mitchell to use the university to train social reform experts. No less than Jane Addams, who made northern settlement workers a staple of public consciousness, Mitchell and Mills helped validate the role of trained experts in social reform. In the process, they justified the dominance of middle-class professionals in the development of social policy. Fourth, the YMCA's interest in college students underscores the importance that at least some southerners attached to the emerging service-oriented university. In search of suitable candidates for its missionary work, the YMCA turned to the largest repositories of intellectual talent and youthful vigor available in the region at the time. As much as other reformers, Mitchell saw the YMCA as a conduit for progressive reform.

An active supporter of social and racial amelioration, Mitchell was conservative on the question of women's education. Coeducation was introduced at the university in 1894, but in 1909 only 10 of 298 students were women. The president admitted that women had been given little encouragement to attend the state school. Coeducation, he submitted to Wallace Buttrick of the GEB, "does not accord with the instincts of the people of the state." Yet Mitchell also had to admit the relentless demand of many women for a college education that would allow them to pursue teaching careers in the state's high schools. But Mitchell did not simply want to separate women from men in state educational facilities. He also wanted to ensure that they received a different form of education, one supposedly suited to their feminine sensibilities. In arguing for a distinctly female brand of education, Mitchell reflected the conventional ideology of separate spheres for men and women.[62]

Like most of his contemporaries, Mitchell had little argument with the assertion that women needed some kind of education. But because "men and women are not unequal, but unlike, it seems to me, therefore, that the training should be nicely adjusted to the functions of each in society." The president criticized southern women's colleges for emphasizing "accomplishment" to the detriment of "discipline and knowledge." Surprisingly, he approved of women being educated in the "scientific spirit," but laboratory research was not what he had in mind. Instead, Mitchell stepped back from the suggestion of equal education by asserting with Victorian self-assurance "that home is the rightful sphere of woman, and everything that prepares here [*sic*] best for that large mission should find a place in the college course."[63]

Mitchell's ideas about women's education harmonized with those of most male educators in the South. John McBryde of the Sweet Briar Institute in Virginia encapsulated these ideas at a meeting of the Richmond Education Association in 1907. He warned southern institutions not to follow the northern tendency to educate women without regard for gender distinctions. When educated as men, women degenerated into "unsexed" matrons "robbed of more than half of her strength and influence." Women's education should be adjusted to cultivate the qualities of "modesty, sympathy, patience, endurance, hope, courage, faith, loyalty," and "devotion to duty." Although women should not be deprived of the liberal arts, they should be encouraged to absorb culture through the study of music and art. McBryde also imagined women grappling with the intellectual "problem" of "house furnishings" as well as "designs for wall papers, and patterns for carpets" and curtains. Instruction in domestic science and the womanly virtues would mitigate the gender-neutralizing influences of a college education. Many progressives would have agreed with McBryde's declamation that a curriculum that "fills a woman's soul with foolish notions of a glorious independence apart from man and apart from home is . . . pernicious."[64]

Mitchell favored some form of coordinate education in which women would be restricted for the most part to their own facilities but would share university resources. The faculty would be drawn largely from professors at the state college with a woman appointed as dean for the separate institution. Pembroke College at Brown University, where he had taught for a year before accepting the South Carolina position, provided a model for a coordinated women's college. In December 1909, the president wrote to Wallace Buttrick to request $2,500 of the GEB to build a women's college. As with other building projects, Mitchell hoped that the board's assistance would provide an impetus to legislative support.[65]

The board made no offers for a women's college, but the president had experienced something of a conversion on the question of coeducation by 1912. Most likely, the two events were related. The economic origin of his change of heart was evident in a letter to D. T. Lauderdale: "Co-education has succeeded in all the Western States. It is more economic. Education is now so costly that it is impossible for a State to build two great universities, one for women and one for men." Despite its apparent fiscal appeal, Mitchell argued that southern gender conventions and the practice of coeducation were incompatible. Like Edwin Alderman at Virginia, Mitchell offered "coordinate instruction" as an alternative "that works best in the older states like South Carolina." The president suggested the University of Virginia's plan to establish a coordinate college as an example of the southern solution to women's education. During Mitchell's brief tenure, though, the board took no action on the proposal.[66]

Mitchell's struggle to accommodate women's education sheds light on the ideological parameters of progressive reform. Although he acknowledged the demand for teachers to staff the South's expanding school system, he adhered closely to the rigid gender distinctions that organized the middle-class cosmos. Women's education was necessary and socially beneficial, but it should be carried out within boundaries circumscribed by traditional notions of domesticity. As he described to D. T. Lauderdale, "The presence of women is refining to men, each intellectually supplement the other, the women being great in intuition, and the men in reason." Women may be equal, Mitchell sullenly admitted, but they were by nature fundamentally different: "Their tastes supplement one another, women delighting in music and art, and men in science and politics; their recreation and social life supplement one another, the women giving social teas and dramas, the men athletics and other manly sports." Deploying women in the education crusade and training them as pedagogical experts should not threaten men's social authority, nor should it challenge traditional conceptions of masculinity. But progressives were on slippery ground because women were not uniformly content to accept the conditions that men attached to their professional ambitions. And ambiguities naturally emerged when men and women promoted the same reforms, demanded the same education, performed the same work, and accomplished the same results. But from the perspective of stated policy, Mitchell insisted that education should not extinguish women's hallowed responsibility for the sanctity of home and hearth.[67]

Although Mitchell spent the majority of his time trying to extend the university's social influence, he also supervised internal changes that reflected his commitment to university modernization. Like Hill, Alderman, and Dabney, Mitchell saw an inextricable connection between internal reform and university outreach. Professionalization of university curricula redefined the university and the faculty who taught it. At the same time, it trained efficiency experts for social service.

The utilitarian impulse was clear in Mitchell's promotion of the social sciences. When the chair of moral and social science was left vacant by the resignation of professor Gordon Moore, Mitchell saw it as an opportunity to modernize the department. The president recommended that the new chair incorporate sociology, government studies, and select history courses under the umbrella of "political and social science." But Mitchell also sought to fulfill the "duty of a State university to offer work in Political and Social Science." Using Francis Lieber's political studies department as a model, which distinguished the college's otherwise lackluster antebellum record, the president planned to "revive and modernize" the chair. Cautious of the implications of critical investigation in the area of sociology, Mitchell assured trustee David R. Coker, in code words for racial conservatism, that the position would be awarded to "a man of our own, thoroughly sympathetic with our people through traditions and purpose."[68] Yet Mitchell's conservatism on racial matters did not prevent him from trying to recruit northerners for the position. Searching for a qualified candidate, he canvassed Howard Lee McBain of the University of Wisconsin, the leading progressive institution in the country.[69]

The creed of social service undergirded Mitchell's call for an improved department of physics. The president was particularly concerned that attention be given to the study of electricity. To this end, he called on the Board of Trustees to hire an adjunct professor of physics to manage the new subdiscipline. Electricity was a subject "vitally related to the development of the South at this time." The president's interest in electricity apparently was sparked by a visit to the Southern Power Company's development at Parr Shoals. At the cost of $3 million, the project was generating power for 175 cotton mills and 25,000 horsepower for Columbia. Presumably, Mitchell imagined professor Bruce Coleman, who would fill the adjunct position, functioning as a liaison between the university and the hydroelectric industry. Mitchell's interest in science was more than cursory. Physical science was nothing less than an "antidote to prejudice, racial, sectional, religious and political." He cheered the inclusion of the pure sciences in college curricula for shifting the focus of state colleges away from an exclusively "literary" pedagogy.[70]

Professionalizing the university's curriculum was central to Mitchell's scheme for modernization. Part of the initiative stemmed from the desire to adjust university courses to the needs of southern commerce and industry. It was also a function of the effort to harmonize university offerings with national professional standards. Like Walter Hill, Mitchell endorsed the elevation of law school standards. He urged that the law course be extended from two to three years, in conformity with the country's leading schools. Unsuccessfully, he also lobbied for the adoption of an international law course. In addition, he proposed improved remuneration to encourage the professionalization of the law faculty. Mitchell and the board also hired a publicist to solicit donations to finance a new building.[71]

Because of its importance to infrastructure development, Mitchell stressed a more professional engineering program. He called on the board to recognize civil engineering "as a separate professional department on a footing of equality with the School of Law and the Department of Education." Pointing to the increasing number of students applying to study civil engineering in graduate school, he stressed the university's obligation to provide training in country road building, a "new career to the young men of South Carolina."[72]

Much more so than Walter Hill, Mitchell pressed the board to increase faculty salaries. Better pay was essential to recruiting and maintaining promising scholars. Impressed with the teaching accomplishments and social service record of J. Bruce Coleman, professor of mathematics, Mitchell recommended his promotion to adjunct professor with a salary of $400. The president warned the Board of Trustees that it would be difficult to retain the popular Coleman without adequate compensation. Similarly, Mitchell requested an additional $1,000 for W. P. Mills, the YMCA director.[73] More urgently, Mitchell alerted the trustees that W. H. Hand, the university's vigilant crusader for improved high schools, had been offered the presidency of Anderson College. Justifying a salary increase, Mitchell focused on his role in promoting educational efficiency:

> It is my firm judgement that the biggest piece of constructive work in the state at this time is the development of the high schools in the various communities of South Carolina. An efficient high school in a community strengthens all of the common schools, and standardizes the colleges of the state. . . . Thus the high school is the keystone to the educational arch of South Carolina. The growth of the high schools under Professor Hand's leadership has been gratifying, and he has really won a national place by reason of his substantial work in developing the high schools of this state. . . . In a word, I should regard it as a calamity, both to the University and to all of the people of the state, for Prof. Hand to be lost to this work.[74]

To prevent Hand's departure, Mitchell recommended that the board increase his income from $2,250 to $3,000 and give the professor a house on campus. Standardizing high school education was the responsibility of professional efficiency experts such as Hand, not dilettante reformers. Increasing Hand's salary would acknowledge his professional status and reward his specialized expertise.

Although Mitchell exhorted the faculty to support university extension, he strongly endorsed research as a valid academic pursuit. Scholarly investigation would offer theoretical guidance to the examination of social issues layered in convention and mystifying folkways. Mitchell pointed to the work of the State Board of Health as an example of how research assisted material development. In response to an inquiry about sabbaticals at South Carolina, Mitchell wrote that they would help the faculty "crawl out of our shell. Everything that will relate us anew to the larger movements of the world in thought and social activity will be an unspeakable gain."[75]

To finance independent research, Mitchell encouraged the trustees to adopt a sabbatical system. Citing the exacting expenses incurred during a research trip taken by associate professor of mathematics E. D. Easterling, Mitchell insisted that the university's interests were served by rewarding ambitious scholars. Independent scholarship was vital to the educational revival: "Imitation, echo, rote, tradition, all this has no more vitality than a mummy." The task for southern higher education was to liberate the "southern mind" from the paralysis of tradition so that it could use the law, scholarship, literature, and medicine for social advancement. Independent research was justified not by the expansion of knowledge or the elucidation of intellectual uncertainties but by its contribution to social service.[76]

But while Mitchell extolled the virtues of a research agenda, he did little to improve the university's admission standards. Before he assumed office the board and the faculty decided to raise the requirements for admission in the

1910–11 session from ten units to fourteen units of high school preparatory work. Echoing the inveterate optimism of the university boosters, acting president A. C. Moore justified the board's decision by citing the rapid improvement in the state's high schools. Rigorous admission standards would benefit the university by ensuring that applicants were prepared for the demands of university courses. The change in requirements would also benefit the high schools by preventing the premature departure of insufficiently educated students. The decision was an eminently progressive one: The university would rationalize education by distinguishing itself from the state's high schools. But as with the other claims of many New South enthusiasts, the material accomplishments failed to meet the optimistic ideals.[77]

A curious entry in the Organization Committee's report for May 1912 suggests the administration's weakening resolve on the admission question. It also highlights the role Mitchell played in relaxing the more stringent requirements. Entrance requirements should be observed, the committee granted, "*except* where the President, for satisfactory reasons, within the next three years, shall deem it best to waive them." To meet the inevitable problem created by admitting underachievers, the committee added the feeble provision that the departments in which the struggling students were enrolled "should see to it that they receive such special help as is needed." In an equally timorous conclusion, the report suggested that "it is the sense of the Committee" that unqualified students should not be admitted except under extenuating circumstances.[78]

By 1913, Mitchell's last year at the university, the administration was confronting the familiar dilemma faced by reformers whose desire for improved standards ran headlong into the inadequacy of the region's high schools. In 1910 the administration justified the revised admission requirements as an effort to "articulate" the university as the head of the state education system. Reversing this policy three years later, the administration explained, in an astonishing example of rhetorical dexterity, that *because* the university is the "head of the public school system of the State," it was under an obligation to "prevent ... an impassable gap between itself and the public high schools." Instead of the "rapid improvement" attributed to high schools in 1910, the administration lamented that less than half of South Carolina's secondary institutions were providing more than ten academic units. Examining this bleak situation, the university refused "to place its entrance requirements at a standard which would result in either shutting out the graduates of more than one-half the high schools or in forcing itself into maintaining a fictitious standard."[79]

Mitchell's modernizing university needed enough students to cover the costs of its expanded programs and to solidify its image as an institution of public service rather than a sanctuary for privileged dandies. These objectives could hardly be met by imposing prohibitive entrance requirements. As a result, the university concluded that it was "unprofitable and unwise" to admit students on conditions that were unenforceable. Instead, the school would "preserve a reasonable minimum entrance for the students of smaller preparation" while offering advanced standing to those better prepared. Clinging to the hope for improved entrance requirements, the university admitted that changes in admission standards depended on the quality of the state's high schools.[80]

The deterioration of admission standards during Mitchell's administration exposed the social context that constrained southern progressivism. Although he supported improved standards for elementary and secondary schools, Mitchell's pedagogical agenda dictated a preference for quantitative over qualitative results. To reach people reared in a culture of rural isolation, local autonomy, and antipathy for state-supported institutions of dubious public benefit, Mitchell and his progressive allies were compelled to make the college more, not less, accessible.

As an agent of class formation, the modernizing university needed experts to direct southern progress. In an address to a conference of public servants, educational bureaucrats, and college presidents, Mitchell observed, "In the university you have already begun to rear up among the students a corps of purposeful men who in their several communities will later execute your purposes on the field." Social advancement required sophisticated institutions of higher education, but not at the expense of regional uplift. Optimism and political exigencies created a powerful sanction for university accommodation to social conditions. University administrators were not obligated to maintain low standards, but their commitment to erasing the provincialism of the antebellum college led them to favor numbers and money over lofty standards.[81]

The president's less than vigilant enforcement of admission standards was emblematic of his program for USC. More so than any of the figures examined in this study, Mitchell embodied the activist impulse at the core of southern educational progressivism. Mired in poverty, illiteracy, provincialism, and political conservatism, the South, according to progressives, demanded deliverance at the hands of the region's best and brightest. The obscure classical college was for many progressives the symbol of what plagued the region. Impractical, elitist, and isolated from the broader intellectual and social currents remaking the nation, the classical college symbolized the detritus of tradition. This depiction was a useful rhetorical weapon in the assault on the region's educational backwardness.

Although Mitchell and others did not abandon the classical curriculum, they subordinated it to a vision of the university as a repository of technical knowledge for a developing region. Attuned to the functional needs of industrial growth, Mitchell turned the university's energies toward cultivating efficiency experts. Committed to the values of social efficiency and coordinated reform, progressives saw the university as the key instrument in southern progress.

A resolution drafted by the Board of Trustees shortly after Mitchell's departure from Columbia underlines the impact of his administration on the university:

> It shall be the policy of the University of South Carolina to serve all the people of the State by the highest cultivation and widest diffusion of every kind of worthy learning and beneficent motive. Its standards, therefore, must be designed to fit existing conditions and to create better conditions. . . . Of the two parts of the University's field—the part within the walls and that without—neither must be neglected in favor of the other. On the one hand it must be understood that no amount of advertising, of enthusiasm, or of inspiration can be a sufficient substitute for genuine, thorough, accurate, strenuous teaching of those things which are worth teaching at all.[82]

If there were antecedents to pedagogical utilitarianism at USC, Mitchell's leadership galvanized those tendencies. The university would no longer define itself by its classical curriculum, character formation, and its retiring faculty. Instead, social service became a legitimate ideal for the state university.

Yet the resolution also suggests that Mitchell's legacy was mixed. Like the trustees at the University of Georgia, the South Carolina board was reluctant to absorb the creed of utilitarianism, research, and professionalism. The early twentieth century was a period of transition for higher education in the South. Rather than a new dispensation for pedagogical utility, the period witnessed an uneasy equilibrium between liberal culture, mental discipline, and practical education. Whereas Mitchell, Hill, and others elevated social service above liberal education, they left the humanities ignored but intact. If anything, the controversies generated by the Mitchell administration illustrate that there was nothing inevitable about the ascendancy of utilitarian education. Yet the board's resistance to Mitchell's program also reflects the peculiar political climate that prevailed in South Carolina at the time. The controversy that set Mitchell on a collision course with Coleman Blease influenced the president's legacy at Columbia as much as the resistance to modernization.

Notes

1. Mitchell, "Phases in the Educational Movement of the Day," 18.

2. Presley, *Samuel Chiles Mitchell.*

3. Hollis, "Samuel Chiles Mitchell," 22.

4. Hollis, "Samuel Chiles Mitchell," 24.

5. Mitchell, "Phases in the Educational Movement of the Day," 20.

6. Mitchell, "Do Our Colleges Pay?" 217; also see Gaston, *The New South Creed,* 85–92; Mitchell, "The Task of the College in the South," 261.

7. Mitchell, "The Task of the College in the South," 259–61.

8. Mitchell to Charles Rylan, January 15, 1912, in folder titled "Personal Correspondence, September 1912–1913," Mitchell Papers, USC.

9. Ibid., 262; Mitchell developed his pedagogical utilitarianism while a professor at Richmond. See Mitchell's "Practical Tendencies in Education," Mitchell Papers, LOC. In his reverence for "special knowledge," Mitchell spoke the language of social efficiency, which historian Daniel Rodgers identifies as one of three "languages of discontent" shared by progressives. The language of efficiency represented the "merger of the prestige of science with the prestige of the well-organized business firm." See Rodgers, "In Search of Progressivism," 126–27.

10. USC's financial distress was by no means an exception among southern schools. For example, the total usable income for the sixty-six universities and colleges in Virginia, North Carolina, South Carolina, Georgia, Alabama, Mississippi, and Arkansas for 1901 was $65,843 less than that available to Harvard in 1901. Woodward, *Origins of the New South,* 437.

11. Presley, *Samuel Chiles Mitchell,* 134. The report of the SEB's field agent to the GEB sheds light on USC's destitution: "Suffered greatly during the Civil War and Reconstruction. Building not modern in appearance and equipment. No endowment. Income $29,000 from State appropriations and $7000 tuition. . . . Entrance requirements low. . . . Two year course in pedagogy reduced to meet ability of 82 holders of state normal scholarships. Location and history promise educational leadership in State if modern ideas will prevail in support, management, and instruction." In "Education in South Carolina, 1904," Report to the General Education Board, folder #106, box 6; "South Carolina, 1904–1911," SEB Papers, UNC.

12. Presley, *Samuel Chiles Mitchell,* 134–35.

13. Mitchell, "The Ideal of the State University," 5–9; see also Mitchell, "An Aftermath of Appomattox," 141; Mitchell to George Darby, October 14, 1909, in folder titled "Personal Correspondence October 1909 to February 1910," Mitchell Papers, USC; Mitchell to W. K. Tate, October 20, 1909, in folder titled "Departments, 1908–1910," Mitchell Papers, USC. In an undated address titled "A Model Community" given at Coker College in South Carolina, Mitchell claimed, "The soul of a college is service, service to all the people in intellectual, moral, and religious ways" (box 9, Mitchell

Papers, LOC). See also Mitchell to H. C. Ritter, February 10, 1911, in folder titled "Faculty, 1911–1913," Mitchell Papers, USC.

14. Mitchell, "Our New College Presidents," unpublished address, July 27, 1910, in folder titled "Addresses, Lectures, Sermons, April 1910–1910," Mitchell Papers, USC.

15. Southern progressives used revivalistic techniques in the education crusade. According to historian William Link, Robert Ogden, architect of the Conference for Education in the South, used its annual "extravaganzas" as a way to "coordinate the opinion of the 'best men' of the North and South and as a staging ground to organize the educational crusade." Progressives used "careful advance preparations, including consultation with local leaders," a well-planned "public event designed to reverse popular attitudes," and a revivalistic presentation designed to "move public opinion toward a dramatic conversion of social sin." In Link, "The Social Context of Southern Progressivism," 63–65.

16. Mitchell, "An Aftermath of Appomattox," 141–42; Mitchell to William MacDonald, December 23, 1909, in folder titled "Addresses, Lectures, Sermons, 1909," USC Archives; Mitchell to David R. Coker, August 21, 1908, in folder titled "Coker Family, 1908–1913," Mitchell Papers, USC.

17. Mitchell, "An Aftermath of Appomattox," 141–42; see also Mitchell to Thomas F. Parker, December 22, 1910, in folder titled "Departments, 1908–1910," USC Archives; Mitchell to Carl Morgan, December 30, 1911, in folder titled "Personal Correspondence, October 1909–February 1910," Mitchell Papers, USC. The president also recruited experts to present the mill problem to the university. Mitchell to Weltner, November 24, 1909, in folder titled "Addresses, Lectures, Sermons, 1909," USC Archives. His intention was to "enlist the strongest and most influential of our men to work on their behalf." Mitchell to Weltner, April 24, 1911, in folder titled "Personal Correspondence, September 1912–1913," USC Archives. On the Sunday school as an example of university social service, see Mitchell to Grace W. Vandiver, December 22, 1910, in folder titled "Faculty, 1908–1910," Mitchell Papers, USC.

Mitchell was one of the "town people" committed to "the organization of society under their leadership." They hoped that education would "tear the mill children away from the anachronistic culture of their fathers and teach them to accept the legitimacy of the new, town-dominated society being built by the middle classes." In Carlton, *Mill and Town in South Carolina,* 173–74.

18. Mitchell, "Annual Report of the Board of Trustees, 1910–1911," *Reports and Resolutions of the General Assembly of the State of South Carolina* 2 (1912): 712–13, SCSL (hereafter abbreviated as *Reports and Resolutions*).

19. "President's Report to the Board of Trustees," December 31, 1909, in "Minutes of the Board of Trustees; Trustees' Minutes," January 10, 1910; see also "President's Report," October 5, 1910, SCL; Mitchell to Douglas McKay, August 27, 1910, in folder titled "Personal Correspondence," Mitchell Papers, USC; "President's Report," December 29, 1910, in "Trustees' Minutes," SCL; Mitchell to Julius Walker, April 12, 1910, in

folder titled "Departments, 1908–1910," Mitchell Papers, USC. The "Good Roads" bulletin enjoyed unusual popularity. The editor of the *Southern Good Roads* journal wrote that it was "one of the best things of its kind that has fallen into my hands in months." A. L. Fletcher to M. Goode Homes, January 10, 1912, in folder titled "Good Roads," Mitchell Papers, USC. See also Tompkins to Mitchell, January 4, 1911, Mitchell Papers, USC.

20. "Annual Report of the Board of Trustees, 1909–1910," *Reports and Resolutions,* 1141.

21. Mitchell to R. B. Herbert, December 3, 1910, in folder titled "Faculty, 1908–1910," Mitchell Papers, USC.

22. Mitchell to W. W. Ball, October 28, 1910, Mitchell Papers, USC; see also Mitchell to R. A. Meares, January 4, 1911, Mitchell Papers, USC.

23. "President's Report," December 29, 1910, SCL; see also Mitchell to Coker, January 24, 1910, in folder titled "Coker Family, 1908 to 1913," Mitchell Papers, USC; Coker to Mitchell, January 26, 1910, in folder titled "Coker Family, 1908 to 1913," Mitchell Papers, USC; "President's Report," June 1911, SCL. The bulletins appealed to interests outside the state. Impressively, the Wisconsin Granite Company wrote to request a copy of the "Good Roads" bulletin. W. J. Lewis to G. Holmes, February 6, 1912, in folder titled "Personal Correspondence, October 1909 to February 1910," Mitchell Papers, USC.

24. Henderson, "E.K.G.," *Raleigh News and Observer,* August 10, 1913, in Snider, *Light on the Hill,* 160.

25. Ibid., 162.

26. Ibid., 163–64, 225–26.

27. Mitchell to Rose, October 29, 1910, in folder titled "Faculty, 1908–1910," Mitchell Papers, USC. Before Mitchell's presidency, professor A. C. Moore functioned as acting president. Responding to the board's application for laboratory space at the school, Moore gave the idea a ringing endorsement: "Their work has a large educational value, and an understanding of what they are doing gained by the students of the University would be the best way of securing the dissemination of a general knowledge of the work throughout the State." Moore added that its connection with the university would bring the board much-needed "prestige." He also suggested that it might "be the entering wedge" for a department of public health. Moore, "President's Report," May 27, 1909, SCL.

28. "President's Report," September 21, 1909, SCL.

29. Office of the Executive Secretary of the SEB to Mitchell, October 15, 1910; Rose to Mitchell, October 19, 1910; Mitchell to Rose, October 24, 1910; all letters in folder titled "Departments, 1908–1910," Mitchell Papers, USC.

30. In 1912, Mitchell suggested these topics for consideration at a conference on higher education in the South: "1. How can the university prove more vitally helpful to the public schools? 2. What forms of public service can the university wisely embrace? 3. The University-State. 4. The University and the changing view of the State, or Science in its relation to the progress of modern society." Reiterating the public service mod-

el of higher education, Mitchell linked the state to the university in a collaborative effort to apply science to social problems. Mitchell to A. A. Murphree, March 27, 1912, in folder titled "Conferences, 1909–1913," Mitchell Papers, USC.

31. Mitchell to A. A. Murphree, December 29, 1910, in folder titled "Conferences, 1909–1913," Mitchell Papers, USC. Mitchell was unambiguous about the benefit of a course on public health and sanitation. Taught by employees of the State Board of Health, the courses manifested the fusion of the university and the state: "These lectures will undoubtedly prove attractive to our students, and a means of informing them as to the subject vital to community building in this state. . . . This step will relate the university vitally to one of the most progressive, potent agencies in the State." "President's Report," October 5, 1910, SCL.

32. "President's Report," December 29, 1910, SCL.

33. Officer to Mitchell, December, 1911, box 4, Mitchell Papers, LOC. A former colleague of Mitchell's at Richmond College praised his program: "I have received safely the pamphlets you sent me. . . . They are in the line of popular service and ought to go far toward convincing the people of your state that the University has a practical side and can be made useful to the plainest of the people as well as the aristocracy." C. H. Ryland to Mitchell, January 11, 1912, Mitchell Papers, LOC. A legislative report applauded university "outreach" and observed, "This spirit of public service shows itself increasingly in a great variety of ways, such as extension work by lectures in all parts of the State; bulletins on practical subjects, and by the presentation of great popular interests, such as good health, good roads, and the enrichment of rural life." "Report of the Legislative Committee Appointed to Investigate the Condition of the State Educational Institutions for 1911," *Reports and Resolutions* 3 (1912): 1052.

34. "Supplement to the President's Report," December 29, 1910.

35. Mitchell, "Aftermath of Appomattox," 145. The president was not the only one who called on the assistance of federal government experts and officials. In 1912, M. Goode Homes, professor of civil engineering, wrote to the U.S. Office of Public Roads to request experts to present a series of lectures on "Dust Preventives, Road Binders, and Road Sanitation." In Homes to L. W. Page, November 20, 1912, in folder titled "Departments, 1911–1913," Mitchell Papers, USC; see also Page to Mitchell, November 16, 1910, in folder titled "Addresses, Lectures, Sermons, April 1910–1910," Mitchell Papers, USC.

36. Mitchell to James A. Hoyt, November 9, 1909, in folder titled "Addresses, Lectures, and Sermons, 1909," Mitchell Papers, USC; Presley, *Samuel Chiles Mitchell*, 145; L. W. Page to Mitchell, November 16, 1910, in folder titled "Addresses, Lecturers, Sermons, April 1910–1910," Mitchell Papers, USC. On Kirkland's commitment to state intervention in education, see Kirkland, "The Teacher and the State," 249–56; for Alderman's insistence on taxation to support "the establishment and maintenance of a system of schools adequate for the needs of a free people," see his article titled "The Southwestern Field" 287–92; Mitchell, "The Coordination of Social Engineers in the South," Address to the Conference of State Supervisors of Rural Schools, High School

Inspectors, Agents of Farm Demonstration, Presidents of State Universities, and School Superintendents, Nashville, April 1, 1912, box 9, Mitchell Papers, LOC.

37. For instance, see McIver, "Current Problems in North Carolina," 293–303; Mitchell, address given at the Conference for Education in the South, *Proceedings of the Conference for Education in the South, Seventh Session, Birmingham, Alabama, 1904* (New York: Committee on Publication, 1904), 160–67.

38. W. K. Tate to Mitchell, October 12, 1909, in folder titled "Personal Correspondence, October 1909–February 1910," Mitchell Papers, USC.

39. Mitchell to Tate, October 25, 1909, in folder titled "Personal Correspondence, October 1909–February 1910," Mitchell Papers, USC.

40. "President's Report," September 21, 1909, SCL.

41. Swearingen to Rose, December 22, 1909; also see Mitchell to Rose, December 23, 1909; Mitchell to Tate, February 8, 1910; all three letters in folder titled "Personal Correspondence, October 1909 to February 1910," Mitchell Papers, USC; Office of the General Agent of the Trustees of the Peabody Education Fund to J. E. Swearingen, April 29, 1910, in folder titled "Peabody Funds, 1909–1913," Mitchell Papers, USC; Trustees' Minutes, January 10, 1910, SCL.

42. J. Q. Davis to Mitchell, January 6, 1910, in folder titled "Board of Trustees, 1908–1910," Mitchell Papers, USC.

43. Link, *The Paradox of Southern Progressivism,* 130.

44. Mitchell to Rose, December 6, 1909, in folder titled "Faculty, 1908–1910," Mitchell Papers, USC.

45. Ibid., 142. Link identifies "an unusual affinity between Progressive Era educational and health reform." For instance, several of the members of the Rockefeller Sanitary Commission for the Eradication of Hookworm Disease, such as Walter Hines Page and James Y. Joyner, also held positions on the SEB.

46. Mitchell to Tate, February 17, 1910, in folder titled "Personal Correspondence October 1909 to February 1910," Mitchell Collection, USC. Brimming with New South optimism, he wrote to the president of Howard University that "it is altogether strengthening to note the increasing spirit of co-operation and unity among educational agencies in the South." Mitchell to W. P. Thirkield, February 28, 1910, in folder titled "Personal Correspondence October 1909 to February 1910," Mitchell Collection, USC. In the interest of coordinating educational agencies, Mitchell supported a proposal to construct a building to accommodate the offices of the state superintendent of education, the elementary and secondary school professors, the School of Education, and a practice school. "President's Report," October 5, 1905, SCL.

47. "President's Report," December 5, 1911, SCL; Mitchell to Watson, January 31, 1912, USC Archives; Watson to Mitchell, January 31, 1912, in folder titled "Departments, 1911–1913," Mitchell Papers, USC. A further impetus to state and university fusion came from the appointment of M. W. Twitchell, professor of geology and mineralogy, to the position of state geologist. The president hailed this innovation as an example of "how a

State university, centrally located . . . can serve all the interests of the people of the State." In "President's Report," June 5, 1911, 3.

48. Grantham, *Southern Progressivism,* xvii.

49. Mitchell, "The Coordination of Social Engineers in the South," April 1, 1912, Mitchell Papers, LOC.

50. Grantham, *Southern Progressivism,* 270.

51. Mitchell to Rev. J. E. Hicks, November 22, 1912, in folder titled "YMCA, 1912–1913," Mitchell Papers, USC.

52. Mitchell, "An Aftermath of Appomattox," 162.

53. "President's Report," December 29, 1910, SCL; see also Presley, *Samuel Chiles Mitchell,* 149.

54. Mitchell to Richard Morse, June 10, 1912, in folder titled "YMCA, 1909–1911," Mitchell Papers, USC; see also Mitchell to Hicks, November 22, 1912, Mitchell Papers, USC.

55. In "In Search of Direction," Joseph M. Stetar argues that southern universities maintained an attachment to discipline, piety, and liberal culture that together formed a coherent and appealing program that endured into the twentieth century. But this may overlook the ambiguities of the change in southern higher education at the turn of the century. Using the Christian motifs of moral uplift and ethical revitalization, Mitchell and others legitimated a secular philosophy of education. They spoke the idiom of a Christianity shot through with the progressive spirit of the age. Urban Protestants absorbed the New South message of material progress and viewed state intervention in social matters as an instrument for accomplishing the moral agenda set down by the churches. See Grantham, *Southern Progressivism,* 15–17. What differentiated southern progressives of the social justice persuasion from their northern counterparts was the cultural conservatism that distinguished southern progressivism from its northern variant.

56. Mitchell to J. P. Coats, March 8, 1912, in folder titled "Personal Correspondence, September 1912 1913," USC Archives; Mitchell to Dr. Henry Cope, November 22, 1910, in folder titled "YMCA 1909–1911," USC Archives; Mitchell to Richard Morse, June 10, 1912, in folder titled "YMCA, 1912–1913," Mitchell Papers, USC.

57. Mitchell to J. P. Coats, March 8, 1912, in folder titled "Personal Correspondence, September 1912–1913," Mitchell Papers, USC.

58. Mitchell to C. K. Obar, November 20, 1910, in folder titled "YMCA 1909–1911," Mitchell Papers, USC.

59. Mitchell to F. W. Obar, November 22, 1910, USC Archives; Mitchell to Henry F. Cope, November 22, 1910, Mitchell Papers, USC; Mitchell to T. F. Parker, December 23, 1910, Mitchell Papers, USC; *Bulletin of the University of South Carolina* 33 (April 1913): 27.

60. Mitchell, "An Aftermath of Appomattox," 162.

61. Mitchell to Richard C. Morse, June 10, 1912, in folder titled "YMCA, 1912–1913,"

Mitchell Papers, USC; see also Morse to Mitchell, June 5, 1912, USC Archives. For all its purported interest in the question of southern race relations, the YMCA demonstrated a limited commitment to reducing southern racial discrimination. See Brundage, *Lynching in the New South,* 221.

62. Mitchell to Wallace Buttrick, December 22, 1909, in folder titled "Personal Correspondence, October 1909 to February 1910," Mitchell Papers, USC.

63. Mitchell to Bessie E. Bloom, November 9, 1909, in folder titled "Personal Correspondence, October 1909 to February 1910," Mitchell Papers, USC.

64. McBryde, "Womanly Education for Woman," 467–84.

65. Mitchell to Buttrick, December 22, 1909, in folder titled "Personal Correspondence, October 1909 to February 1910," Mitchell Papers, USC.

66. Mitchell to D. T. Lauderdale, January 4, 1912, in folder titled "Personal Correspondence, September 1912–1913," Mitchell Papers, USC; see also "Memorandum for the Board of Trustees, January 16, 1913," Board Minutes, SCL.

67. Mitchell to Lauderdale, January 4, 1912, in folder titled "Personal Correspondence, September 1912–1913," Mitchell Papers, USC.

68. Mitchell to D. R. Coker, April 30, 1912, in folder titled "Coker Family, 1908–1913," Mitchell Papers, USC. Clearly Mitchell was concerned about finding a candidate suitably respectful of southern racial orthodoxies. As he wrote to a prospective candidate for the job, "I am more particular in making a recommendation to the Board as to this chair than in any that has come before me, for I feel that while the right man will do great good, the wrong man might do untold mischief in these two subjects. Commonsense and invincible sanity are the absolute prerequisites to the teaching of these subjects in this State." Mitchell to Percy S. Flippin, May 20, 1912, Mitchell Papers, USC.

69. Mitchell to McBain, March 15, 1912, in folder titled "Departments, 1911–1913," Mitchell Papers, USC. Writing in response to a group of British students who wanted to study southern race relations, Mitchell remarked that because black people constituted 58 percent of South Carolina's population, the university would provide an excellent place for such study. "Indeed," he wrote, in language that anticipated Howard Odum, "the South is a fine laboratory today for social study in general, and this institution is located in the heart of the South." Mitchell to Henry W. Crees, March 15, 1911, in folder titled "Departments, 1911–1913," Mitchell Papers, USC.

70. Mitchell to J. E. Swearingen, May 22, 1912, in folder titled "Departments, 1911–1913," Mitchell Papers, USC; Mitchell to Coleman, December 2, 1912, in folder titled "Departments, 1911–1913," Mitchell Papers, USC; Mitchell to Philander P. Claxton, December 20, 1909, in folder titled "Personal Correspondence, October 1909–February 1910," Mitchell Papers, USC. Because of Clemson's dominance, agricultural instruction did not figure prominently in Mitchell's program. Consistent with the New South enthusiasm for scientific agriculture, he did support training for teachers in the agricultural and mechanical arts. Mitchell to Swearingen, May 22, 1912, in folder titled "Departments, 1911–1913," Mitchell Papers, USC.

71. "President's Report," December 29, 1910, SCL; Law Faculty to Mitchell, March

2, 1912, in folder titled "Departments, 1911–1913," Mitchell Papers, USC; Mitchell to F. W. Cappelmann, June 22, 1912, in folder titled "Faculty, 1911–1913," Mitchell Papers, USC.

72. "President's Report," December 29, 1910, SCL.

73. Ibid.

74. Mitchell, "Memorandum for the Board of Trustees of the University of South Carolina at their meeting on January 16, 1913," in "Trustees' Minutes," SCL.

75. Mitchell to John G. Bowman, June 26, 1909, in folder titled "Personal Correspondence, 1909," Mitchell Papers, USC; see also "President's Report," December 29, 1910, SCL.

76. Mitchell to W. K. Tate, October 20, 1909, in folder titled "Departments, 1908–1910," Mitchell Papers, USC; see also "President's Report," December 29, 1910, SCL. See also Mitchell's support for professor Gordon B. Moore's leave of absence to conduct sociological research in Europe. The president endorsed the professor's still novel decision to specialize in sociology and acquiesced to his request for a separate chair of sociology. "President's Report," December 29, 1910, SCL.

77. "President's Report," May 27, 1909, SCL; see also *Bulletin of the University of South Carolina* 16 (1909–1910): 3–4. Students were admitted on the basis of entrance examinations or certificate from an accredited school. As in Georgia, the list of accredited high schools was determined by the state high school inspector.

78. "Report of Committee on Organization," May 9, 1912, "Trustees' Minutes," SCL.

79. *Bulletin of the University of South Carolina* 33 (April 1913): 16–17.

80. Ibid. Improved schooling was obstructed by influential textile interests and pervasive political conservatism. The prospect of increased taxation and the social implications of black schools led many South Carolinians to resist the education crusade. Grantham, *Southern Progressivism,* 255; Link, *The Paradox of Southern Progressivism,* 281.

81. Mitchell, "The Coordination of Social Engineers in the South," April 1, 1912, box 9, Mitchell Papers, LOC.

82. "Minutes of the Board of Trustees," June 10, 1913, SCL.

7

Progressivism Besieged: Governor Coleman Blease's Attack on Samuel Mitchell

At first glance, Samuel Mitchell considered the political climate of South Carolina hospitable to educational progressivism. Legislative appropriations had more than doubled by the time Mitchell assumed office. With the cooperation of governor Martin Ansel, a supporter of Mitchell's program, they increased incrementally during his first two years as president.[1] The election of Coleman L. Blease to the governorship in 1910 signaled a challenge to the progressive consensus that united urban boosters, merchants, industrialists, and professionals. Far more than a familiar episode of petty political wrangling, Blease's attack on the president was an offensive in his war against progressivism.

Although the South was still predominantly agrarian, rapid industrialization after 1880 transformed the southern economy but left in place many of the region's traditional social institutions. Class polarization accompanied the aggressive expansion of the textile industry after the Civil War. Upcountry poor whites, jolted by declining agricultural fortunes and subject to new, impersonal market relations, sought their livelihoods as propertyless wage workers in the whirring cotton mills.[2] At the same time, entrepreneurs and professionals of the mill towns forged a common identity in their commitment to economic growth and the domestication of the mills' fiercely independent workers.[3]

Exponents of the creed of material progress believed a compliant labor force was needed for economic development. With inflammatory excess, Blease articulated the discontent of a proletariat who felt themselves "circumscribed and persecuted by arbitrary mill officials and meddlesome reformers alike."[4] For Blease and his supporters, Mitchell's activist university, no less than progressive programs for compulsory education and moral uplift, expressed the new paternalism of the town people. Blease persecuted Mitchell for reasons deeper than a penchant for retribution against the university that had dismissed him for plagiarism.[5] The scandal that erupted when the governor accused Mitchell of persuading the Peabody Education Fund to allocate money originally intended for the education of white women to the instruction of black men highlights the social landscape that defined southern progressivism. The Blease-Mitchell incident also suggests the formidable obstacles that confronted university modernization.

Blease rode to power on a wave of class antagonism muted since the upheavals of the 1890s. The traditional sectional and class divisions between the tidewater plantation region and the predominantly poor white upcountry resurfaced after the war. During the New South period, the piedmont attracted the greatest industrial and urban growth. Factory workers and poor farmers came to share with their antebellum predecessors an antipathy for the Bourbon landowning elite of the low country, who dominated the state legislature. Agrarian radicalism, fostered by currency contraction, declining cotton prices, and the organizational skill of the Southern Alliance, found low country Bourbonism a prominent target. Benjamin R. Tillman, a plantation owner known for persecuting blacks and Republicans in Edgefield County, became the unlikely champion of dispossessed upcountry farmers and workers. He also helped solidify the racial and class divisions that brought Blease to power in 1910.[6]

Tillman catapulted himself to political prominence in South Carolina by denouncing agricultural peonage and the tidewater plutocrats. He advocated a primary system to break the Democratic oligarchy and an agricultural college to teach the sons of farmers. Like Blease, Tillman included the South Carolina College in his indictment. His rhetoric deliberately linked the "drones and vagabonds" who graduated from the college with the low country's privileged elites. A vigorous proponent of an independent agricultural and mechanical college, he was elected to Clemson's first board of trustees. In an effort to increase his political exposure, Tillman traveled throughout the state debating the Democratic leadership. In Charleston, he maligned what he considered the city's dissolute and haughty residents. The city paper responded in kind, disparaging Tillman as typical of the people who "carry pistols in their hip pockets, who expectorate upon the floors, who have no tooth brushes, and comb their hair with their fingers." According to historian Edward Ayers, it was this kind of derision that confirmed for Tillman and his supporters that the low country elite harbored nothing but disdain for the "crackers" of the piedmont.[7]

Tillman was elected governor in 1890 on the strength of Alliance support, but his commitment to the Populist agenda was cursory at best. However, his legislative record reflected enough concern for the state's disadvantaged to maintain the core of his white farm support. Along with James K. Vardaman and Tom Watson he earned his stripes as one of the most notorious race-baiting politicos of the day. Under Tillman's leadership, South Carolina held a constitutional convention that, despite spirited opposition from black delegates, disfranchised most of the state's eligible black voters. He also polarized South Carolina politics into two clear factions: conservatives and Tillmanites. Financial, business, and professional interests uniformly opposed Tillman. Most would have agreed with the editor of the Columbia *State*, who warned that "the integrity of the commonwealth was threatened by the hegemony of the back country proletariat."[8]

Although Tillman failed to measure up to the standards of the Alliance, his voice resonated with the grievances of the average farmer. As Ayers describes, "Few farmers could hope to send their sons to an agricultural college even if it were built, but they could applaud Tillman's relentless laceration of the South Carolina 'aristocracy' and its soft-handed sons."[9] Silenced by his departure to the Senate and by the Populist debacle of 1896, the dissident strain returned more virulently in the form of Coleman Blease in 1910.

Blease was educated at Newberry College and the Georgetown University law school. He built his popular appeal by affecting the appearance of the unread demagogue hostile to colleges and their anemic occupants. But his contempt for the University of South Carolina (USC) was rooted in personal experience. Attending the law school in 1887–88, he was dismissed from the Clariosophic Society when it was learned that he had plagiarized a submission to an essay contest. "Overbearing and defiant" about the plagiarism incident, he was expelled from the university in 1888. He served in the General Assembly before entering the campaign for governor in 1906.[10]

Blease's election brought to the surface class and regional tensions submerged since 1896. A flamboyant political opportunist skilled in using incendiary oratory, a distinguished dresser with a magnetic personality capable of igniting an audience's passion, Blease captured the support of the Tillmanites and wielded it against the state's respectable elements. Although Governor Blease gained support from Tillman's former followers, his strongest endorsement came from the upcountry mill workers, whom Tillman had dismissed as "that damned factory class." As a legislative representative from the upcountry, Blease supported Tillman. As a gubernatorial hopeful, he invoked "Pitchfork Ben" as his political role model.[11]

Much like Tillman, Blease exploited his constituents' deeply entrenched class and race prejudices. Typical of his racial views was his 1906 assertion that "God never intended the Negro to be anything but the servant of the white man."[12] Yet in manipulating racial bigotry, a contemporary reporter observed, he "articulated the poor man's unexpressed emotions, ambitions and disgruntlements; did it garishly, did it sentimentally, did it courageously." Whereas the class divergences of the Tillman era separated the tidewater from the upcountry, Blease's regime sharpened the antagonism between the mill and town people. In general, however, Blease, like Tillman, alienated the business and propertied classes with crude rhetorical salvos. At the same time he provided conservative state newspapers enough fodder for a continuous stream of indignant editorials.[13]

Legislative obstruction distinguished Blease's governorship. His opposition to child labor laws and compulsory education reflected the suspicion shared by mill workers that progressive reform threatened the independence of poor whites. Workers resented the coercive overtones of progressive social uplift. Blease captured the character of this protest in his 1911 inaugural address: "Much has been said about the enactment of laws in regard to the labor in our cotton mills. These people are our people; they are our kindred; they are our friends, and in my opinion they should be let alone, and allowed to manage their own children and . . . their own affairs."[14] As the sharecroppers and tenant farmers found a voice in "Pitchfork" Ben Tillman, so the mill workers found a defender in Coleman Blease.

The antagonism between the Bleasites and the town people reflected political divisions, but it also illuminated the cultural chasm separating middle-class southerners from a rural yeomanry. Whereas Blease endorsed lynching as an appropriate response to the "unspeakable" crime of rape, Mitchell deplored it as an act of irrational brutality subversive of the social order.[15] Contributing to the rising tide of racial extremism between 1890 and 1915, Blease advocated violent suppression of the "Negro Beast." Mitchell, on the other hand, subscribed to the "accommodationist" racism popular among southern liberals, which combined paternalism and humanitarianism in the belief that black progress was best served by racial separation.[16]

The progressive aversion to racial demagoguery reflected more than a difference in style. It was grounded in the cultural values at the core of southern Victorianism. Like their northern counterparts, New South intellectuals embraced the "underlying ethos of Victorian thought," which enshrined a rigid distinction between "savagery and civilization." To Mitchell and his contemporaries, Bleasite extremism manifested the "animalistic" impulses of savagery that stood in the way of progress and the march of civilization.[17] Never far from the minds of middle-class southerners was the danger racial extremism posed to social cohesion and material progress.

The cultural distance separating Blease and Mitchell also was evident in attitudes toward alcohol. In his first inaugural address, Blease treated the temperance movement to his biting sarcasm: "I . . . beg leave to call your attention to the evil of the habitual drinking of coca cola, pepsi cola, and such like mixtures, as I fully believe they are injurious. It would be better for our people if they had nice, respectable places where they could go and buy a good, pure glass of cold beer than to drink such concoctions." Blease continued his assault on "respectable" people and their pious certitudes at night rallies in the industrial districts.[18] Mitchell, on the other hand, was a teetotaler. His son Broadus once observed that his father "couldn't relax. It would have been good if he had been a smoker or if he had a drink before dinner, but he never smoke or drank." The Mitchell home on the campus of USC was a place of intellectual pursuits, moral restraint, and rigidly enforced good behavior. Often irascible from nervous exhaustion, the president created a domestic environment that was, according to Broadus, "almost painfully serious and earnest."[19]

A temperance advocate, a Protestant with evangelical sensibilities, an introspective intellectual who yearned to exercise social authority, Mitchell could hardly have been expected to greet Blease's rise to power with equanimity. While Blease inveighed against the mill town parvenu and their claims to social leadership, Mitchell intoned his conviction that "lawlessness ought to be . . . attacked and public opinion braced in behalf of the necessity of order."[20] Optimistically he commented in 1909, "Everything in the South is quiet, political stagnation everywhere. . . . For the first time in many, many decades the race question seems to have retreated into the background, greatly to the relief of all sensible people."[21] Brandishing extremist rhetoric and calculated working-class sympathies, Blease sought to disrupt the comfortable status quo that Mitchell and his progressive allies had built. Ultimately, the two were divided by ideological values that organized their ideas about social and political change.

From the beginning of his administration, Blease made educational modernizers a target for his rhetoric and his executive veto. In his January 17, 1911 inaugural address, Blease condemned the use of school textbooks not written by southern authors. At the same time he assailed public support for black education. More ominously for Mitchell and his allies, the governor railed against what he considered the exorbitant cost of funding public higher education. He intimated that reductions in appropriations for state colleges might lay in the future. He also vehemently opposed compulsory education. Blease castigated "those men who go around in the State or outside the State and parade figures to show the percentage of the ignorance of our people." More than likely, the governor had in mind the consciousness-raising techniques of South Carolina's own state supervisor of rural schools, W. K. Tate, and Samuel Mitchell. By no means the only object of the governor's recrimination,

Mitchell and the education reformers belonged to the class that threatened Blease's authority.[22]

The governor made good on his threats against higher education. In his December 29, 1910 report to the Board of Trustees, Mitchell had strongly recommended that the university request a $50,000 legislative appropriation to build a new auditorium. The president claimed that the new building would provide needed classroom space and help the school "radiate" progressive ideas throughout the state by providing a forum for public speakers. The president also requested an additional $10,000 to finance the extension of steam pipes from the central heating plant to the college's buildings. Passed by the House ways and means committee and approved by the Senate finance committee, though shorn of $5,000 intended for the heating plant project, the bill was endorsed by the Senate. But the governor vetoed the bill. The House joined Blease in opposing the steam pipe request but gave its approval by a close margin to the auditorium appropriation. However, the Senate failed to overturn the governor's veto. Consequently, the university's appropriation for 1911 amounted to $74,709, almost $20,000 less than that of the previous year.[23]

If Blease's inaugural address and his veto of the university appropriation were not enough to cause Mitchell misgivings, a speech the governor gave at Spartanburg in 1911 was. Reiterating his suspicion that public institutions of higher education were a financial sinkhole, Blease suggested that, in comparison to the denominational schools, the state-funded universities produced inferior graduates. College professors, he claimed erroneously, were receiving financial support for summer trips to Europe. Most disturbing for Mitchell was Blease's invidious comparison between Mitchell and Henry Snyder, the president of Wofford College. Acerbically, Blease suggested that the president of the Spartanburg college had "more sense and education than Dr. Mitchell has brains enough to learn." The governor's vitriol may have won him support among the mill people of Spartanburg, but it elicited the opprobrium of most of the state press sympathetic to the progressive agenda.[24]

Despite Blease's invective, Mitchell remained optimistic about his plans for the university. Stoically, he wrote to a friend that "the remarks of the Governor at Spartanburg have had no appreciable effect. I take for granted that he will hold up a running fire of comment of this kind so long as he holds that chair, but I am guided by your own dignified course under somewhat similar circumstances, preserving absolute silence."[25] Mitchell was also prudent. Responding defensively to the governor's ad hominem would only have fanned the flames and tarnished his image as a disinterested advocate of educational progress. Although the governor's remarks were without warrant, they were not inexplicable. Blease lumped Mitchell and the "diplomaized [*sic*] mollycoddles" in the same category as the mill magnates, professionals, and reformers, who threatened the independence of the mill people and Blease's political fortunes.[26]

The president evidently understood the relationship between progressivism and Bleasite extremism. "The energies of the people are going to practical things, heavens be thanked! The progress which the State is actually making in thought as well as material development is best registered in the faint response which the occasional cry of the demagogue awakens."[27] As a proponent of compulsory education and temperance, Mitchell and his missionary university were not unlikely targets for Blease. Whereas the governor vilified stiff-backed Victorian reformers and their self-serving morality, the progressives focused on "uplifting" and "civilizing" illiterate mill hands, the core of Blease's supporters. As Mitchell's wife, Alice, commented buoyantly to her mother in 1912, "We stepped into one of the hardest educational jobs in the country, owing to the peculiar combination of caste feeling, backwardness, and Tillmanism, and it is thrilling to tug away and see progress." To Blease and his supporters, the progressive crusade challenged local autonomy and a moral order at odds with middle-class discipline.[28]

Hopeful that his silence would deter further aggression, Mitchell was disappointed by Blease's 1912 annual message to the legislature. Once again he asserted that public funding for the university was excessive: "Our higher State institutions are receiving entirely too much money. . . . The idea of one of your State colleges [USC] receiving seventy-five thousand dollars for the number of students which it has is preposterous." For Blease, the issue—at least officially—was inequitable taxation. "I would not injure any State college," he contended disingenuously, "but extravagance is wrong anywhere, and especially when the people are paying more taxes now than they can well afford." Reducing the school's appropriation was only one part of his program for fiscal retrenchment. Consistent with his policy to curb public spending, Blease claimed in the same message, "We are paying too much for water and lights for the public institutions in Columbia," and, "You are paying too much money to the Catawba Indians." He reminded his constituents of the promise he had made to "fight for reduction of expenses and to veto extravagance, and [I] have done everything that I said I would do in my campaign promises."[29] Accurate or not, Blease reinforced the traditional aversion to taxation and opposed government expansion. In fact, as historian David Carlton points out, educational progressives of the post-Blease era were forced to draft propaganda that would nullify the widespread opposition to taxation that the governor's tirades against government excess had solidified.[30]

To the governor, Mitchell's university was emblematic of the progressive drive for bureaucratic control. To counter creeping progressive control, Blease advocated eliminating the state bank examiner, the Bureau of Agriculture (which had established close ties to the university), the state game warden, and the insurance commissioner. In addition, he called for abolishing the post of state geologist, which he himself had authorized the previous year. (The office of the state geologist was located on the Columbia campus and was occupied by professor M. W. Twitchell.) President Mitchell greeted the governor's decision to establish the post with enthusiasm, suggesting that it was "only another evidence of how a State university, centrally located like this, can serve all the interests of the people of the State."[31] Blease's hit list of agencies is important not only because it included two departments closely connected with the university but also because it demonstrated the association he made between the university and an intrusive, regulatory state. To Blease, the administration's efforts to forge links between the university and the mill communities reflected its complicity in a program of government coercion.

Fortunately for the university, the General Assembly opposed Blease's plan to reduce the university's appropriation. The legislature allocated $25,000 for school maintenance, bringing its income for 1912 to $98,298. Mitchell's hope that the university would be protected by the election of the moderate progressive Ira B. Jones in 1912 was crushed when Blease, after a campaign marred by race baiting and invective, was reelected. Noted for racial extremism in his first term, he made racial issues an obsession in his second. At a conference for southern governors in Richmond, Blease endorsed lynching as a form of retributive justice. The governor insisted that he would not muster the South Carolina militia "to shoot down their friends engaged in taking the life of a black man who had dared to lay his hand upon a white woman."[32] Already the recipient of Blease's unsolicited scrutiny, Mitchell became embroiled in a scandal of the governor's making that exhibited both his racial antagonism and his antipathy for progressives.

In his second inaugural address of January 21, 1913, Blease ordered an investigation into alleged financial improprieties involving the president and the Peabody Education Fund. According to Blease, President Mitchell, on learning of the imminent dissolution of the Peabody Fund, negotiated with the Peabody trustees to secure a portion of the money for USC already assigned to South Carolina's Winthrop College. The president reportedly made the agreement on the condition that if the fund accepted his petition, he would allocate the remaining funds to support black educational institutions. Based on no more solid evidence than the testimony of professor D. B. Johnson, the president of Winthrop College, the governor called for a legislative investigation into the matter. The governor was certain that it would reveal "a pretty dirty transaction on the part of somebody." Encouraged by Johnson, Blease came to believe that Winthrop College would have received "considerably more" than the $90,000 it did had it not been for Mitchell's treachery. More than administrative indiscretion, the governor cast the scandal in terms of a deliberate affront to white supremacy. "And, if it is true, certainly the president of the South Carolina College has no place in the educational department of South Carolina. If he would rather take that money to educate negroes than to give it to the white girls of South Carolina, he certainly has no place during my administration in any department of the government."[33] Exploiting racial prejudice, Blease hoped to vilify Mitchell as an enemy of southern social conventions. Inauspiciously, the governor asked Josh Ashley, strident Blease partisan and ringleader of a lynching at Honea Path, to introduce the resolution requesting the investigation.[34]

The investigation followed a series of events that began when W. K. Tate, state supervisor of rural schools and professor of elementary education at the university, shared a train ride with F. H. McMaster, a Winthrop College supporter, from Washington, D.C., to South Carolina. Tate told McMaster that he had heard that D. B. Johnson had prevailed on former governor Martin Ansel, a member of the Peabody board, to support a motion redirecting $40,000 intended for USC to Winthrop College. In June 1911 McMaster wrote to Johnson, related Tate's story to him, and asked him to confirm Tate's information.[35]

Johnson's response sheds light on his efforts to discredit Mitchell. It also exposes the intercollegiate rivalry that plagued efforts to coordinate higher education in the South. Johnson told McMaster that several representatives of southern state universities, including Samuel Mitchell, had signed a proposal requesting that any money remaining after the general distribution of the Peabody funds to the various state schools be allocated to "the negroes of the South instead of to the State Normal Schools representing the higher education of the white women of the South." Johnson was outraged because the petition failed to acknowledge Winthrop's allegedly privileged relationship with the Peabody trustees. According to Johnson, the Peabody trustees had led him to believe that the state normal school could expect more than $50,000 when the fund was distributed. Much of this hopefulness was built on self-delusion. He believed that Winthrop College was cherished by the Peabody trustees because the school was named after Robert Winthrop, the first chair of the Peabody Trust and a close associate of George Peabody. Through a deluge of letters over a twenty-year period, the president of the Rock Hill college "waged a single-minded—almost obsessive—campaign . . . to secure the money for Winthrop."[36]

President Johnson indignantly claimed that the state university, "knowing as it did Winthrop's prospects for receiving a large appropriation from the Peabody Board, might have refrained from joining in such an attack upon the State Normal Schools of the South, including Winthrop." The oversight in his account was that Mitchell had signed the petition at an educational conference in Atlanta in April 1909 while he was still at Brown University.[37] Conveniently, Johnson failed to correct the oversight when Governor Blease obtained a copy of Johnson's letter from a trustee of the college in September 1911. Although Mitchell had been elected president in 1908, he remained at Brown for the year 1908–9, taking over the job at USC in the summer of 1909. Mitchell knew nothing of South Carolina's byzantine educational politics, let alone the "special" relationship, which may have existed only in Johnson's imagination, between Winthrop College and the Peabody Fund when he signed the petition in the spring of that year.[38]

Furthermore, although Mitchell did sign a petition requesting that any money remaining after a distribution of funds be donated for educating black teachers in the designated states, this request was entirely in keeping with the conditions of the fund laid down by its benefactor, George Peabody. A report filed by a committee on the distribution of the Peabody Fund in 1906 reaffirmed the biracial intentions of the fund's donor: "It is the conviction of your committee that the remainder of the Fund, presumably about $400,000, should be contributed to the education of the negro." A report submitted in May 1911 by Wickliffe Rose, the general agent of the Peabody board, endorsed the plan of distribution outlined in the 1906 report, which included a $40,000 appropriation to USC and $350,000 for black students.[39]

Mitchell did write to Wickliffe Rose in January 1909 to request that the trustees consider a gift to USC of $50,000 to finance a School of Education. The request almost duplicated the amount that the Peabody board had itself recommended, both in 1906 and 1911, for use by southern state universities to establish schools of elementary education. Mitchell's request was not intended to undermine Winthrop College but to improve elementary school instruction at the university level. In fact, Mitchell cooperated with Johnson's request of August 1908 for support in electing Governor Ansel as a trustee of the Peabody Fund.[40]

Although Mitchell's support for the petition to the Peabody Fund was free of malice toward Winthrop College, the document he signed and his justifications for financial aid to schools of education reflected the gender biases that shaped progressive educational policy. In turn, they mirrored the deep-rooted attitudes about gender that pervaded middle-class southern society.

The resolution drafted by the six university presidents and four heads of educational schools called attention to the pressing need for professional teachers to staff the region's multiplying high schools. The underlying assumption was that only men would be hired for the secondary school system. The signers believed that university-based schools of education were the most cost-efficient means of training high school teachers and that separate teachers' colleges were economically unfeasible. The normal schools, on the other hand, supplied "a training insufficient in extent" and often rejected male applicants. Despite the liabilities of the normal schools, women graduates found teaching an avenue of opportunity into the world of professional work outside the home. Through teaching, some women experienced for the first time a sense of personal fulfillment and economic independence. Although grossly underpaid, the number of women in the teaching profession doubled after 1880. By the late 1880s, women were in the majority among teachers in the South's public schools. By 1900, the percentage of women in southern schools was almost equal to that of their counterparts in the North.[41]

Invisible to the college presidents at the Atlanta conference were the issues of equitable pay and professional opportunity for women teachers. The presidents confidently concluded that "the young man trained in the State University and having taken the course in its School of Education is best prepared to serve his State as a high school teacher."[42] Writing in response to a letter from Wickliffe Rose, in which Mitchell was asked to make recommendations for distributing the Peabody Fund, he declared that "the prime need of education in the South is trained *men* to serve as superintendents in states, counties and cities, and as principals and teachers in the multiplying high schools." Clearly, Mitchell and his counterparts believed that men were needed in positions of authority in the education system.[43]

Yet filling positions of power with steady-handed men was a concomitant of Mitchell's conviction, undoubtedly shared by male progressives, that educational advancement and male dominance were inseparable. Intrinsic to progressivism were ideological assumptions about the connection between power and gender. "When the public school system was first inaugurated in the South," Mitchell wrote, "the initial need was for trained women in the common schools. Recognizing this, our Board wisely helped normal schools for women. Further progress hinges on the supply of trained *men* as teachers and superintendents."[44] Delineating the nurturing female sphere from the competitive male sphere, a cognitive reflex central to the middle-class ethos of the period, Mitchell justified his recommendation that the Peabody Fund assist men only. By associating the predominantly female, common school teachers with the image of the maternal caregiver, the president reinforced the idea that a woman's primary function was to prepare children for the Spencerian world of market competition and manly independence.

Some educators considered female dominance in the field of teaching a threat to masculinity. In a letter to Martin Ansel, trustee of the Peabody board, Edward Joynes, professor emeritus of USC and trustee of Winthrop College, wrote, "Now it is the concurrent opinion of all ablest educators that the great want of our public schools is more and better men as teachers, and the greatest danger of our public education is its excessive *feminization*." To balance the disproportionate number of women in the field, Joynes recommended that the Peabody Fund strengthen the male-only education departments.[45]

According to the legislative committee examining the Peabody-Mitchell affair, a national consensus held that the state universities should use the remaining funds to train men. The movement for university-based colleges to train male high school teachers was a response to larger social forces in the region: The change in the Peabody board's policy was a function of the development of the public university "as the permanent educational fortress in each commonwealth and [of] the necessity of securing through the State University trained men to officer and teach in the public school system of the South."[46] The decision not to contribute to southern normal schools in the latest round of allocations was a product of the "massed wisdom of the educational leaders of America." To hold Mitchell responsible for this decision was "too idle for consideration, and no one knows this fact better than Dr. D. B. Johnson."[47] Likewise, Mitchell, Joynes, and the other college presidents who signed the Atlanta petition acknowledged women's contribution to the development of southern education. However, they were convinced that further "progress" required male leadership, particularly in the high school, the university's incubator.

If the "feminization" of teaching troubled some progressives, the issue of racial "adjustment" cast a shadow over all discussions of education in the South. On hearing that the trustees had decided that the $40,000 assigned to USC instead would be given to Winthrop College, Mitchell wrote an indignant letter to Wickliffe Rose asking him to confirm the rumor: "It has doubtless occurred to you that in this distribution provision is made in every Southern State for the training of white men as teachers, principals, and superintendents, except in South Carolina. Yet so far as my knowledge of the South goes, there is greater need in no commonwealth for the training of just such men than in this State, where the conditions are stressful, because the proportion of negroes is here greatest."[48] Separate but egregiously unequal, public education for blacks suffered at the hands of southern white legislators whose enthusiasm for racial separation was inversely proportional to their willingness to pay for it. Two years after Mitchell left USC, the state superintendent of education inquired, "Is it too much to hope for a minimum of $25 per white child and $5 per negro child?" Partial compensation for the disparity came from General Education Board as well as the Slater, Jeanes, and Peabody funds.[49] Unable to rely on state appropriations, the president and the university hoped that Peabody funding would underwrite a new education department.

Curiously, Mitchell had not previously brought up the issue of black education in correspondence relating to the Peabody Fund. He and other educators certainly were interested in black education, particularly the kind that would encourage social and economic stability. But fearing the loss of the funds on which he had hinged his hopes for an education building, the president was prepared to invoke racial imagery to win over like-minded northerners. As he wrote to the Peabody board, "It is unnecessary for me to speak of the difficulties that the progress of education has met in this state, having perhaps the largest percentage of negroes in any State in the South."[50] The issue of black education could serve a useful rhetorical purpose. Although Mitchell and Blease were divided on the issue of racial policies, they were united by their willingness to exploit racial prejudice to accomplish political objectives.[51]

The president's worst fears about the distribution of the Peabody funds were confirmed in December 1911. Former Governor Ansel, a member of the Peabody board, voted to have USC's $40,000 allocation given to Winthrop College, which brought its total gift from the board to $90,000. The university received an exiguous $6,000 for scholarships. Accused of taking money away from the education of white women and giving it to black men, Mitchell and his struggling university suffered the greatest injustice when USC became the only state university not to receive $40,000. With the exception of the George Peabody School at Nashville, which taught both men and women, Winthrop College was the only normal school to receive Peabody money. Understandably disappointed by this turn of events, Mitchell and a delegation from the university met with Ansel. The former governor gave the delegation his perfunctory assurance that he would try to redress their grievance. In November 1912, two months before Blease leveled his accusations against the president, Mitchell and his delegation appeared before the Peabody board in New York City to plead their case. Losing no opportunity to beg on behalf of Winthrop, and concerned that Mitchell's appeal might do some detriment to the normal school, Johnson went before the board the same day. Neither institution received any additional funding.[52]

The investigation, which lasted from February 5 until February 14, 1913, brought to light both the details of the affair and Mitchell's innocence. The president, along with state superintendent of education J. E. Swearingen and August Kohn, trustee of the university, were called to testify. It was Wickliffe Rose, general agent of the Peabody board, who untangled the complex matter. Rose clarified the Peabody Fund's biracial granting policy. He described the plan he had drafted in 1906 to direct the bulk of Peabody funding to state universities for training male teachers. He also clarified the 1906 decision, reaffirmed in 1911, to allocate $350,000 to educate black teachers. He reassured the investigating committee that the Peabody Fund had been abundantly generous to the normal schools, including Winthrop, between 1875 and 1906. Testifying before the committee, D. B. Johnson denied any knowledge of the 1906 report. He also reiterated his conviction that the university presidents' petition of 1909 had derailed Winthrop's opportunities for a substantially larger appropriation.[53]

Defiantly, Governor Blease ignored Rose's testimony and sent a message to the General Assembly highlighting the provision in the resolution signed by Mitchell (which the governor had not seen when he made his initial accusations) endorsing financial aid to black education: "Did you catch the words, 'AND THE REMAINING FOR THE TRAINING OF NEGRO TEACHERS IN SAME STATES?' Did you see the second name to the paper, '*S. C. Mitchell, President, University of South Carolina?*' If this agreement is carried out, where would your girls' college, the great Winthrop, come in for her share of this money?"[54] Despite Blease's animosity for the president, a majority report submitted by the joint investigating committee exonerated Mitchell of any deliberate attempt to divert money from Winthrop College to the university or to black schools. Not surprisingly, the minority report submitted by Josh Ashley, Blease's sycophant, declared that Mitchell's behavior warranted "the censure of every white man in South Carolina who is opposed to educating negroes, of every white man who is in favor of Winthrop College, and of every white man who believes in white supremacy."[55]

Lacerated by Blease and Johnson, Mitchell still enjoyed the support of some prominent southern progressives. J. H. Kirkland, president of Vanderbilt and a leading southern proponent of improved university standards, wrote, "I am indignant beyond expression. I do not know that I ever saw anything so little or contemptible." Offering to write a letter of support to the South Carolina

General Assembly, Kirkland hesitated, fearing that he might damage "a cause one wishes to serve by imprudent venture."[56] Also from the ranks of southern higher education, George Denny, president of the University of Alabama, wrote pledging his support to his South Carolinian counterpart.[57] C. G. Wyche, a South Carolinian then working at the U.S. Senate, also endorsed Mitchell. "Were this sentiment to come from no heart but my own," he wrote, "it would mean very little to you but I believe I represent the men of Carolina."[58]

Of course, Mitchell garnered the approval of people such as J. E. Swearingen, August Kohn, and Wickliffe Rose. However, the most unexpected voice of approbation came from Benjamin R. Tillman, U.S. senator for South Carolina. Learning in April 1913 that Mitchell was considering leaving Columbia, Tillman wrote to persuade him to stay. Even for Tillman, Blease's race-baiting had gone too far: "I am certain that Governor Blease, in his crusade against you, does not voice the sentiment or wishes of any considerable number of people. He is only making the negro question an issue in everything he says or does to inflame the passions of his more ignorant followers." With an element of irony befitting an agrarian tragedy, Tillman, the demagogue who had castigated USC as a haven for effete intellectuals and catalyzed many of the social forces that culminated in Bleasite extremism, was urging that Mitchell continue at the state college. It was Tillman's hope that "the elements of progress, enlightenment, and statesmanship, now in the state, shall remain to combat Blease's further progress toward pulling down what has been accomplished by other Governors."[59]

If Mitchell enjoyed the support of the "better people" during the trial, he was deluged by sympathetic outpourings when it was learned that he was planning to leave South Carolina for a job at the Medical College of Virginia in Richmond. The father of one student attending USC wrote to the president praising his work in promoting education and citizenship. Political conditions were unfavorable to progress, he warned, because of the "dark period in the history of our State," but he insisted that Blease "does not hold his position from the best people of South Carolina. It was the immoral liquor drinking people of our State that made him governor."[60] J. J. M. Graham, a dry goods merchant from Cades, wrote to express empathy for Mitchell's persecution at the hands of "the low down ledicilious [*sic*] character one Cole L. Blease whom I feel is a disgrace to the good name of south carolina [*sic*]." Graham feared that Mitchell's departure would create the entering wedge for Blease to "break down the old state collage [*sic*] which he has been trying to crush out ever since he first intered [*sic*] public life."[61]

Supporters suggested that the governor's crusade against Mitchell was part of Blease's larger program to undermine the school. A Columbia architect wrote, "While his [Blease's] attacks are directed at you individually, they are intended for the Institution you represent, and you are selected merely as the most conspicuous mark."[62] The owner of a hardware store in Yorkville chimed in his support for Mitchell as well. "The University can ill afford to give you up, I know you have had a lot to contend with. That Scoundrel of a Gov has tried to hurt you by lieing [*sic*] and doeing [*sic*] every thing else against you, but the people are at your back and know what you are 'All OK.'"[63] Mincing no words, an employee of the Abbeville County Court summarized the contempt of many of South Carolina's "respectable" people for Blease's antics: "You stand today a head and shoulders above any other man in this state. You cannot possibly be influenced by that little abortion, called governor, of S.C."[64] Unfortunately for proponents of university activism, Blease's assault was more than enough to drive Mitchell away from the opportunity that South Carolina presented for southern progressivism.

Mitchell's ordeal also gained him the approval of some middle class blacks. Channing Tobias, secretary of the Colored Men's Department of the YMCA's International Committee, whom Mitchell had met during a conference, regretted his decision to leave: "I want you to know that the thinking men of my race believe in you. . . . My only hope is that in our endeavor to express our appreciation we have not embarrassed you in your work."[65] For Tobias and other sympathizers, the president's departure was a blow to the movement for social uplift, economic progress, and educational reform. Writing to Mitchell in April 1913, W. H. Mills of Clemson College suggested that in realigning higher education to serve the movement for state-directed reform, Mitchell had created "the antidote to Bleasism." Only the university, Mills argued, could "fully set forth those principles which are antagonistic to, and finally destructive of, those principles incarnated at the present in Gov. Blease. For this reason, you bear the brunt of his hatred. He strikes more or less blindly at all that the University ought to stand for." Although Mitchell's position was no doubt "unpleasant," Mills assured him that he was the standard bearer for "the thinking men of the State" who looked to the besieged president for "redemption from the bonds of ignorance."[66]

Along with Mitchell's disheartened supporters, *The State*, South Carolina's leading progressive newspaper, lamented the president's ignominious departure. The paper's editorials on the Blease-Mitchell controversy lucidly captured prevailing middle-class opinion about the meaning of the governor's assault and the purpose of higher education. *The State*'s encomium for Mitchell suggests that the "town people" considered the Peabody affair a cultural conflict between defenders of order and the minions of ignorance.[67]

In an article unambiguously titled "The Builder—The Destroyer," the editor suggested that on arriving in Columbia, Mitchell found an antiquated university, "a passive spectator rather than a leader of . . . thought." The president revitalized the university by adding new lecture halls and new dormitories and increasing student attendance from 285 in 1909 to 500 in 1913. More than these material improvements, Mitchell "brought the State to the university; he brought the university to the State." According to the editor, the president succeeded in making the university a conduit of "practical culture," the vital center for "the forces of uplift and education." The effort to extend the influence of the university into the state at large was the central theme of Mitchell's administration: "He fashioned the university into an instrument of State-wide influence for the welfare of the people. He held up the light in hundreds of dark places; he was a missioner of progress."[68]

Blease, on the other hand, was the prince of southern darkness. When elected governor he found the state "progressing slowly, but if it moves at all today, that movement is retrogression." An opponent of compulsory education, Blease had made South Carolina the pariah of the United States. "He has gone among the people as their governor, stirring up prejudice, creating a spirit of lawlessness and standing between the people and the light." Clearly then, Mitchell was a messenger of the "light" for rational progress and responsible leadership.[69] The editor claimed that educational development in South Carolina was inexorable, and Blease's "incendiarism" was but the crude expression of a political style discredited by the intelligent leadership of the state.[70]

Although there is little doubt that D. B. Johnson hoped to entangle Samuel Mitchell in a scandal, the episode should be viewed against the backdrop of rivalry among southern educational institutions. Winthrop and USC were chronically dependent on outside financial support. Notwithstanding the shibboleths about "fraternal cooperation" sprinkled throughout the official documentation on the Mitchell affair, the two institutions were competitors for philanthropic largesse. Edward S. Joynes, emeritus professor and Winthrop trustee, provided some insight into the tensions inherent in the education system. The Peabody board's decision to divert money originally intended for USC to Winthrop was an act "invidious and even degrading to the University. . . . Such an act, if consummated, would breed a jealousy and antagonism between the sister institutions and other respective friends, the evil effects of which would last, most injuriously, for more than a generation."[71] Although rivalry between educational institutions for external funding was not peculiar to the South, its intensity was, for the simple reason that the stakes were higher than in the North. Grossly underfunded by state governments and derided as extravagant shelters for "diplomaized mollycoddles," it is not surprising that southern colleges looked ravenously at the windfall promised by the Peabody Fund.[72] And, as Edward Joynes put it bluntly in his letter to Ansel, "Winthrop College has already received so many favors from the Peabody Board that there is less excuse for robbing in its behalf a sister institution which has never received now [*sic*] asked for any."[73]

Despite Joynes's dubious claim of university selflessness, his remarks point to the function of northern investment in the evolution of southern education. Dependency on northern financial support reflected the parsimony of state support for public education. Yet it also bred institutional competition that militated against progressive dreams of cooperation. The spectacle of Mitchell and his entourage pleading before the Peabody board to reconsider its decision on the same day that Johnson made his appeal illustrates the distance between the claims of educational advancement and the realities that shackled progressive reform in the South.

The controversy starkly illustrates the awkward situation in which southern educators found themselves. In January 1912, Mitchell stood accused of endorsing the appropriation of money from a private charity to educate black students. The president was then charged with conspiring to acquire the money by depriving Winthrop Normal College, a state institution for educating white women, of the funds it had anticipated from the same private charity. At no time was Mitchell ever charged with mishandling public money. As a result of the investigation, a leading southern educator faced the prospect of a ruined career, public humiliation, and the taint of official and racial impropriety because of a deliberate distortion of a pledge he had signed that related to a northern-based charity. If the Peabody fiasco reveals nothing else, it demonstrates the connection southern progressives made between northern philanthropic support and southern educational reform.[74]

The governor's assault on Mitchell was the culmination of a general anti-university program. In fact, Blease consolidated his hold over the mill electorate in 1912 with campaign rhetoric that featured acrimonious denunciations of the state university.[75] By no means did Blease destroy the university. In 1913, the school received an appropriation of $137,000, the largest in its history.[76] The result of the investigation, according to Hollis, was the strengthening of the policy of "gradualism" popular before Mitchell's time.[77] The cautionary approach that the trustees adopted after 1913 only highlights how the Mitchell administration exemplified the cultural and social forces most despised by Blease and his followers. In its programs for university extension, YMCA activism, mill village uplift, and bureaucratic rationalization, the university became the harbinger of a bureaucratically administered social order.

Despite overtures from a legion of middle-class supporters, Mitchell decided to accept an offer of the presidency of the Medical College of Virginia. The trustees of the new college were familiar with the embattled president of USC, who had maintained close contact with many of Richmond's educational elite during his sojourn in South Carolina.[78] He had turned down requests from Johns Hopkins, Washington and Lee, Virginia Polytechnic Institute, and the University of Arkansas, so it is unlikely that he would have accepted the Medical College offer had it not been for the Peabody scandal. Suffering nervous exhaustion and frustrated by opposition to his program for university regeneration, Mitchell looked to the Medical College as a more promising terrain for progressive education. The USC appointment had also been a financial hardship. The $5,000 salary offered by the Medical College provided an additional incentive to leave Columbia.[79]

The Peabody Fund scandal illustrates the social constraints on progressive efforts to transform southern universities into instruments of state service. No less than advocates of health reform and racial harmony, progressives in higher education regularly encountered resistance to their plans for technocratic leadership and administrative centralization. Often this opposition came from those strongly attached to the traditions of southern autonomy. Sometimes, as in the case of the Blease episode, political culture, class, and partisanship intersected in a powerful challenge to middle-class social leadership. Bringing the university to the state, Mitchell also brought to it progressive ideas about standardization and university support for state regulatory agencies. If these plans appeared benign to progressives, they seemed threatening to mill workers and others suspicious of outside interference. It was from their fear and distrust that Blease drew support for his crusade. The Mitchell-Blease incident demonstrates that modernizing universities, far from being isolated from the political mainstream, were agents of social change as well as symbols of a new and ominous leviathan that had little in common with traditional customs. Under the leadership of men such as Mitchell and Hill, the interventionist university became a leader in the progressive movement, defining for a New South a new relationship between government, education, and social reform.

Notes

1. In 1906, when the school's status as a university was restored, the legislature appropriated to it $40,502. In 1908, when Mitchell was elected president, the university received $70,038. By 1910, when Ansel left office, the college's appropriations had risen to $93,853. Data from *South Carolina Reports and Resolutions* in Crow, *The Control of the University of South Carolina,* 270, with exception of figure from 1910, in *Acts and Joint Resolutions of the General Assembly of the State of South Carolina,* 1910, SCSL.

2. The conflict between preindustrial social values and the structures of industrial capitalism affected the South no less than the North and England. As historian Herbert Gutman explains, Gilded Age cultural friction resulted from the infusion into the working class of "peasants, farmers, skilled artisans, and casual day laborers who brought into industrial society ways of work and other habits and values not associated with industrial necessities and the industrial ethos." See Gutman. "Work, Culture, and Society in Industrializing America," 541. Textile workers and tenant farmers were integrated into a market economy that seemingly deprived them of independence while failing to deliver economic security. Historian Steven Hahn elucidates the transformation of Georgia's upcountry yeomanry into marketplace-driven tenant farmers and sharecroppers in *The Roots of Southern Populism.*

3. Carlton, *Mill and Town in South Carolina,* 8–9; Woodward, *Origins of the New South,* chapters 1, 5, and 14. The town was the locus of industrialization and middle-class self-definition. As Carlton argues, the town "provided an opening wedge with which modern forms of social organization, including corporate enterprises, elaborate and hierarchically ordered divisions of labor, and bureaucracy could penetrate a South whose economic and social life had long revolved around autonomous white planters and small farmers." The bureaucratically organized university was an expression of "modern forms of social organization." For interpretations emphasizing the persistent power of a planter elite, see Wiener, "Class Structure and Economic Development in the American South," 970–92; and Billings, *Planters and the Making of a New South.* For a review of the literature on the question of southern continuity or discontinuity, see Woodman, "Economic Reconstruction and the Rise of the New South," 254–307; and Woodman, "How New Was the New South," 529–45. In an essay that attempts to resolve the dichotomy of planters and industrialists, James Cobb argues that both found common ground in certain economic policies that tended to mitigate their differences, in "Beyond Planters and Industrialists," 45–68.

4. Carlton, *Mill and Town in South Carolina,* 11.

5. Presley seems to suggest that Blease was prompted by a desire to retaliate against the school for the plagiarism incident. Presley, *Samuel Chiles Mitchell,* 168–70. He also argues that Blease "played on the resentments of the illiterate mill workers" (p. 171) who had nothing but contempt for higher education. Along a similar line, Hollis suggests that Blease made "political capital" by his assault on the university. Too impov-

erished to take advantage of higher education, Hollis argues, mill workers and poor whites relished Blease's invective against the university, in *University of South Carolina*, 249. This interpretation gives too much credit to Blease and not enough to the mill workers. Clearly, Blease was a gifted rhetorician who fastened on symbols of privilege as targets for his political campaign. Yet the class character of Blease's supporters and their endorsement of his opposition to progressive legislation suggests that Blease represented the legitimate concerns of people who considered the government and the progressive campaign to extend its reach a threat to their way of life.

6. Grantham, *Southern Progressivism*, 56; Ayers, *The Promise of the New South*, 225.

7. Ayers, *The Promise of the New South*, 227.

8. Grantham, *Southern Progressivism*, 56.

9. Ayers, *The Promise of the New South*, 227.

10. Hollis, "Samuel Chiles Mitchell," 31–32.

11. Woodward, *Origins of the New South*, 394. According to Woodward, Blease was Tillman's "understudy" who "imitated the master but improved his technique and expanded his appeal."

12. Hollis, "Samuel Chiles Mitchell," 31.

13. Grantham, *Southern Progressivism*, 58. For evidence of solid support for Blease and his candidates among millworkers, see Carlton, *Mill and Town in South Carolina*, 216–20. According to F. Peters, a black schoolteacher from Graniteville, South Carolina had always been divided between three classes: aristocrats, blacks, and poor whites. After the war the mills "began to draw all of this class together from all parts of this and other states." Concentrated in the mill towns, poor whites were even more susceptible to demagoguery, which exacerbated their antagonism toward aristocrats and blacks. "This hatred against the negro, the aristocrat and the north was still taught and kept up, and today we have Senator Tillman, Governor Blease, our State Supt. of Education and many others in office who fully oppose negro education." Peters to Robert Ogden, box 12, Ogden Papers, LOC.

14. Carlton, *Mill and Town in South Carolina*, 233–34.

15. For an analysis of lynchings that emphasizes the role of the South's peculiar form of land ownership and labor control after the Civil War, see Brundage, *Lynching in the New South*.

16. For a discussion of the accommodationist racism that enjoyed wide currency among progressives, see Fredrickson, *The Black Image in the White Mind*, 283–97. For a largely psychoanalytical explanation of the emergence of racial extremism after 1890, see Williamson, *The Crucible of Race*, chapters 4–5.

17. Singal, *The War Within*, 26–27.

18. South Carolina House of Representatives, *Journal*, 1911, 94–95, quoted in Carlton, *Mill and Town in South Carolina*, 222.

19. Quoted in Presley, *Samuel Chiles Mitchell*, 187; see also Singal, *The War Within*, 60.

20. Mitchell to John M. McBryde, October 20, 1909, in folder titled "Personal Correspondence, October 1909–February 1910," Mitchell Papers, USC.

21. Mitchell to Otto Dunkel, December 15, 1909, in folder titled "Personal Correspondence, October 1909–February 1910," Mitchell Papers, USC.

22. *Journal of the House of Representatives of the General Assembly of the State of South Carolina* (January 17, 1911): 92–93, quoted in Presley, *Samuel Chiles Mitchell*, 169–70.

23. Hollis, *University of South Carolina*, 250; "President's Report," December 29, 1910, "Trustees' Minutes," SCL.

24. Presley, *Samuel Chiles Mitchell*, 171–72.

25. Mitchell to J. M. McBryde, September 25, 1911, in folder titled "Personal Correspondence, 1911–September 1912," Mitchell Papers, USC. For another letter along the same lines, see Mitchell to G. B. Moore, September 1, 1911, in folder titled "Personal Correspondence, September 1912–1913," Mitchell Papers, USC.

26. Blease's quote, which appeared on a campaign poster and is included in the Tillman scrapbooks at Clemson College Library, is taken from Hollis, *University of South Carolina*, 251.

27. Mitchell to A. J. Montague, July 15, 1910, in folder titled "Personal Correspondence, May 1910–December 1910," Mitchell Papers, USC.

28. Alice Mitchell to her mother, March 10, 1912, folder #7, box 1, Mitchell Papers, UNC.

29. *Reports and Resolutions* 1, January 9, 1912, 654–55, South Carolina Department of Archives and History.

30. Carlton, *Mill and Town in South Carolina*, 266. Blease was not uniformly antitaxation. He supported general state appropriations for public schools for the purpose of restoring a balance between allocations made for town and rural schools. However, he reversed his position when the anti-Blease General Assembly funneled most of the appropriation to the already well-supported town schools. Ibid., 232. The governor's reduction of support for higher education exemplified his antipathy for progressive control. In the minds of Blease and his supporters, progressive programs for university extension and centralized control over education were inseparable from efforts to regulate child labor and compel school attendance. Each militated against the traditional southern opposition to concentrations of power and authority. Ibid., 224.

31. "President's Report," June 1911, SCL.

32. *Richmond Times Dispatch*, December 4, 1912, in Presley, *Samuel Chiles Mitchell*, 177.

33. *House Journal*, January 22, 1913, 154–55, in Crow, *The Control of the University of South Carolina*, 249–50.

34. Hollis, *University of South Carolina*, 252; Carlton, *Mill and Town in South Carolina*, 246.

35. Crow, *The Control of the University of South Carolina*, 253–54. On Johnson's admission of the influence he had on Ansel's decision to secure $90,000 for Winthrop College, see p. 260.

36. Presley, *Samuel Chiles Mitchell*, 181, footnote.

37. Ibid., 183.

38. Hollis, *University of South Carolina,* 255. Johnson's letter to McMaster, dated July 15, 1911, appears in Crow, *The Control of the University of South Carolina,* 254–55.

39. "Report of the Committee of the Peabody Board," 1906, 6; see also George Peabody, deed of gift establishing Peabody Education Fund, March 15, 1867; "Report of the General Agent of the Peabody Board," May 1911, in "Memoranda of the Relations of S. C. Mitchell to the Peabody Education Fund," 13, box 9, Mitchell Papers, LOC (hereafter abbreviated as "Memoranda"). Although this collection of documents is not identified in the Mitchell collection at the Manuscript Division in the Library of Congress, it seems to be the transcript of the legislative investigation launched by Blease and Ashley into the Peabody affair. See also "Proceedings of the Trustees of the Peabody Education Fund," fifth meeting, November 1, 1911, box 16, Mitchell Papers, LOC.

40. Mitchell to Wickliffe Rose, January 22, 1909, "Memoranda," Mitchell Papers, LOC.

41. Ayers, *The Promise of the New South,* 212.

42. "To the Trustees of the Peabody Education Fund," April 16, 1909, "Memoranda," Mitchell Papers, LOC.

43. Mitchell to Wickliffe Rose, March 15, 1911, "Memoranda," Mitchell Papers, LOC.

44. Ibid.

45. Joynes to Rose, October 31, 1911, "Memoranda," Mitchell Papers, LOC.

46. Legislative Investigation Committee, "Memoranda," Mitchell Papers, LOC, 67.

47. Ibid., 9.

48. Mitchell to Rose, August 4, 1911, "Memoranda," Mitchell Papers, LOC, 31.

49. Cooper and Terrill, *The American South,* 584.

50. Mitchell to the Board of Trustees, Peabody Fund, October 18, 1911, "Memoranda," 36, Mitchell Papers, LOC.

51. On racial paternalism in the New South and its relationship to black education, see Doyle, *New Men, New Cities, New South,* 269–78.

52. "Memoranda," 66, Mitchell Papers, LOC; "Trustees' Minutes," March 4, 1912, USC; Presley, *Samuel Chiles Mitchell,* 185. In addition to the $40,000 Winthrop received indirectly from USC, it also got $50,000 originally meant for the Peabody Institute of Boston.

53. Legislative Investigation Committee Report, February 27, 1913, box 8, Mitchell Papers, LOC.

54. *House Journal,* February 7, 1913, 498–99, in Presley, *Samuel Chiles Mitchell,* 186.

55. Legislative Investigation Committee Report, February 27, 1913, box 8, Mitchell Papers, LOC; quote from *House Journal,* March 1, 1913, 1426–28, in Presley, *Samuel Chiles Mitchell,* 187. The report acknowledged the compatibility between the university presidents' 1909 recommendations for distribution and the policy of the Peabody trustees on financial support for black education and state universities.

56. Kirkland to Mitchell, February 14, 1913, in folder titled "Governor of South Carolina 1907–1913," Mitchell Papers, USC.

57. Denny to Mitchell, January 23, 1913, box 8, Mitchell Papers, LOC.

58. Wyche to Mitchell, February 10, 1913, box 8, Mitchell Papers, LOC.

59. Tillman to Mitchell, April 10, 1913, box 8, Mitchell Papers, LOC.

60. W. C. McDaniel to Mitchell, April 14, 1913, box 8, Mitchell Papers, LOC.

61. J. J. M. Graham to Mitchell, April 14, 1913, box 8, Mitchell Papers, LOC.

62. Charles Wilson to Mitchell, April 11, 1913, box 8, Mitchell Papers, LOC. Echoing the sentiments of many of the "town people" who gave Mitchell their support, Wilson believed that the interests at stake in retaining the president at USC were the university, the common schools, and the state's "ignorant masses." Of equal importance, Wilson acknowledged Mitchell's role in making the university an instrument of the state: "The University stands now, as never before, for the common schools, for the uplift of the masses, and has come in contact, for the first time, with all the people of the State."

63. George Brown to Mitchell, April 12, 1913, box 8, Mitchell Papers, LOC.

64. T. C. Green to Mitchell, April 11, 1913, box 8, Mitchell Papers, LOC.

65. Tobias to Mitchell, April 14, 1913, box 8, Mitchell Papers, LOC.

66. Mills to Mitchell, April 11, 1913, box 8, Mitchell Papers, LOC. Numerous other letters were sent to Mitchell expressing regret at his decision to leave USC and support for his efforts to rejuvenate the university. Uniformly, these letters came from the ranks of South Carolina's middle class: professionals, entrepreneurs, and anti-Bleasite politicians. For example, see letters of W. Renwick Bradley, superintendent of education for Abbeville County, to Mitchell, February 15, 1913; Lewis W. Perrin, lawyer from Spartanburg, to Mitchell, April 12, 1913; Robert Moorman, lawyer from Columbia, to Mitchell, April 10, 1913; and C. T. Woods, member of the State Supreme Court, to Mitchell, April 10, 1913, all in box 8, Mitchell Papers, LOC.

67. David Carlton describes *The State* as "the leading spokesman for the 'Progressive' element among the 'town people.'" This Columbia newspaper spearheaded many key progressive reform initiatives and became Blease's principal adversary. *Mill and Town in South Carolina,* 282.

68. *The State,* April 28, 1913, Mitchell Papers, LOC.

69. Ibid.

70. Ibid. Others were convinced that D. B. Johnson's motives were purely selfish. Alice Mitchell believed that he had "watched the Peabody Board for years as a cat watches a mouse. [He] should have corrected any false impression as to what Mr. Mitchell had done, instead of using it in the jealous over-ambitious way that he did." Alice Mitchell to her mother, Mrs. Broadus, March 10, 1913, folder #8, Mitchell Papers, UNC. T. O. Mabry of Verona, Mississippi believed that Johnson's motives were "sufficiently obvious." Mabry, a former head of the department of natural sciences at Winthrop whom Johnson had allegedly dismissed arbitrarily, reassured Mitchell that nothing more could be expected of a college president "who will *obtain money under false pretenses from the Legislature.*" Mabry to Mitchell, February 10, 1913, Mitchell Papers, LOC. Mitchell also held Johnson responsible for insinuating that the president was guilty of racial impropriety, the one transgression guaranteed to send Blease into a rage. Presley, *Samuel Chiles Mitchell,* 188.

71. Joynes to Ansel, October 31, 1911, "Memoranda," Mitchell Papers, LOC.

72. The bitter institutional rivalry paralleled the acrimony of state politics. Writing in 1893, one Dabney correspondent offered a commentary that could easily have been applied to 1911: "It is a small state . . . politics are indescribable . . . and each institution seems to be *fighting for its existence.*" Henneman to Dabney, August 5, 1893, folder #77, box 5, Dabney Papers, UNC.

73. Joynes to Ansel, October 31, 1911, "Memoranda," Mitchell Papers, LOC.

74. The importance of the Peabody Education Fund to education in the South after the Civil War should not be underestimated. As one historian notes, "To negate its existence is to remove the foundation stone upon which rested all subsequent philanthropic effort in the South. It was the first private multimillion dollar foundation in American history with a positive approach toward the prevention of social ills." Parker, "George Peabody's Influence on Southern Educational Philanthropy," 70.

75. Hollis, *University of South Carolina,* 251.

76. Presley, *Samuel Chiles Mitchell,* 190.

77. Hollis, *University of South Carolina,* 262.

78. Presley, *Samuel Chiles Mitchell,* 192–93.

79. Alice Mitchell to her brother, April 13, 1913, folder #8, box 1, Mitchell Papers, USC.

8

Visions of Grandeur: Edwin Alderman and the University of Virginia, 1904–15

Of southern progressives in higher education, Edwin Alderman was one of the more successful in transforming the university into an instrument of state service. Alderman promoted a multitude of reform initiatives, but two themes dominated his administration: the professionalization of higher education and the unification of the state's educational system in the interest of social progress. His administration represented the major ideological impulses generated by the educational wing of the southern progressive movement in the crucial period of 1899–1915.

He was more active than most in regional and state reform organizations. He was also more outspoken than other progressives about the function of the university in the New South. If Mitchell's South Carolina exemplifies progressivism besieged, Alderman's Virginia illustrates successful university progressivism. But like Mitchell and the others, he linked university development to the social needs of the New South. And more aggressively than others, he used the campaign to coordinate education as a vehicle for promoting university dominance.

Born in 1861 in Wilmington, North Carolina, Alderman showed few signs in early life of the distinction he would later achieve. After attending private school, he enrolled at the University of North Carolina (UNC) in 1878. There, he led an undistinguished but respectable scholarly life.[1] Although Alderman shared the ambition of most young, middle-class southerners for a life in politics, he settled for a career in education and never left. Working as a public school teacher in Goldsboro, he became superintendent after his mentor, Edward P. Moses, resigned. In 1886 Alderman was elected president of the North Carolina Teacher's Assembly. In 1889 he joined Charles McIver in a highly orchestrated campaign for public education that lasted until 1892. Traveling throughout the state, Alderman and McIver sponsored weekly teachers' institutes and rallies that promoted public support for education. The campaign achieved an increase in state appropriations to public schools. It also established the North Carolina Normal and Industrial School, of which McIver subsequently became president.[2]

The education campaign quickly convinced them of the need to adjust school reform to the culture of the rural South. Speaking of McIver, Alderman commented, "His task was to plead with an individualistic and conservative community, hating overmuch, by reason of robbery and suffering, the very word 'tax,' for a democratic and communal institution costing large sums of money and a world of patience."[3] The campaign's success depended on their ability to conciliate local opinion. In an address to the Conference for Education in the South in 1906, Alderman noted the balance that reformers had to strike between administrative centralization and local control. Executive control was necessary in the transitional period from postwar minimalism to modern efficiency. But the "local interest in the school must grow so strong that the legislative power will finally touch only what is general and vital," while the "directing power shall be local." By generating grassroots support and local leadership for public education, they minimized the threat of intrusive control.[4]

The evangelical-style educational rallies gave them an opportunity to polish their oratorical technique. They also crystallized Alderman's ideas about the relationship of education to the state. His experience as an educational propagandist convinced him that the South's social conditions demanded "men with faith in education as a great agency for moulding social and economic forces," capable of exercising influence over the "most majestic of all human agencies—public opinion."[5]

In 1893 Alderman was elected to the recently established chair of history and philosophy of education at Chapel Hill. After serving as president of UNC from 1896 to 1900, he took over the executive position at Tulane. There, Alderman was active on the Southern Education Board (SEB) and in state educational campaigns. In 1904 he became the first president of the University of Virginia (UVA). Although Thomas Jefferson had prohibited the election of a president, the university's Board of Visitors decided in 1902 that the system of appointing rotating faculty members to the executive position was cumbersome and inefficient. In an effort to promote efficiency the board departed from tradition and unanimously elected him over such notables as Woodrow Wilson, Charles Dabney, and Francis P. Venable of UNC.[6]

In his inaugural address the new president lucidly outlined his administrative agenda. To transform the university into an institution that could meet the challenges of an expanding southern economy, the school would have to increase its annual income by $100,000.[7] The university also would assume responsibility for organizing the state's education system. To shed rational light on social problems, the university would cultivate the social sciences. As a corollary, Alderman insisted that the university offer technical expertise to the region's burgeoning industrial sector. The president was particularly interested in improving the school's engineering department and establishing a School of Business. Finally, he suggested that the university preserve literate culture by adding a School of English Composition.[8]

Echoing reformers across the South, Alderman placed the creed of university service at the center of his program. The university had an obligation to apply its expertise to social problems when called upon by the state: "If a state comes to the conclusion that its public health must be conserved, or its roads improved, or its economic resources developed . . . it has a perfect right to turn to the university for help and direction."[9] The value of higher education was its ability to deliver social service. It was imperative that the modern college "provide as well experts in every phase of expansion in a complex new line, in engineering, in commerce, agriculture, the domestic arts, in public health, in public transportation, and public welfare generally." A state university should not only disseminate knowledge but also direct "the surest ethical and economic insights to practical problems of co-operation and relief."[10] The university would advance social efficiency by training professionals for southern industry and commerce. "I mean by the engineer and the business man," he announced in a 1906 address, "a man who may be relied on to create a clean city, or build a bridge, or erect a factory, or build a public building."[11] Like other progressives, Alderman connected university modernization to the larger task of transforming southern culture. Casting the university as an adversary of "particularism" and "localism," the university would mold public character in a "peculiar organic sense."[12]

Southern progressivism was laced with regional peculiarities, but its model for the modern university came from the North. In 1909, Alderman suggested the importance of president Charles Van Hise's University of Wisconsin as a prototype for the modern university. "To speak objectively," Alderman wrote to Frederick T. Gates of the General Education Board (GEB), "I desired to change its ideals somewhat from the ideals of Oxford to the ideals of Wisconsin; to transform it from an aristocratic University to a democratic University," and to mold the school into an agency of social service leading "a great region entering into an industrial democracy." Just as Walter Barnard Hill did, Alderman looked to it as a shining example of progressive education and social outreach.[13]

The new president brought his creed of practical education to a college with a small enrollment and a meager income. Walter Hines Page concluded in 1904 that UVA had "remained local and provincial and poor during the expansive period in which nearly all our other universities have broadened their spirit and become national." The president probably would not have quarreled with Page's description. To Alderman, the school was "poor." Almost any college in the region would have compared unfavorably with Tulane, his former employer and one of only two universities in the South with a million-dollar endowment.[14]

The university's annual income is a telling measure of UVA's relative stature in Alderman's first year. For the year 1903–4, UVA received $31,000 from the state. Added to students' fees, tuition, and donations, the total income amounted to $153,000. The University of Georgia, by comparison, had just secured $22,500 that year, its first state appropriation. Together with the rest of the university's revenue, the total income was $105,430. Tennessee, on the other hand, received no state appropriation for 1903 and only $10,000 in 1904. Compared to Louisiana, which received only $77,543 that year, Virginia was wealthy. Compared to the majority of northern institutions, however, which southerners looked to as the standard of higher education, southern schools appeared uniformly impoverished.[15]

To finance expansion and improve the school's fiscal situation, the president set out to increase its endowment. At the time of Alderman's election, the Washington alumni chapter initiated the Jefferson Memorial Fund, an endowment drive for $1 million. The campaign soon fell under Alderman's direction. His aggressive solicitation of northern philanthropy was rewarded by a $500,000 contribution from Andrew Carnegie. The endowment drive also netted an unconditional gift of $100,000 from the GEB for a School of Education to be named after southern educator J. L. M. Curry. Carnegie's half million dollars became the endowment for the James Madison School of Law and the James Monroe School of International Law.[16]

Unlike most of his contemporaries, Alderman enjoyed unusual success in his efforts to increase the university's legislative support. Alderman benefited from a legislature favorably disposed to educational improvement and a highly organized alumni who contributed to the campaign endowment. Also critical was the role of the May Campaign in generating political support for public education in Virginia.[17] Euphoric over the university's improved fortunes, the president wrote to George Foster Peabody in March 1906 that the school's victory had been "complete and unclouded." It was certainly formidable. The annual appropriation, which had not been increased since 1880, was raised from $50,000 to $75,000. Even more momentous was the approval of an $85,000 appropriation for improvements and equipment.[18]

Like Chancellor Hill's experience at Georgia, the windfall signaled a change in the relationship between the university and the state. "The university received the largest appropriation of any institution," Alderman commented to Peabody, "and the State acknowledges its responsibility for its life and growth." In fact, the state's generous appropriation was part of a large package of funds allocated for public education that year. With additional assistance from the GEB, Alderman mused, "I would be a pretty happy man in the consciousness of having an institution rapidly forging to the front." In the meantime, he rejoiced that the university had secured a more solid footing with the legislature.[19]

Soliciting support from the GEB later the same year, Alderman outlined his plan to infuse the university with the tenets of southern progressivism. Efficiency, departmental reorganization, the coordination of state education agencies, and the promotion of professional schools were central to his program. "The great struggle" in the region, he wrote to the board's Wallace Buttrick, was for "a co-ordinated and efficient system of education" that connected primary schools with high schools under the direction and leadership of universities. Alderman linked the coordination of schools to the movement for public roads, libraries, rational systems of taxation, and rural uplift. Together, he argued, these initiatives were propelling society toward "self-realization." Using the familiar organic imagery of progressivism, he observed that "these movements as yet are chaotic or atomistic, characterized by lack of harmony and symmetry and oneness of purpose, and needing to be correlated and fused and welded into one effective agent of social amelioration." The southern education movement would help crystallize just such an agency.[20]

Alderman explained that social conditions necessitated "fuller endowment of a small number of the larger and stronger universities along the lines of sociological and industrial instruction." Passing as it was through a "social and industrial revolution," he argued, the South needed to "get power to guide it wisely."[21] The establishment of the Curry Memorial School of Education had augmented the school's social science offerings. He suggested to the board that an annuity of $6,000 for six years would further improve this area by facilitating the expansion of the departments of history, economics, sociology, and political science.[22]

Translating rhetoric into reality, Alderman promoted academic professionalization. In executive fashion, he planned the expansion of the school's academic offerings in consultation with department heads. The faculty proliferated with new professors of education, secondary education, economics, surgery, mechanical engineering, and chemistry, among others. The president also endorsed the idea of sabbaticals, a measure designed to advance professional research. Alderman believed that a paid leave of absence for a professor loaded down by classroom obligations would advance faculty professionalism. It was also easy to endorse sabbatical leaves when the financial stimulus came from the Carnegie Foundation.[23]

Academic professionalization was most evident in the law faculty's efforts to protect its professional status. Anticipating the addition of a fifth professor to the law school, the faculty sent a list of suggestions to assist the president in selecting candidates. The new appointment should be an adjunct professor hired on probation. The "double advantage" was that the adjunct could be paid less and could be dismissed easily if he "should prove unsuccessful, or otherwise undesirable."[24]

The faculty then classified potential candidates as either teachers in other law schools, experienced practitioners, or recent graduates. Law school teachers would be precluded by the unattractive remuneration and insecurity of the adjunct position. Attention should then be focused on recent graduates from law schools or career teachers. But why not recommend hiring a hardened lawyer weathered by years of litigation? The faculty admitted that in the "olden days" the law office seemed to offer the best training for future lawyers. Legal apprenticeship had been attractive at a time when law schools had offered instruction only in "practicioners' methods." In recent years, though, legal instruction had evolved into "a science and a profession."[25]

Like most other late nineteenth-century academic disciplines that sought to consolidate their professional status, the Virginia law faculty shrouded itself in the mantle of science. They also differentiated themselves from practicing lawyers. The faculty argued that practitioners disregarded the application of "sound principle" to a "given state of facts" and ignored "the reasons upon which it rests." Instead, they conducted themselves as "partisans" who used "astute argument" in the effort to manipulate principle for a particular case. The practicing lawyer was a theoretical dilettante, studying "isolated propositions of a particular topic" rather than "the topic in its entirety." The practitioner examined the law "not as a science, but rather as a collection of isolated rules." Hardly a flattering portrait of the profession for which law students were preparing. The teacher, on the other hand, was a theoretician who, Comte-like, related the intricate branches of law to each other in "its entirety, and with judicial impartiality"—the objectivity of scientific investigation. Law was no longer a matter to be trifled with by amateurs but an academic discipline requiring sober scholarship.[26]

The faculty also appended a flimsy caveat about teaching proficiency. The practitioner accustomed to the excitement of the courtroom would need periodic infusions of "enthusiasm" to maintain his interest in daily teaching. On the other hand, the professional teacher, well accustomed to classroom drudgery, would need much less external stimulation. Despite the questionable logic, the law faculty used the hiring as an opportunity to assert its professional status. Their recommendations were an effort to solidify the exclusionary and self-regulating functions of a professional guild. Hiring an adjunct would give the faculty more latitude in determining the candidate's suitability. It would also ensure that he posed no economic threat to the department or the faculty. Distinguishing between narrow-minded practitioners and disciplined theorists leading "a sort of monastic existence" in the cause of scientific truth, Virginia's law faculty accelerated the process of specialization driving late nineteenth-century professionalization.[27]

While faculty set themselves off from amateurs, the administration moved toward separating liberal from technical education. The new organization registered the trend toward departmental rationalization. The "Academic Departments" included the college and the department of graduate studies. The "Professional Departments" included law, medicine, engineering, and agriculture. The college offered not only the bachelor of arts but two additional degrees, the "cultural" and "vocational" bachelor of science.[28]

The new degrees were the product of a controversial attempt by the faculty to eliminate the Latin requirement for the bachelor of arts degree. Proficiency in at least one of two classical languages had long been an essential feature of a college education in the South. According to historian Philip A. Bruce, the "fixed system" of classical education had been undermined before Alderman's administration. Latin stood as one of the final monuments of the antebellum tradition. But the faculty was "now intruding into the immemorial temple of the Latin and Greek languages, and calling for the reduction of those scholastic deities to a footing of equality with humbler studies."[29] Newspapers accused the school of lowering its standards to those of inferior colleges.

Some of the stiffest opposition to the faculty proposal came from alumni groups. The Maryland Alumni Association submitted a resolution to the administration calling for the preservation of the Latin requirement. In response to one disgruntled New York alumnus, Alderman wrote that the decision was the product of sober deliberation. In fact, the president had written to several academics at leading northern universities for their comments on Virginia's proposal. He also asked their advice on how to present the proposal to the Board of Visitors and alumni. According to Alderman, the decision reflected the demands of southern progress. He argued that instead of commercializing the degree, the administration had vigilantly raised university standards across the board. In fact, the university's efforts to raise standards qualified it for membership in the Southern Association of Colleges and Secondary Schools in 1905. In 1912, it became the only southern university admitted to the Association of American Universities.[30]

In 1908 the Board of Visitors decided to leave the existing bachelor of arts requirements intact. Yet a compromise was reached with the addition of the two degree streams. The new bachelor of science degrees would accommodate students interested primarily in practical and technical instruction. Students unable to manage the classical languages were eligible for the cultural bachelor of science, whereas the vocational bachelor of science was "designed for those who desire to fit themselves for some vocation for which special training in one of the Natural or Mathematical Sciences is necessary." Although the board's decision accommodated a more specialized, technical instruction, it was no categorical victory for the progressives. The classical requirement was circumvented but not eliminated. If anything, the episode illustrates the ideological differences between the faculty and the university's alumni. The Alderman administration may have set a progressive agenda, but many university constituents chose to defend tradition and continuity.[31]

Alderman signaled the emergence of the utilitarian ethic at Virginia in his support for academic specialization. In March 1905 Richard Heath Dabney, history professor at Virginia, responded to Alderman's request for suggestions on university development by insisting on realignment of the School of Historical and Economic Science. Expecting one instructor to teach subjects handled by at least ten at most other institutions was "preposterous." At most advanced universities in the country, Dabney argued, three times as many instructors taught the "historico-economic group of sciences" as Latin. At Virginia, however, "we have a professor and three assistants for this one dead language while a single professor must attempt, unassisted, to teach the two great vital subjects of History and Economics with such incidental scraps of Political Science and Sociology as he can manage to add, as flavoring to others." A full professor of economics was needed to modernize the social sciences at Virginia. Apparently Alderman agreed, making Dabney's recommendations a priority in his appeal to the GEB. With funds from the alumni drive the president was able to adopt Dabney's recommendations. In the 1905–6 session, Alderman established a separate chair of economics with a full professor.[32]

Although determined to achieve his entire reform agenda, the president was vigilant about advancing professional education. The professional departments grew considerably in the president's first three years. From an enrollment of 58 in the 1903–4 session the department of engineering had doubled to 124 in

1907. In 1907 the department had two more professors, three more adjunct professors, and four more instructors than it had in 1903–4. Additions to the department of medicine were no less impressive. In three years the school had acquired a renovated anatomy building, new laboratories for histology, embryology, physiology, and clinical diagnosis, and additional professors for pathology, physiology, and histology. According to Alderman, it had received "the largest share of expansion in the extension of its laboratories and teaching force," a remarkable "growth in efficiency." To accommodate those advancing to professional degrees, the administration allowed students to apply the first year of professional courses to their degree in lieu of academic electives.[33]

In his recommendations for development that year, he stressed the improvement of professional and practical education. The South's demand for professional experts in chemistry and education was as pressing as the need for engineers and lawyers. Emboldened by his success with the legislature in 1906, he asked for a $75,000 chemistry building, explaining that this discipline was "the great basic subject of the modern industrial world." Chemical experts would be in "demand throughout the South for the next decade," and the president wanted Virginia to maintain what he claimed was its lead among southern institutions in this field.[34]

To this shopping list Alderman added a request for a $75,000 law building. As one of the nation's leading departments of law and the most prestigious law school in the South, it deserved better accommodations. In addition to a new building, the president called the legislature's attention to the administration's decision that the law course be expanded from two to three years in conformity with the "larger and more important law schools in America."[35] Invoking the idea of social service, Alderman requested yet another $75,000 to pay for a new medical building: "Our hospital is a state hospital, owned and controlled by the state, and its facilities are at the call of the people." The president also called on the legislature to make appropriations for library improvements and property maintenance. However, the bulk of his requests in 1907 were earmarked for the professional departments and the enhancement of practical education.[36]

If there was any ambiguity about the direction Alderman wanted the university to take, it was cleared up in the section of his report titled "Our Task." The touchstone of university expansion in the coming years would be technical education for social service. "The industrial and technical schools must be maintained and perfected. . . . The University must be made equal to the work of training leaders in all forms of productive activity for a new and difficult era." The engineer, the businessperson, and the scholar were "the men we want."

Equally important, the university "must breed them." The university wanted to "get close to the life of the people and to serve that life practically." The modern college was no mere polytechnical institute but an incubator for trained professionals in the fields of law, medicine, agriculture, and business. Pedagogical utilitarianism would be the guiding principle of university development.[37]

Southern industry demanded trained chemists, but the benefits of scientific chemistry extended beyond the factory. With the development of scientific agriculture it was imperative that farmers have working knowledge of chemistry, physics, botany, zoology, entomology, and other sciences. Mining and metallurgy also demanded advanced knowledge in chemistry. The chemist and the engineer would be captains of industry. As the South's efficiency experts, they would coordinate resources and maximize productivity. But the South was drastically deficient in trained chemists and engineers. If southern universities could not provide them, it would be necessary to attract them from the North and West. Southern economic autonomy demanded instruction in the applied sciences.[38]

No department had a more legitimate claim to social service than the medical school, but financial insecurity plagued it throughout Alderman's tenure. Relentlessly, Alderman reminded the legislature that the medical school was a public institution that delivered palpable social service. "There is no more practical servant of the State than the doctor, and it is fast becoming . . . recognized that his greatest function in our civilization is not only to cure and restore to economic efficiency those who are sick, but to keep the community at large in a normal condition of health." Echoing the progressive theme of public health, Alderman connected improved medical care to increased social efficiency. More than a teaching institution, the hospital was a social agency for community health and economic productivity. In 1911 the legislature responded to Alderman's ineluctable pressure by increasing the medical school's annual appropriation from $10,000 to $18,000. Sensing that the tide had turned for the hospital, Alderman asked the legislature to rescue the medical department with a $21,000 appropriation in 1913.[39] Although the president could not sweep away the department's financial troubles, he did solidify the notion that the department was an extension of the state. By offering practical education and social assistance, the university hospital justified its claim to public support.

The development of the department of education illustrated the progressive synthesis of professionalization and social service. The president persuaded the GEB to launch the department in 1905 with a $100,000 donation to the J. L. M. Curry School of Education. Following the GEB's program for southern state universities, Virginia used Rockefeller money to hire a high school inspector. The inspector would also hold an appointment to the university as professor of secondary education. Alderman appointed Bruce R. Payne, recipient of an M.A. from Trinity and a Ph.D. from the Teacher's College at Columbia, to the new position.[40]

Payne traveled throughout Virginia promoting the development of secondary education. Inspecting high schools for university accreditation, addressing meetings of teachers and administrators, and mobilizing community support for public education, Payne translated Alderman's plan of university extension into reality. Cooperating with state and county superintendents, inspectors, and teachers, Payne promoted secondary education and solidified the foundations of the "Social Efficiency State."[41] His work in coordinating curricula helped justify the university's role in managing the state education system. According to Alderman, Payne built "the nexus between the college and the common school." Yet as a paid agent of the GEB he also functioned as an advocate of business efficiency and bureaucratic management.[42]

By northern standards, Virginia's education system was abysmal. Although the Reconstruction era public school system was sustained under the watchful administration of superintendent William H. Ruffner, it declined in the 1890s during what historian Louis Harlan described as "a public school famine." Opposition to school spending from the deeply entrenched political machine of senator Thomas S. Martin blocked efforts at educational reform until 1902. That year, the SEB turned its attention to Virginia.[43]

Spurred by board support, education reformers established the Cooperative Education Association of Virginia. In 1905, the association launched a massive state campaign to construct a genuine system of public education. Following on the heels of the crusade, Payne, along with Joseph Eggleston, state superintendent of public instruction, prepared a bill for a state-supported system of high schools. In 1906 the legislature passed the measure. But it was the collaborative efforts of Alderman, Payne, Samuel Mitchell, and the Cooperative Association that made the May Campaign successful. Throughout the campaign, Payne maintained a steady barrage of propaganda in weekly and daily newspapers. According to Charles Dabney, the campaign was "epoch-making in that it secured the enactment of laws for the betterment and extension of the schools authorized under the new constitution, which marked the beginning of a new era in public education in Virginia."[44] By 1908 the education forces had secured the passage of forty of the forty-three pieces of legislation submitted to the legislature.[45] Through the work of associational agencies and experts such as Payne, the university extended its reach and fused itself to an expanding bureaucratic state.

Paralleling the efforts of modernizers at several other southern universities, Alderman promoted the elevation of university standards. In 1909 the president reported that the entrance requirements had been raised to fourteen units (a unit representing 180 days of class in a given subject) from eleven the previous year. This change brought Virginia into conformity with the leading members of the Association of Colleges and Preparatory Schools of the Southern States. Applicants to the Academic College were expected to be graduates of a four-year high school. The administration made corresponding improvements to the entrance requirements for law and medicine between 1909 and 1912.[46]

The new entrance requirements exemplified the progressive impulse to conform to regional and national standards of higher education.[47] They also illustrated the reformers' program for rationalizing southern education. As J. M. Page, dean of the university, explained in a report to the legislature in 1913, "In this way competition between the University and the State public high schools is absolutely prevented."[48] Alderman suggested to the rector that the new entrance conditions guaranteed that "those presenting themselves for instruction are prepared for the work; and, what is more to the point, the high schools are not robbed but protected in their normal growth and thus given a chance to become great instruments of training in themselves and great feeders of the proper sort to colleges and to universities."[49] Compared to other progressives, Alderman was acutely conscious of the connection between university standards and southern educational development.

Defining university standards was essential to the effort to coordinate the public education system. Progressive educators confronted high schools that claimed to be colleges and colleges that called themselves universities. Few acknowledged any uniform standard for distinguishing a high school from a college. It was to this institutional confusion that Alderman and other progressives directed their coordinating efforts.

Progressives set out to define the function of each level of education. In 1910 the Virginia General Assembly created the Education Commission to coordinate state higher education. The panel included President Alderman, state superintendent of public instruction Joseph D. Eggleston, and John R. Saunders, member of the state Senate. As Charles G. Maphis, the commission's secretary, described the condition of higher education at the time, "The present tendencies of these institutions appear to be toward educational duplication and consequent financial waste." Although commissioned to examine higher education, the panel also had to define the relationship between college development and secondary education. Their conclusions emphasized the primacy of education in southern progress, efficiency, and government-university cooperation. Through the efforts of Alderman and his associates, the Virginia Education Commission became an important agency of educational progressivism in the state.[50]

The public high schools stood in "organic relation" to the elementary schools and higher education. While training students for "civic, commercial and industrial life" they cultivated a "higher degree of social efficiency and leadership than the elementary schools."[51] As much as the elementary school and the high school, the university was an integral part of a coordinated system of education. According to the commission, it was the culmination of the state-supported system, the servant of the Progressive State. "The State and all of its departments should consider its university as the primary source for all guidance and information based on scholarship and research, and its should demand of its chiefest public service corporation constant helpfulness and direction."[52]

The Education Commission also formed a committee to investigate the engineering programs at Virginia colleges. Presumably, the information would help rationalize educational spending by identifying areas of curricular overlap. However, administrators at some institutions considered it a scheme to solidify the UVA's hegemony over state higher education. P. B. Barringer, president of the Virginia Polytechnical Institute (VPI) and former dean of the university, accused the committee of trying to lure students away from VPI and the Virginia Military Institute.[53]

Despite Alderman's protestation that he wanted "no advantage for this branch of the State's educational life located here at the University," Barringer was onto something. If Alderman's motives were not as cynical as Barringer implied, Alderman at least had a vested interest in establishing the superiority of the UVA engineering program. Writing to Barringer, Alderman highlighted the differences between VPI's and UVA's engineering curriculum. Whereas the former required only two years of high school for admission, the UVA required four. At VPI students pursued a four-year degree, much of which was taken up by "military tactics and rudimentary humanistic studies." At Virginia, Alderman pointedly remarked, engineering students were required to endure four years of residence "devoted exclusively to technical and scientific studies." Acerbically, Alderman added, "Is there no difference in the results? If there be none, then there must exist some strange educational magic, by which two years out of a student's school life may be saved. Can you reveal to us where the magic lies?" Alderman smugly implied that VPI might offer a reasonable introduction to engineering, but UVA was the state's preeminent engineering school. In fact, he argued that the university ranked among the nation's best engineering schools, including Cornell, Columbia, and the Massachusetts Institute of Technology.[54]

Extending his claims of educational superiority to the university's entire field of applied sciences, Alderman asserted that its standards conformed to those of "all American universities and technological schools of the better class." Alderman warned that the trend toward standardization would force colleges with lower requirements to justify their policies or admit the inferiority of their degrees. Despite his thinly concealed antagonism, Alderman assured Barringer that the committee was interested only in promoting institutional harmony: "The recommendation of the Committee that the three schools represented in it should ascertain by frank and frequent conferences the exact facts as to the courses given and their relative academic value . . . seems to me the true road to harmonious co-operation." Infringement on competing institutions, Alderman seemed to suggest, was an acceptable price to pay for "progress."[55]

The Education Commission is important for what it suggests about state-university cooperation in the New South. The commission galvanized the cooperative relationship between the government and state institutions of higher education. It made experts out of academics, inviting institutions of higher education to take part in formulating public policy. As Alderman explained to Wickliffe Rose, the commission represented a "step forward in standardizing and systematizing and reorganizing education in the State."[56] In doing so, it contributed to the emergence of the modern centralized state. Universities were not simply the beneficiaries of public support but the architects of a regulated system of education. They had a special obligation to state development as well as a special claim on state assistance.

The administration's medical school program also reflected Alderman's determination to coordinate education in Virginia. A nagging deficit and inadequate legislative support had crippled plans to expand the department. Alderman believed that rationalizing the state's medical education was the best way to ensure cost-efficiency and progress. In June 1911 the commission recommended amalgamating the medical school at UVA with the Medical College of Virginia and the University College of Medicine. The proposed institution would be located in Richmond, the site of the Medical College.

Like other episodes of Alderman's administration, the movement for medical school union reflected the multiple forces of progressive efficiency, resistance to centralization, and the university's drive for dominance. The Education Commission submitted five recommendations on the proposed amalgamation to the legislature. Promoting academic professionalization, the commission called for a medical school faculty devoted exclusively to teaching. In addition, it requested the establishment of a genuine medical college in Virginia. Centralizing medical education would reduce the surplus of poorly trained doctors in the state. The commission also admitted that the decision was dictated by financial considerations: Funding three medical schools was exceedingly expensive. Competition, duplicate faculties, and the division of students had impaired the quality of the state's health care. One well-funded institution was enough.[57]

Opposed to educational duplication, Alderman and the commission objected to a proposal to place the university's medical school and the Medical College of Virginia on a mill tax basis. Regular appropriations would only create two separate and equally underfunded institutions. More importantly, it would destroy the movement for unification. "If [the Medical College] of Virginia is put upon such a basis, it has a club with which to destroy this whole unifying idea." The measure would alienate university supporters, but it would also bolster "the medical college people who will set up absurd conditions for entrance into any such amalgamation." The president had little difficulty subordinating the interests of the Medical College to the juggernaut of unification.[58]

Part of the explanation for Alderman's vigorous support of unification is that the university stood to benefit from the merger. The new school, the commission's second recommendation insisted, "should be absolutely under the control and a Department of the University of Virginia."[59] The Alderman administration, well represented on the Education Commission, hoped to use the medical school issue to assert itself as the sole arbiter of educational quality in Virginia. As the commission's 1912 report asserted, "one of the chief functions of a State university is to set up educational ideals and to fix educational standards." Professionalization would also enhance the school's prestige: "It is not a university unless it supports adequately one or more professional schools. Chief among the professional schools are law and medicine."[60] Presumably, it would also enjoy a larger percentage of the state education budget. Evidently, medical school unification was motivated as much by the Alderman administration's determination to bolster the university's status as by the concern for educational efficiency.

One of the factors propelling the merger was the expectation of donations from the Carnegie Foundation and the GEB. This "enormous sum of money," Alderman explained in a letter to the dean, H. R. Whitehead, could be guaranteed only if the university demonstrated its willingness to "control the medical situation" by removing the school at Charlottesville to Richmond. "They will not touch us if we stay at Charlottesville," the president warned the dean. The familiar refrain of northern philanthropic influence played once again in the history of the southern education.[61]

The president was also concerned about regional competition and prestige. Alderman explained to Whitehead that Vanderbilt University had just received $1 million from the board. "Now it seems to me," the president confided, "looking far ahead—unless we are perfectly willing to surrender leadership to Vanderbilt and to be simply a small restricted school that there is but one thing for us to do, and that is to attempt to control the situation at Richmond." The president was adamant: "We must control it absolutely. . . . It must be a University School—controlled by us." If the northern philanthropists were willing to give money to the school at Charlottesville, he would be tempted to consider the offer. Yet even a financially sound school at Charlottesville might not be satisfactory, he admitted. Only amalgamation would give the university control over medical education in the state. If the university allowed the plan to be undermined by political jockeying, it would have to be content with "playing second fiddle forever."[62]

The attempt by Richmond politicians to place the new school under the authority of the Medical College provoked Alderman's wrath. Writing to Whitehead in December 1913, the president threatened to discontinue negotiations if local interests persisted in trying to make the new institution a Richmond school. Alderman was not interested in a power-sharing arrangement with two institutions. Executive authority should be administered by the dean of the university's medical department, subject to the direction of the president and Board of Visitors.[63]

Alderman saw his role in the medical school issue as progressive educator for the unenlightened. Describing two board members as "intensely ignorant of medical education" and "influenced by local considerations," Alderman insisted that they be "taught and instructed." Apparently, the president had relinquished none of the paternalistic condescension that had alienated educators in North Carolina. Encouraged by the promise of philanthropic largesse, the Alderman administration became the leading proponent of amalgamation. However, the plan was defeated by the university's Board of Visitors when it failed to secure an endowment from the Carnegie and Rockefeller foundations.[64]

One of the school's greatest contributions to state service was the development of Virginia's educational infrastructure. Largely through the efforts of Bruce Payne, secondary school supervisor, the university helped erect a system of secondary education that in 1911 included more than 100 high schools and 15,000 students. Payne informed Alderman that in 1905 the state had spent approximately $150,000 to maintain high schools. By 1910, that figure had climbed to $453,403. Alderman appreciated Payne's efforts. In an article for the *Alumni News* in 1915, the president included the School of Secondary Education in his litany of university agencies promoting educational cooperation.[65]

The administration also duplicated the plans of university modernizers across the South to improve the skills of public school teachers. In 1906–7 it established a Summer School for the benefit of elementary and secondary school teachers. That year, the school attracted 208 attendants. By 1910 the attendance had catapulted to 1,263, which prompted Alderman to request that the Summer School be made a regular university department. The Board of Trustees acquiesced and the school's courses were granted credit. The Summer School became an unexpected but vital example of Alderman's program for university social service. Administrators hoped that it would transform shabbily educated teachers into reasonably broad-minded professionals: "I feel that through the means of the Summer School it is reaching out and touching helpfully the life of our people in ways that it could not hope to do if its activities were confined to the work of the regular term."[66]

The president saw the Summer School as an achievement for university extension. Together with faculty involvement on boards of education, educational institutions, and industrial commissions, the Summer School demonstrated the policy of university social service.[67] Charles G. Maphis, director of the Summer School and professor of secondary education following Bruce Payne, agreed with Alderman's assessment. According to Maphis, the Summer School was the only state institution that offered high school teachers the opportunity to improve their education.[68] Like Charles Dabney's Summer School of the South, which set an example for university extension, Virginia's reflected the progressive emphasis on practical education and social service.[69]

The president found other opportunities for university outreach. With a newly established geology department, Alderman took the lead in creating the State Geological Commission, an organization based at UVA.[70] The administration also established the department of public health and sanitary science. According to the president, this department would allow the university to contribute to preventive medicine in the state. The creation of a School of Forestry in 1908 gave further evidence of the university's commitment to social service.[71]

Alderman came to believe that university extension would be the measure of progress in southern higher education. Writing to Hollis Frissell, principal of the Hampton Institute and member of the SEB, he suggested that university cooperation with the state and private enterprise constituted "the next big thing the [General Education] Board can do to serve the advance of southern education in the field of higher training." Universities had to establish links with public and private organizations promoting social improvement. Critical among these were public health, good roads, and civic improvement clubs. Educational coordination required universities to cooperate in extension work. Secondary school development was only the start.[72]

Legislators opposed requests for financial assistance because they failed to see the social benefits of proposed spending. When presented with evidence of university service to the state, they would "clamor for it." State universities were particularly responsible for supervising the fields of public health, preventive medicine, school inspection, library improvement, "social gatherings," community debates, and economics. But whereas "western" states (primarily Wisconsin) demanded that universities deliver social service, the southern states "have neither expected nor desired the universities and colleges until recently to obtrude their helpfulness."[73]

On the premise that a state university should make its "instruction and resources . . . more available and serviceable to the whole state," the plan called for a University Extension Bureau comprising three departments.[74] The department would offer correspondence courses in academic or technical subjects. It would also sponsor community discussion at high schools, through state contests, and in information bulletins. Topics of discussion would be those most on the minds of southern progressives: good roads, taxation, compulsory education, and commission government.[75] In addition, the Extension Bureau would conduct research on subjects of "community and State importance" as well as offer expert advice to municipal boards, commercial clubs, and "economic betterment associations."[76]

The plan for university extension work resonated with progressive themes. Publishing information, generating public discussion, and forming liaisons between university experts and government organizations, the social service college would intervene for the welfare of the New South. It would mold southern economic and social development in the image of social efficiency. Just as high schools would train efficient laborers, universities would train professionals and offer faculty expertise to business and government. Each level of the education system would contribute energetically to economic progress, class stratification, and racial harmony, thus reconfiguring the region according to progressive hopes.

The president's plan became the framework for the university's Extension Bureau.[77] In 1915 he informed university alumni that the new bureau would soon become an independent department for the dissemination of knowledge "not only by public lectures but by organized service, so that no community in need of expert advice can fail to know where to ask for it." The university had already made dramatic progress in developing the extension idea. Professors had participated in the Education Commission, the Geological Commission, the State Cooperative Association, the State Board of Education, the State Highway Commission, the State Tax Commission, and the Federal Tariff Commission, among others. In addition to cooperating with these agencies, faculty members had contributed to the improvement of public health and the work of the YMCA. They also moderated public discussions at high schools and civic organizations.[78] Contrary to what some critics charged, the university was not "meddling with the State's affairs" when it offered technical expertise to government agencies. When government initiatives "based on scientific needs, affecting the public good" were undertaken, the modernized university should be "commandeered" to assist the state. No longer the ward of the state, the social service university was at the disposal of the region's governments.[79]

If the president played the zealot for university extension, he was the consummate diplomat on women's education at UVA. Like many progressive administrators, he gave tacit assent to the idea of women's higher education but preferred not to disturb the political waters to achieve it. Instead, he entrusted the creation of an atmosphere favorable to women's higher education to the gradual evolution of public opinion. Alderman never gave serious thought to the idea of integrating women at Charlottesville. Instead, he preferred the idea of a separate or "coordinate college."

In response to a request from Alice Kyle for a statement on the efforts of the Virginia Federation of Women's Clubs to draft legislation for a women's college, Alderman blandly admitted that "modern states" had long neglected it. One wonders how comforting Kyle found President Alderman's acknowledgment that women were "necessary to civilization." In principle, at least, he endorsed the idea of an institution of higher education for women. With the rhetorical evasiveness perfected by educational progressives, Alderman advised Kyle that the movement for a women's college be undertaken "wisely" and built on a "structure of usefulness and power." He encouraged Kyle that discussion of the issue would prove "inevitably victorious," but he cautioned that it "must be patiently presented, and time is required for their patient presentation." It was certainly not "wise" in his estimation to present the issue to the current General Assembly. It was unfortunate, he conceded, that this "great undertaking" was not on the list of priority reforms. But it was necessary that the development of normal schools and the expansion of the high school system "be solidly grounded before any large new undertaking is attempted." Instead,

Alderman suggested that Kyle and the Virginia Federation concentrate on raising public consciousness of the need for a women's college.[80]

Over the next five years, faculty support for the idea of a coordinate college grew, but the same concerns inhibited Alderman's approval. In 1915 legislation was proposed for establishing a coordinate college. Although the school would be affiliated with the university and share its resources, it would remain independent. Despite declaring himself "unalterably in favor" of the renewed proposal, Alderman hoped that the issue would "not be made the focus of all the energy and striving of everybody." The Board of Visitors was divided on the issue, he suggested, and the governor was downright "unfriendly" to the measure.[81]

The crucial issue, Alderman claimed, was university finances. The school was in "vital need of substantial appropriations." He confided to A. C. Gordon that he would not jeopardize the university's interests at a time when it faced yet another "crisis of its development." Furthermore, the "emotional" opposition of the Board of Visitors and the General Assembly made selling the idea even more difficult. Considering the political climate, the president was reluctant to establish another underfunded college. Counseling patience until a governor favorable to the measure was elected, Alderman once again declined to be a partisan for the women's college. Ambivalent on the issue of women's education in 1915, the president made a more public demonstration of his support for the idea of the coordinate college in a speech the following year.[82]

The plan for a coordinate college was governed in part by Alderman's conventional ideas on gender. The president opposed coeducation because it failed to provide for "the need of the two sexes for different kinds and methods of instruction suitable for their careers." Assimilation at UVA was particularly unthinkable to Alderman, considering its "habits for nearly a century . . . its spirit, the very genius of the place." A separate but coordinated college, on the other hand, would allow the university to shape society by cultivating "the mothers who make the homes, the scholars, the great citizens that womanhood is to contribute to our civilization." And separate from the university, the college would develop departments of art, music, and home economics, disciplines suited to the "peculiar" educational needs of women. The proximity of a separate but equal women's college would also have a civilizing effect on men. Educated women would not threaten men's social authority because only men would "lead the splendid future of this commonwealth." But they would acquire "a more common-sense chivalry" as well as the comfort of knowing that when women "who bear and rear the race" needed assistance in their educational pursuits, men had not abandoned them.[83]

Progressive efficiency was also a consideration in Alderman's support for the coordinate college. Financing a separate college would strain the state's resources and compromise the movement for cost-efficiency in education. Alderman reasoned that costs could be controlled by making university libraries, laboratories, and faculty available to the women's college. Unlike its struggling private counterparts, a women's college supported by university resources would enable it to maintain college standards.[84]

But progressive efficiency covered a multitude of sins. As in his management of the medical school issue, Alderman invoked efficiency to justify the university's claim to educational primacy in Virginia. He echoed the concerns of alumni and benefactors when he warned that a separate college would encourage a "distinct cleavage" in the university fold. According to the president, a women's college would foster unseemly "antagonisms and hostile educational camps." Replicating his argument for coordinating Virginia's schools of engineering, Alderman opposed any solution that would generate institutional rivalry. But rationalizing medical instruction, engineering, and women's education meant asserting university authority. "To direct and control such an undertaking [women's education] seems to me to be its right, its opportunity, and its duty." A coordinate women's college would invariably mean an institution under the university's "supervision and control."[85]

Into this mixture of motives for the coordinate college, Alderman also injected social service, the first principle of his philosophy of education. Reaching out to women, the university would advance its democratic agenda by incorporating "one half of our life never before reached by it." At the same time, it would serve the cause of public education by supervising the education of future high school teachers.[86] Accepting women would confirm that the university had repudiated its elitist and patrician ways in favor of "the greater concept of duty to society as the chief end of a university."[87]

Despite his temporizing, Alderman espoused a philosophy of reform that assumed an expanded sphere of social engagement for women. He shared the progressive conviction that women were essential to the project of educational reform and rural uplift. But it was women who were pressing the issue into the public forum, insisting on new opportunities of social expression: "The demand for this college is a part of a world-movement which has reached Virginia, and which perceives that women must be given adequate training, if they are to fulfill their destinies in an era marked by new and insistent, economic and civic, as well as domestic demands upon womanhood." Alderman made it clear that a consensus had developed in favor of some form of higher education for women beyond normal school training. The question now was one of method, not principle. Although constrained by traditional gender orthodoxies, Alderman believed that the university was obligated to reconcile with the genesis of a "new human type," the "trained, cultivated, capable woman engaged in civic and economic, as well as domestic, duties." By encouraging the work of the Cooperative Education Association, in which women were key organizers and activists, promoting the professionalization of grade school teaching, and supporting the establishment of the North Carolina Normal and Industrial School for Women, Alderman advanced a new conception of women in the modern South. Although on balance he was no champion of women's education, he did endorse a gradualist approach that validated the argument for women's higher education. He assimilated his views on women's education into a larger scheme of social reform that saw women as coparticipants but not equal partners.[88]

Yet he was an advocate of progressive reform, and his administration helped build the framework of what would become a "centralized educational polity."[89] In a letter to Henry Higginson of Boston, Alderman explained that when he arrived at Virginia he found it in need of money, better organization, and a "more democratic attitude." Throughout his administration he "sought to enrich it, and to organize and democratize it, as its Founder intended, by so relating it to all the other phases of education as to achieve unity of purpose in our whole educational order, and to introduce into it the concept of service to the State and Nation." As a progressive, Alderman labored to infuse the university with the idea that education should be modified to meet practical social needs.[90]

In his efforts to recast the university according to the social service ethic, Alderman mirrored progressives in higher education throughout the South. If the ideal of social service was accepted as a legitimate goal of higher education in the North, it became the pedagogical gospel at state universities in the South. Despite the competing claims of liberal culture and research, utility gained ascendancy in the region. Alderman almost certainly spoke for other progressive educators when he suggested, "The doctrine that education is one whole process for the service of the State has been the guiding principle of my administration."[91]

No academic himself, Alderman endorsed the ideal of research not as an end in itself but as an instrument for public service. In fact, the president jubilantly proclaimed, "There is scarcely a Commission or a Board or a great social enterprise in the State on which some of them [faculty members] are not serving." University professors had a responsibility to teach, but they also had an obligation to spread their expertise beyond the campus. Alderman believed the school had cultivated the social service habit by pushing education "in the direction of public health," fostering professional training by establishing the Geological Survey with its "economic increase upon the State's life," and creating the Summer School. The movement for coordinating university and high school curricula was the pinnacle of progressive efficiency.[92]

Yet Alderman imagined that modernizing education would construct a society managed by progressives, not the people. Not all institutions of higher education subscribed to Alderman's gospel of efficiency. Those that did not he dismissed as retrograde and small-minded. Coordination extended the reach of the public school system, but it also extended the influence of efficiency experts often inimical to rural life. At the same time, it expanded the control of a state university that acted as an agent of government authority and "scientific" philanthropy.

Alderman's UVA fostered the process of middle-class formation in the New South. University faculty blazed a path out of the academical village and into positions as expert advisers on state agencies and commissions. Faculty and department heads actively encouraged the growth of a professional ethos in their respective disciplines. The administration obliged by promoting research, raising standards, expanding professional departments, and encouraging specialization. At the same time the university grafted itself onto an emerging education bureaucracy. At Alderman's prompting, the university followed the lead of other state universities in crusading for better rural schools and state support for public education. Yet it also helped solidify a system of education stratified by race and steeped in traditional notions of gender. In both, the university fulfilled the promises of the New South.

Notes

1. Malone, *Edwin Alderman,* 19.

2. Bailey, *Liberalism in the New South,* 134–35; Eaton, "Edwin Alderman," 207–10; Grantham, *Southern Progressivism,* 250–51.

3. Alderman, "Charles D. McIver of North Carolina," 105.

4. Alderman, "The Achievement of a Generation," 241; see also Link, *The Paradox of Southern Progressivism,* 131–33. Alderman saw the campaign as a model for other educational crusaders. Writing in response to a request for a biographical sketch of his role in the campaign, Alderman commented on the example that he and McIver set for reformers: "The work done by McIver and me was more or less taken as a model in arousing and organizing public opinion but improved on, of course, by the Southern Education Board in providing similar crusade forces in all the states." Alderman to Mark Sullivan, July 3, 1926, in folder titled "Correspondence with E.A.A. Regarding Reconstruction and Educational Revival," Alderman Collection, UVA. See also Sullivan to Alderman, May 19, 1926, Alderman Collection, UVA.

5. Alderman, "Charles D. McIver of North Carolina," 108. Also see Alderman, "Northern Aid to Education," 2411.

6. Quantz, "Edwin Alderman and the Founding of the University of Virginia School of Education."

7. Malone, *Edwin Alderman,* 200.

8. Ibid., 201. Little was done to promote literature with the exception of the founding of the *Virginia Quarterly Review* several years later.

9. "University in the Service of Democracy," Commencement Address at UNC, June 1912, in *Edwin Alderman,* Rare Virginia Pamphlets, vol. 43, 36, Special Collections, UVA.

10. Alderman, "The Achievement of a Generation," 251.

11. Alderman, "The Spirit of the South," in folder titled "Charter Day Address," March 23, 1906, Alderman Collection, UVA.

12. Alderman, "Education and Public Service," in folder titled "Address at Inauguration of Edward Kidder Graham, 1876–1918," 368, Alderman Collection, UVA; see also "University in the Service of a Democracy," 30. Alderman had this to say about the relationship between society and the state university in an address to the National Education Association at Jacksonville: "At this stage of our culture, when millions are to be impressed with the importance of knowledge, the Southern scholar must forego his office of prophet and seer and become ruler and reformer. Southern universities and colleges must do the work of social regenerative forces, reaching out directly into the life of the people, making known how much better light is than darkness." "The University and the South," in *Edwin Alderman,* Rare Virginia Pamphlets, vol. 23, Alderman Collection, UVA.

13. Alderman to Frederick T. Gates, January 22, 1909, Alderman Collection, UVA.

14. Page, "The University of Virginia and Its President," 5224.

15. "Statistics for the Years 1903–04, Collected by Order of the National Association of State Universities," box 7, Hill Collection, UGA; Woodward, *Origins of the New South,* 436–37.

16. "A Statement of Accomplishment and Recent Growth," *University of Virginia Record* 3 (April 1910): 8, in "Edwin Alderman," Rare Virginia Pamphlets, vol. 43, *Edwin Alderman* 82, UVA (subsequent references to *Record* are found in Rare Virginia Pamphlets cited here); "Minutes of Rectors and Visitors," April 13, 1905, vol. 7, p. 41, UVA.

17. On the significance of the May Campaign for the university appropriation, see Harlan, *Separate and Unequal,* 158.

18. Alderman to Peabody, March 13, 1906, box 3, Peabody Papers, LOC.

19. Ibid.

20. Alderman, "Northern Aid to Southern Education," 2412; see also Alderman to Wallace Buttrick, November 14, 1905, box 57, Peabody Papers, LOC. For evidence of the GEB's efforts to encourage better business management at schools that applied for funding, see General Education Board, *The General Education Board,* 116, 147–48.

21. Alderman, "Northern Aid to Education," 2411.

22. Ibid.; Alderman to Buttrick, December 7, 1905, Alderman Collection, UVA; Alderman to Buttrick, January 11, 1906, in folder titled "Wallace Buttrick to Alderman, 1855–1926," Alderman Collection, UVA.

23. Alderman, "A Statement of Recent Growth," *University of Virginia Record* 3 (April 1910): 13–14; Alderman to J. G. Bowman of Carnegie Foundation, June 25, 1909, in folder titled "Carnegie Foundation, 1 of 3," box 7, President's Papers, UVA; Alderman, "A Statement of Recent Growth," *University of Virginia Record* (June 1907): 10.

24. Department of Law to Alderman, undated letter, 1–2, folder titled "Law," box 15, Alderman Collection, UVA.

25. Ibid., 3–4.

26. Ibid., 4–5.

27. UVA Department of Law to Alderman, no date, in folder titled "1907–1912 Law," box 15, President's Papers, UVA. As historian John Higham points out, professions had always existed, playing an important function in society even before 1860. However, the "reorganization of the professions in such a way as to vest new authority in emerging academic groups" was not simply the result of professionalization but the consequence of accelerated specialization. "The multiplication and differentiation of bodies of esoteric knowledge made the new professions possible." The "institutional matrix" emerging from this process of specialization included exclusive scholarly organizations, procedures regulating research, standardized entrance requirements, and the egalitarian university department. See Higham, "The Matrix of Specialization," 3–18.

28. Ibid., 17–18.

29. Bruce, *History of the University of Virginia,* 154.

30. Ibid. "Resolution of Maryland Alumni Association of the University of Virginia," in folder titled "Degrees," box 9; Roger Wood to Alderman, December 7, 1907; Alderman to Wood, December 17, 1907; Morris Tilley of University of Michigan to Alderman, November 4, 1907; Alderman to Jacob G. Schurman of Cornell, September 25, 1907; Alderman to James B. Angell of University of Michigan, September 25, 1907, in folder titled "Degrees," box 9; all letters in President's Papers, UVA. For opposition to the proposal from the Board of Visitors, see Eppa Hunton to Alderman, January 4, 1908, President's Papers, UVA.

31. "A Statement of Recent Growth," 1910, Rare Virginia Pamphlets, vol. 43, *Edwin Alderman,* 18–19, UVA.

32. Dabney to Alderman, March 20, 1905, President's Papers, UVA.

33. "Statement of Conditions and Needs," *University of Virginia Record* (June 1907): 20–21.

34. Ibid., 18–19.

35. Ibid., 18–19; the president was also in contact with William R. Vance of George Washington University on elevating law school standards. Alderman to Vance, December 16, 1907, in folder titled "Law," box 15, President's Papers, UVA; "A Statement of Recent Growth," June 1907, 11, 12, Alderman Collection, UVA.

36. "A Statement of Recent Growth," June 1907, 19–22, Alderman Collection, UVA.

37. Ibid., 23–24; see also "Education and Public Service," in folder titled "Address at inauguration of Edward Kidder Graham, 1876–1918," Alderman Collection, UVA.

38. "A Brief Statement of Conditions and Needs," 1910, 12–13, President's Papers, UVA; "A Brief Statement of Conditions and Needs," December 20, 1909, 40–41, in folder titled "Legislative Program, 1 of 2," box 15, President's Papers, UVA.

39. "A Brief Statement of Conditions and Needs," 1910, Rare Virginia Pamphlets, vol. 43, *Edwin Alderman,* 9, UVA; see also Alderman to A. C. Gordon, October 9, 1911, in folder titled "Annual Reports" box 4, President's Papers, UVA; Alderman to Governor William Hodges Mann, December 2, 1911, President's Papers, UVA; Alderman to the Finance Committee of the Senate of Virginia, December 18, 1912, in folder titled "Legislative Program, 2 of 2," box 15 President's Papers, UVA.

40. Dabney, *Universal Education in the South,* 415–16; Quantz, "Edwin Alderman and the Founding of the University of Virginia School of Education," 5–6. In 1912, Alderman again prevailed on northern charity to improve the department of education. That year, he secured a $40,000 grant from the Peabody Fund for a new building to house the department. Alderman to A. C. Gordon, October 28, 1912, in folder titled "Annual Reports," box 4, President's Papers, UVA.

41. Link, *The Paradox of Southern Progressivism,* chapter 7.

42. For Alderman's comments on Payne, see Alderman to Henry L. Higginson, February 6, 1909, in folder titled "Miscellaneous Alderman Correspondence, 1903–1910," Alderman Papers, UVA; Link, *A Hard Country and a Lonely Place,* 116–18; Payne was aware of the importance of his position in solidifying the relationship between the progressive university and the expanding educational network: "I have worked hard and more hours during the past two years than I have ever done before in a similar period of time, and I believe I can state it as a fact that as a result *the University is not only in closer touch with the public school system of the State and exercises more influence on that system than ever before,* but the University itself has been liberalized and its viewpoint much modified through its contact and co-operation with the public high schools." Payne to Wallace Buttrick, May 15, 1914, in folder titled "Secondary Education, 1906–1914," box 20, President's Papers, UVA.

43. On education and the political climate in Virginia at the turn of the century see Harlan, *Separate and Unequal,* 135–69, and Moger, *Virginia.*

44. Dabney, *Universal Education in the South,* 327.

45. Grantham, *Southern Progressivism,* 252.

46. "President's Report," October 29, 1909, *Annual Report of the Superintendent of Public Instruction of the Commonwealth of Virginia, 1908–09,* 549 (hereafter abbreviated as *Annual Report*); "Report of the President," October 28, 1912, *Annual Report, 1911–12,* 357–58, Alderman Library, UVA.

47. As Hugh Hawkins argues in *Banding Together,* xi–xii, universities shared in the progressive drive for national coordination. Administrators were concerned by the "disarray threatening academic institutions—overproliferation, fraud, and corruption

by special interests. They saw institutional isolation as breeding poverty and powerlessness, arbitrariness and poor education." Associations promised uniformity, rational procedure, and collective power.

48. "Report of the Dean," September 20, 1913, *Annual Report of the Superintendent of Public Instruction of the Commonwealth of Virginia, 1912–13,* UVA.

49. Alderman to Gordon, October 28, 1912, in folder titled "Annual Reports," box 4, President's Papers, UVA.

50. "Report of the Virginia Education Commission to the General Assembly of the Commonwealth of Virginia, 1912," *Edwin Alderman,* Rare Virginia Pamphlets, vol. 43, 6, UVA. See also "Meeting of the State Education Commission," February 9, 1909, folder titled "Education Commission," box 9, President's Papers, UVA.

51. "Report of the Virginia Education Commission to the General Assembly of the Commonwealth of Virginia, 1912," *Edwin Alderman,* Rare Virginia Pamphlets, vol. 43, UVA.

52. Ibid., 46.

53. Alderman to Barringer, May 31, 1911, in folder titled "Education Commission, 1910–1913," box 9, President's Papers, UVA. See also undated letter from Alderman to Barringer in same file.

54. Alderman to Barringer, May 31, 1911, in folder titled "Education Commission, 1910–1913," box 9, President's Papers, UVA.

55. Ibid.; see also Alderman to E. W. Nichols of VMI, June 1, 1911, box 9, President's Papers, UVA; Alderman to Governor William Hodges Mann, December 9, 1911, box 15, President's Papers, UVA. For another of his efforts at conciliation, see his letter to E. W. Nichols of VMI, June 6, 1911, in folder titled "Education Commission, 2 of 2," box 9, President's Papers, UVA.

56. Alderman to Rose, September 14, 1909, in folder titled "Education Commission," box 9, President's Papers, UVA.

57. Alderman to Eppa Hunton, June 10, 1911, in folder titled "Medical College," President's Papers, UVA; "Report of the Virginia Education Commission to the General Assembly," Rare Virginia Pamphlets, vol. 43, UVA.

58. Alderman to Eppa Hunton, June 10, 1911, President's Papers, UVA.

59. Ibid.

60. "Report of the Virginia Education Commission to the General Assembly," Rare Virginia Pamphlets, vol. 43, p. 51, UVA.

61. Alderman to R. H. Whitehead, June 5, 1913, in folder titled "Medical College," box 16, President's Papers, UVA.

62. Ibid.

63. Alderman to Whitehead, December 6, 1913, in folder titled "Medical College," box 16, President's Papers, UVA.

64. Alderman to Whitehead, June 5, 1913; see also Alderman to Whitehead, December 6, 1913; Alderman to Eppa Hunton, February 10, 1912; Alderman to James M. Page, September 11, 1913; "Copy of a Resolution Adopted at a Meeting of the Board of Visi-

tors, February 18, 1914"; "Copy of Extract from Minutes of Board Meeting, January 29, 1914"; all documents in folder titled "Medical College," box 16, President's Papers, UVA.

65. Payne to Alderman, May 6, 1911, in folder titled "Board of Visitors Meetings," box 21, President's Papers, UVA; Alderman, "The Need of Co-Operation between the University and the State," *University of Virginia Alumni News* 3 (March 31, 1915): 174, in folder titled "Need of Cooperation between the University and the State," Alderman Collection, UVA.

66. Alderman to A. C. Gordon, October 9, 1911, President's Papers, UVA; also see Bruce R. Payne to Alderman, May 6, 1911, in folder titled "Board of Visitors' Meetings," box 21, President's Papers, UVA.

67. Alderman to A. C. Gordon, October 29, 1909, in folder titled "Armistead Gordon Correspondence, 1909–28," Alderman Collection, UVA.

68. Maphis to Wickliffe Rose, May 15, 1914, folder titled "Secondary Education," box 20, President's Papers, UVA.

69. Ibid.; report in folder titled "Alderman's Report to the Southern Education Board, 1905–06," Alderman Collection, UVA.

70. Alderman to Frederick T. Gates, Secretary of the General Education Board, January 22, 1909, in folder titled "Frederick T. Gates Correspondence, 1906–22," Alderman Collection, UVA.

71. Alderman to R. Walton Moore, April 5, 1909, in folder titled "Miscellaneous Correspondence," Alderman Collection, UVA; Addendum on School of Forestry, n.d., in folder titled "Legislative Program," box 15, President's Papers, UVA.

72. Alderman to H. B. Frissell, October 14, 1911, in folder titled "University Extension," box 21, President's Papers, UVA.

73. Alderman to Gates, October 14, 1911, President's Papers, UVA.

74. "University Extension Work—University of Virginia," in folder titled "Extension Work, 1913–14," President's Papers, UVA.

75. Ibid.

76. Ibid.

77. Alderman, "The Need of Co-Operation between the University and the State," *University of Virginia Alumni News* 3 (March 31, 1915): 174, in folder titled "Need of Cooperation between the University and the State," Alderman Collection, UVA.

78. Ibid., 175; see also "Report of the President," October 28, 1912, *Annual Reports, 1911–1912*, Alderman Library, UVA.

79. Alderman, "The Need of Co-Operation between the University and the State," *University of Virginia Alumni News* 3 (March 31, 1915): 174, in folder titled "Need of Cooperation between the University and the State," Alderman Collection, UVA.

80. Alderman to Mrs. James R. Kyle, January 13, 1910, in folder titled "Miscellaneous Alderman Correspondence, 1903–1910," Alderman Collection, UVA.

81. Ibid.

82. Alderman, untitled address, in folder titled "Women's College Speech, 1916," Alderman Collection, UVA.

83. Ibid., 5, 8–9.

84. Alderman, "Women's College Speech, 1916," 7, Alderman Collection, UVA.

85. Ibid., 3, 7, 10.

86. Ibid., 9.

87. Ibid., 10.

88. Ibid., unnumbered preamble and page 2.

89. Link, *A Hard Country and a Lonely Place,* 198.

90. Alderman to Henry L. Higginson, February 6, 1909, in folder titled "Miscellaneous Alderman Correspondence, 1903–1910," Alderman Collection, UVA.

91. Ibid.

92. Alderman to Edwin Mims, November 24, 1911, in folder titled "1911 Alderman Correspondence," Alderman Collection, UVA.

Epilogue: Universities in the Service of the South

> Mr. Leonard was on sure ground here. He understood the value of the classics. "It teaches a man to appreciate the Finer Things. It gives him the foundations of a liberal education. It trains the mind."
>
> "What good's it going to do him when he goes to work?" said "Pap" Rheinhart. "It's not going to teach him how to grow more corn."
>
> "Well—I'm not so sure of that," said Mr. Leonard with a protesting laugh. "I think it does."
>
> —Thomas Wolfe, *Look Homeward, Angel*

If Mitchell and Dabney had joined Alderman in his survey of southern higher education in 1914, they might have had reason to celebrate their accomplishments. Climbing attendance, expanding departments, new faculty, social influence, and financial improvement stood as testaments to the educational activism of southern university progressives. But by 1914 Dabney had fled the South, Mitchell had been driven out of South Carolina, Alderman was burdened by an inadequately financed hospital and medical department, and Hill was dead from exhaustion-induced pneumonia. Such a meeting might have tempered their seemingly indefatigable optimism. It might also have reminded them that for all their claims of progress, the schools they administered were not the modern research universities they had hoped to create with public money and enthusiasm. If measured by the material standards of which New Southerners were fond, southern schools continued to lag behind their northern counterparts. In 1927–28 Harvard allocated more money to its library than the cumulative total of eleven southern state universities. In 1931–32 faculty salaries at southern colleges ranged from \$3,131 to \$4,370. By comparison, northern and western institutions paid their faculty \$3,841 to \$6,421 on average. Universities of the South had not escaped the region's fate as the "Nation's number one economic problem" leading into the 1930s.[1]

A letter written by Leonard Baker, president of the University of South Carolina (USC) in 1936, sheds some light on the persistent hardships of state higher education in the New South. The letter was written in the city of Columbia's sesquicentennial year as a time capsule for the university president of 1986. As a result of financial neglect, Baker reported, the university's physical plant and resources compared unfavorably with those of other institutions of higher education in the state. Echoing southern university presidents since Dabney's time, Baker noted that the school's buildings and library were shabby and in need of repair. Improvements depended on the election of a legislature more responsive to the needs of public higher education. Of course, the president attributed some of the school's adversity to the financial stringency imposed by the Depression. But sounding remarkably like Dabney in his many exhortations to the Tennessee legislature, Baker called for a more reliable system of financial support. In essence he advocated the depoliticization of university support: "Instead of an annual appropriation varying from year to year reflecting the attitude of successive legislatures toward higher education, and often affected adversely by the opposition of political or independent education agencies toward the University, a definite proportion of state revenue should be designated for the support of the institution." Even in 1936, the state university was not as immune from political vicissitudes as Mitchell and others had hoped. At the same time, Baker pointed to the university's entanglement in the bureaucratic competition of the modern regulatory state. Although the Progressive Era university was responsible for establishing much of the framework of bureaucratic governance, it found that it could not always maintain its dominance in the system it had created.[2]

Nagging financial distress was compounded by the continuing gap between high school and university standards. "The present educational policy of admitting all graduates of our public high schools who obtain a diploma representing what we call fifteen units of credit constitutes a serious handicap on scholarship." Despite the accrediting system and the disappearance of the preparatory department, the university still faced the dilemma of accommodating graduates ill prepared for college, and this in an institution that allegedly approximated regional university standards. The presence of the academic underachievers "tend[ed] to pull down the standards to the level of mediocrity." Writing in 1930, University of North Carolina (UNC) historian Edgar Knight corroborated Baker's dismal review of academic standards. According to him, one representative university had found that 40 percent of its first-year students could not meet the requirements of first-year English courses and had to take secondary-level remedial studies to qualify. By national standards, the same school ranked its average first-year student at the level of a second-year high school student. Knight also observed that no southern graduate school could be considered on par with the best national schools. Progressive optimism about rising standards and scholarly achievements struck Knight as little more than hollow claims.[3]

Equally distressing to Baker was the eclipse of academic pursuits by the rising popularity of intercollegiate athletics. He lamented the professionalization of varsity sports and the tendency of alumni and students to measure universities by the strength of their intercollegiate teams. Examining the USC campus today, with its football stadium built to accommodate 80,000 people, and its countless university-licensed retail outlets selling official Gamecocks merchandise, it is difficult not to smile when reading Baker's hope that in "fifty years from now commercialized and professionalized sports will be but a memory of a condition to be regretted." The progressive dream of transforming the university into an instrument of social leadership has sometimes been overshadowed by the growth of the state college as a mirror of popular culture.[4]

Baker's letter suggests something of the enduring problems of southern state universities in the early twentieth century. The University of Georgia's (UGA) fiscal adversities continued at least until World War II. The agricultural depression of the 1920s hit the region and its state universities hard. Yet in addition to the South's economic misfortunes, Georgia as well as other schools continued to struggle under a regressive tax structure founded on low property taxes. Despite countless legislative initiatives for a revised tax system, politicians protected the southern tradition of minimal taxation. The university suffered as a result, but so did elementary and secondary education.[5]

University operations continued to be subject to legislative caprice, which at times made it difficult to guarantee faculty salaries or pay for college maintenance. Destitution finally drove politicians and the administrators of Georgia's several institutions of higher learning to form the University System in 1931. The reorganization brought Georgia's colleges under the authority of a central Board of Regents, which set the course of educational development in the state for years to come. Chancellor Hill's vision of the "collective university" finally was realized, albeit under duress. Despite administrative changes, though, state institutions of higher education continued their downward financial spiral. It would take the federal government's wartime investment in military construction projects to improve appreciably the school's physical plant. Wartime army and navy expenditures on campus improved the school's financial solvency. Returning veterans flooded the university, channeling more federal money into the system. Comparable to the American experience at large, only war-generated spending could alleviate the financial distress of the Depression era.[6]

The University of Tennessee, on the other hand, benefited from New Deal programs of the 1930s. The Tennessee Valley Authority (TVA) turned to the university for assistance in establishing training programs for its employees. Faculty and TVA staff cooperated in expanding the school's engineering department to meet the needs of TVA employees. The TVA's Department of Personnel promoted the development of courses in public administration by offering to pay 75 percent of the salary of faculty hired to teach the new classes. The TVA plan accelerated departmental specialization as well. The political science department, under whose auspices the public administration courses were taught, became independent in 1941. TVA support for archaeological research spawned the development of this discipline at Tennessee. Together with the Tennessee Emergency Relief Administration, the TVA funded the hiring of two archaeologists who were appointed temporarily to the history department. TVA support did not revolutionize the university's financial position; it was not until 1943 that Tennessee could match its 1929 level of legislative support. Yet at a time of fiscal contraction for most state universities, and particularly Georgia, Tennessee enjoyed the fruits of New Deal largesse. A beneficiary of several northern philanthropic donations and a million-dollar endowment, the University of Virginia (UVA) simply was not in the same financial league as Georgia or Tennessee.[7]

The experience of Tennessee and Virginia illustrates the crucial function of external financial support in the development of southern higher education. Like the southern economy and those trapped in the cycle of debt peonage, southern state universities were transformed less by southern initiative than by federal intervention. Southern colleges became the modern research universities that progressives had dreamed of when the federal government funneled its resources into struggling schools such as Tennessee. The relationship historians often overlook between state universities and the New South is their shared experience of poverty, regional isolation, and economic dependence on the North. While the region was revolutionized by government agricultural programs, rural depopulation, labor legislation, and a minimum wage law, its state universities began to take the shape of institutions funded on a large scale for the purpose of conducting advanced technical research. War and the federal government ushered in the sophisticated university envisioned by progressives. A political culture more hospitable to federal spending eased the transformation.

What happened, then, to the southern state university under the administrations of Alderman, Mitchell, Hill, and Dabney? First, modernizing educators established the framework of progressive efficiency in the state universities of the New South. Through professionalization, the emergence of the business-minded college president, bureaucratic reform, academic specialization, administrative reorganization, and tentative steps toward research, state universities paralleled the experience of northern universities. The university mirrored the structural changes that transformed the American political economy in the Progressive Era. Despite resistance, they became modern colleges, if not research universities.

Second, rather than peripheral observers, state universities and their enterprising presidents were at the forefront of the southern progressive movement. Through extension programs, support for educational revitalization, agricultural programs, the fusion of university and state agencies, and university involvement in regulatory commissions and advisory bodies, public universities fostered the development of an activist state. In the capacity of technical experts, faculty and university administrators attached themselves to the regulatory machinery of the state. The specialized, professional departments they built expanded the influence of a new middle class. According to Dewey Grantham, universities became "an integral part of a reform structure" that guided southern development.[8] State legislatures continued to undermine universities such as Georgia. But university discontent often was the result of rising expectations of public support. State governments never abandoned the reciprocal relationship forged by progressive educators. If anything, they consolidated it when social conditions permitted.

Educational reform was the centerpiece of the southern progressive movement, and it bore the marks of progressive ambivalence. Progressives were not interested in promoting social realignment, as evidenced by their conception of democracy. They led no assaults on the South's racial conventions. They also accepted the dominant political and economic configuration in the region. Progressives in higher education represented the urban, commercial middle class that underwrote southern "conservative modernization." Dabney's and Hill's agricultural programs suggested little desire to erase the staple crop economy. The reform movement did not threaten the low-wage, low-tax environment and the plantation economy it served. As historian James C. Cobb argues, disfranchisement, along with "better schools, expanded health facilities, and prohibition promised healthier, more productive, and controllable workers."[9] Although the progressive impulses of social justice and corporate regulation weakened after World War I, the ideals of social efficiency and service lived on in the form of "business progressivism." As historian George Brown Tindall points out, progressivism in the 1920s was indistinguishable from the Atlanta spirit itself.[10]

At the same time, progressivism was a movement of reform, and progressives did promote change. Fusing the New South creed to the gospel of efficiency, progressives advocated economic development, corporate regulation, public service, social efficiency, and the idea of a rejuvenated South.[11] Educational reform undergirded these initiatives. Progressivism was the medium for southern reintegration into national political currents. The presidency of southerner Woodrow Wilson and the influence of the southern contingent in Congress during his terms gave testimony to a revitalized South.

Most importantly, however, progressivism discredited the southern tradition of government minimalism. In its place emerged an embryonic regulatory state. By no means was the state prepared to intervene in social affairs to promote fundamental change. Rather, government activism was channeled into initiatives for material progress and social stability. Even so, the educational framework of the Efficiency State gave thousands of southerners the opportunity to learn and to take some control over their lives, and, for those privileged enough to attend one of the state colleges, an avenue of social mobility. Progressives adopted the Hampton idea of industrial education as the solution to race relations in the South. However, they did not capitulate to racial extremism. Instead, they encouraged the development of organizations committed to racial harmony. Southern progressives carved out an intellectual sphere hospitable to more humane race relations.

While New South university administrators embraced progressivism, they disparaged the antebellum southern college and its classical curriculum. Charles Dabney enunciated platitudes about balancing classical education with technical instruction, but his administration gave cursory attention to the liberal arts. Positivism, bureaucratic thought, and the ethic of business efficiency added intellectual layers to the pedagogical utilitarianism they drew from the New South creed. Promoting a utilitarian agenda, progressive educators eased traditionalist anxieties by paying lip service to liberal culture. They validated an educational formula that measured knowledge by the accumulation of data. The learning that mattered most was the learning that could be quantified, hitched to the wagon of efficiency, not burdened by the task of living the good life. Education linked to commerce, marketplace relevance, assumptions about universities as patrons of technocracy—these are some of the legacies of the progressive era.

Whereas progressives raced to adopt practical course offerings, many historically black colleges preserved the liberal curriculum as an intellectual shield against racism and class oppression. Yet while the utilitarian pedagogy underlying educational progressivism helped to cultivate a professional middle-class and separate the New South college from its traditional moorings, it fostered a modernist sensibility favorable to a more objective examination of southern problems. The progressive ethos paved the way for the Commission on Interracial Cooperation, the Southern Conference for Human Welfare, and the Southern Sociological Congress.

The social service ideal central to progressive educational reform continued to influence southern universities in the postwar period. The advancement of the social sciences was part of a larger intellectual reorientation in the modern South. The study of cultural anthropology, economics, and sociology at UNC and UVA encouraged a critical temperament that slowly eroded the pillars of racism and southern defensiveness. The ethic of social service made it acceptable for UVA to welcome Phelps-Stokes funding to establish a chair in sociology for the study of race relations. During the administration of David Barrow, Chancellor Hill's successor, UGA participated in the University Commission on Southern Race Relations, an organization dedicated to racial reform. At USC, Samuel Mitchell endorsed the program of racial conciliation sponsored by the YMCA. No doubt these were tentative steps well within the prevailing racial consensus. But they suggested the elasticity of racial thought in the South and helped sustain an intellectual climate in which more trenchant questions could be asked.

After the war, the social service ideal was most in evidence at UNC. The school that had exported so many reformers to institutions throughout the region became the embodiment of the progressive university. On the strength of alumni generosity, sizable donations, and legislative bounty, the university grew exponentially.[12] Much as Chancellor Hill had planned, UNC established a school of engineering in 1922 that supplied the state's growing public utility companies with electrical engineers. The department also satisfied the State Highway Commission's increasing demand for civil engineers. Under the leadership of president Harry Woodburn Chase, a proponent of the social sciences, the university launched a department of psychology and a department of sociology. The department of sociology, in turn, gave rise to the School of Public Welfare and the Institute for Research in Social Science.[13]

Under the leadership of Howard Odum, the School of Public Welfare and the Institute for Research in Social Science became engines of regional analysis. Working with state agencies, funded by philanthropic support, and addressing immediate social problems, Chapel Hill's sociologists realized the progressive dream of state service. But thinkers such as Rupert Vance and Guy Benton Johnson broke the progressive mold. Through empirical studies aimed at exposing the cultural roots of southern stagnation, they went beyond the banalities of progressive uplift. They wielded environmentalism and cultural relativism against the certitude of New South optimism. Assisted by a robust university press and Odum's own *Journal of Social Forces,* their work went from the speculative realm into the living rooms of literate Americans. Titles ranging from Arthur Raper's *The Tragedy of Lynching* to Rupert Vance's *Human Factors in Cotton Culture* testify to the breadth and vitality of the university press. Chapel Hill created an intellectual environment that stretched the conception of social service beyond participation in local reform committees.

Social responsibility came to include critical explorations of the culture that sustained persistent backwardness. UNC's innovative sociology was not a departure from progressive education but a fulfillment of its logic. By promoting the ideal of social service, progressive educators laid the groundwork for increasing university involvement in social affairs.[14] Despite UNC's educational leadership, it did not tear down the foundations of southern race and class inequality. However, it did merge more closely with a bureaucratic state. A school of public welfare, university cooperation with the State Board of Health in the training of county health officials, a Division of Public Health funded by the state and the Works Progress Administration, and a state-funded medical center and teaching hospital exemplified the assimilation of the university into the machinery of government.[15]

The history of public higher education is tied to the destiny of the New South. The accomplishments and failures of the progressive movement it fostered are those of the state university as well. They reflected the aspirations of the new men who bestrode the New South. For Alderman, Mitchell, Dabney, and Hill, there were no ivory towers, no splendid academic isolation. Education meant outreach and social uplift, not character building and cultural refinement. Thomas Wolfe's "Pap" Rheinhart would have had little complaint with Dabney's Tennessee, where corn growing was no mean academic pursuit. Rheinhart would have looked in vain, though, for a South transformed by its lessons in progress.

Notes

1. Tindall, *The Emergence of the New South,* 267–68.

2. Leonard Baker to the President of the University of South Carolina, 1986, March 23, 1936, in Vertical File titled "Leonard Baker—Biography," University Archives, USC. Corroborating Baker's argument, historian Clyde Barrow points out that "in no oth-

er region did universities maintain as close and direct a linkage to political or state elites as one finds in the South." In *Universities and the Capitalist State,* 51.

3. Leonard Baker to the President of the University of South Carolina, 1986, March 23, 1936, in Vertical File titled "Leonard Baker—Biography," University Archives, USC; see also Knight, "Education in the South," 48–49.

4. Leonard Baker to the President of the University of South Carolina, 1986, March 23, 1936, in Vertical File titled "Leonard Baker—Biography," University Archives, USC. The history of intercollegiate athletics at southern universities is a particularly under-examined subfield of southern educational history. A book that deals with the emergence of organized university sports at the national level is Smith, *Sports and Freedom.*

5. Dyer, *The University of Georgia,* chapters 9 and 11.

6. Ibid.

7. Montgomery et al., *To Foster Knowledge,* chapter 8.

8. Grantham, *Southern Progressivism,* 268.

9. Cobb, *Industrialization and Southern Society,* 146–47. The theory suggests that the southern middle class accepted a model of economic development premised on planter values and of benefit "primarily to a small but powerful coalition of planters, merchants, and industrialists," 146.

10. Tindall, *The Ethnic Southerners,* 144–48.

11. Grantham, *Southern Progressivism,* 418.

12. Much of the impetus for increasing legislative support came from an alumni campaign to improve the school's physical plant. Concerted giving and lobbying persuaded the state in 1921 to offer the school $925,000 for permanent improvements over two years. That year, the General Education Board gave the university $50,000 to raise teachers' salaries by 25 percent. Critical to the development of the social sciences was Mary Lily Kenan Flagler Bingham's gift of $75,000 annually in perpetuity to improve the salaries of Chapel Hill professors. The first endowment was made in 1922. See Snider, *Light on the Hill,* 160–61, 174–78.

13. Ibid., 178–80.

14. On the "modernist" sensibility and its relationship to regionalism, see Singal, *The War Within,* 6–10, 261, 302–38; for the importance of the new sociological orientation to the study of lynching, see Brundage, *Lynching in the New South,* 215–17.

15. Snider, *Light on the Hill,* 178–79, 200, 226–27, 231.

Bibliography

Manuscripts and Archives

Papers of Edwin Anderson Alderman (MSS 1001), Special Collections Department, University of Virginia Library. [Alderman Collection, UVA]

President's Papers (RG 2/1/2), Special Collections Department, University of Virginia Library. [President's Papers, UVA]

Papers and Addresses Delivered by Edwin A. Alderman, F 221 v.23 and v.43, Special Collections Department, University of Virginia Library.

Memoir of Charles Dabney (MSS 3308), Special Collections Department, University of Virginia Library. ["Memoir"]

Charles Dabney Papers, University Archives, University of Tennessee. [Dabney Papers, UTK]

Charles W. Dabney Papers, #1412, Southern Historical Collection, Wilson Library, The University of North Carolina at Chapel Hill. [Dabney Papers, UNC]

General Education Board Papers, Early Southern Program, microfilm roll #103, University of South Carolina Archives. [GEB Papers, USC]

Hargrett Rare Book and Manuscript Library/University of Georgia Libraries.

Walter Barnard Hill Presidential Papers, Manuscript Department, University of Georgia. [Hill Collection, UGA]

Walter Barnard Hill Family Papers, Manuscript Department, University of Georgia. [Hill Family Papers, UGA]

August Kohn Papers, South Caroliniana Library, University of South Carolina Archives. [Kohn Papers, USC]

Samuel Mitchell Papers, Administrative and Personal, Office of the President University of South Carolina Archives. [Mitchell Papers, USC]

Samuel C. Mitchell Papers, #1003, Southern Historical Collection, Wilson Library, The University of North Carolina at Chapel Hill. [Mitchell Papers, UNC]

Samuel Mitchell Papers, Library of Congress. [Mitchell Papers, LOC]

Robert Ogden Papers, Library of Congress. [Ogden Papers, LOC]

George Foster Peabody Papers, Library of Congress. [Peabody Papers, LOC]

South Carolina State Library. [SCSL]

South Carolina Department of Archives and History.

South Caroliniana Library, University of South Carolina. [SCL]

Southern Education Board Papers, #680, Southern Historical Collection, Wilson Library, The University of North Carolina at Chapel Hill. [SEB Papers, UNC]

University of Georgia Board of Trustees Correspondence and Reports, Hargrett Rare Book and Manuscript Library/University of Georgia Libraries. [Trustees' Correspondence, UGA]

Reports

"Annual Report of the Board of Trustees, 1909–1910." *Reports and Resolutions of the General Assembly of the State of South Carolina* 3 (1911), South Carolina State Library.

"Annual Report of the Board of Trustees, 1910–1911." *Reports and Resolutions of the General Assembly of the State of South Carolina* 2 (1912), South Carolina State Library.

Biennial Report of the Board of Trustees for the Year Ending December 20, 1898, in *University of Tennessee Record* 8, January 1899.

Biennial Report of the Board of Trustees of the University of Tennessee to the Forty-Sixth General Assembly of the State of Tennessee, 1887–1888, University of Tennessee at Knoxville Archives. [*Report of the Board of Trustees*]

"Chancellor's Annual Report to Board of Trustees, June 14, 1900," *Bulletin of the University of Georgia* 1 (October 1900): 12–13.

Proceedings of the Conference for Education in the South, Seventh Session, Birmingham, Alabama, 1904. New York: Committee on Publication, 1904.

Report of the Board of Trustees at the University of Tennessee to the General Assembly, December 20, 1890, University of Tennessee at Knoxville Archives.

"Report of the Committee on Development of the University to the Board of Trustees." *Bulletin of the University of Georgia* 5 (1 January 1905).

"Report of the Legislative Committee Appointed to Investigate the Condition of the State Educational Institutions for 1911." *Reports and Resolutions of the General Assembly of the State of South Carolina* 3 (1912), South Carolina State Library.

"Report of the Virginia Education Commission to the General Assembly of the Commonwealth of Virginia, 1912." *Edwin Alderman,* Rare Virginia Pamphlets (43) 6, University of Virginia Archives.

Books, Articles, and Dissertations

Adams, David. "Philanthropists, Progressives, and Southern Black Education." *History of Education Quarterly* 23 (Spring 1983): 99–110.

Alderman, Edwin. "The Achievement of a Generation." *South Atlantic Quarterly* 5 (July 1906): 236–53.

———. "Charles D. McIver of North Carolina." *Sewanee Review* 15 (1907): 100–10.

———. "Education for White and Black." *Independent* (November 7, 1901): 2647–49.

———. "The Growing South: A Comprehensive Statement of the Status and Forces of This Emerging Era." *World's Work* 16 (1908): 10373–83.

———. "Northern Aid to Southern Education." *Independent* 53 (October 1901): 2411–13.

———. "The Southwestern Field." *Annals of the American Academy of Political and Social Science* 22 (July–December 1903): 287–92.

Anderson, James D. *The Education of Blacks in the South, 1860–1935.* Chapel Hill: University of North Carolina Press, 1988.

———. "The Hampton Model of Normal School Industrial Education, 1868–1900." In *New Perspectives on Black Educational History,* ed. Vincent. P. Franklin and James D. Anderson. Boston: G.K. Hall, 1978.

Andrew, Rod, Jr. "Soldiers, Christians, and Patriots: The Lost Cause and Southern Military Schools, 1865–1915." *Journal of Southern History* 64 (November 1998): 677–710.

Ayers, Edward. *The Promise of the New South: Life after Reconstruction.* New York: Oxford University Press, 1992.

Bailey, Hugh C. *Liberalism in the New South: Southern Social Reformers and the Progressive Movement.* Coral Gables, Fla.: University of Miami Press, 1969.

Barrow, Clyde. *Universities and the Capitalist State: Corporate Liberalism and the Reconstruction of American Higher Education, 1894–1928.* Madison: University of Wisconsin Press, 1990.

Biddiss, Michael. "Progress, Prosperity, and Positivism: Cultural Trends in Mid-Century." In *Themes in Modern European History, 1830–1890,* ed. Bruce Waller. New York: Routledge, 1990.

Billings, Dwight, Jr. *Planters and the Making of a New South: Class, Politics, and Development in North Carolina, 1865–1900.* Chapel Hill: University of North Carolina Press, 1979.

Bledstein, Burton. *The Culture of Professionalism: The Middle Class and the Development of Higher Education in America.* New York: W.W. Norton, 1976.

Brooks, Robert Preston. *The University of Georgia under Sixteen Administrations, 1785–1955.* Athens: University of Georgia Press, 1956.

Brough, Charles Hilman. "Work of the Commission of Southern Universities on the Race Question." *Annals of the American Academy of Political and Social Science* 49 (September 1913): 47–57.

Bruce, Philip A. *A History of the University of Virginia,* Vols. 4 and 5. New York: Macmillan, 1921.

Brundage, W. Fitzhugh. *Lynching in the New South: Georgia and Virginia, 1880–1930.* Chicago: University of Illinois Press, 1993.

Bush, Robert. "Dr. Alderman's Symposium on the South." *Mississippi Quarterly* 27 (1973–74): 3–19.

Carlton, David. *Mill and Town in South Carolina 1880–1920.* Baton Rouge: Louisiana State University Press, 1982.

Cell, J. W. *The Highest Stage of White Supremacy: The Origins of Separation in South Africa and the American South.* New York: Oxford University Press, 1982.

Claxton, Philander P. "Educational Ideals." In *History of the Social Life,* ed. Samuel

Chiles Mitchell, Vol. 10 of *The South in the Building of the Nation,* ed. Julian Alvin Carroll Chandler et al. Richmond, Va.: Southern Historical Publication Society, 1909, 398–427.

Clayton, Bruce. *The Savage Ideal: Intolerance and Intellectual Leadership in the South, 1890–1914.* Baltimore: Johns Hopkins University Press, 1972.

Cobb, James C. "Beyond Planters and Industrialists: A New Perspective on the New South." *Journal of Southern History* 34 (February 1988): 45–68.

———. *Industrialization and Southern Society, 1877–1984.* Chicago: Dorsey, 1984.

Colton, Elizabeth Avery. "Standards of Southern Colleges for Women." *School Review* 20 (September 1912): 458–75.

Conkin, Paul. *Gone with the Ivy: A Biography of Vanderbilt University.* Knoxville: University of Tennessee Press, 1985.

Cooper, William J., and Thomas Terrill. *The American South: A History,* Vol. 2. New York: McGraw-Hill, 1991.

Crow, Orin F. *The Control of the University of South Carolina, 1801–1926: A Case Study of State University Control.* Ph.D. diss., George Peabody College for Teachers, 1931.

Dabney, Charles William. "As Is Education So Is Production." University of Tennessee *Record* (January 1901): 3.

———. *Universal Education in the South,* 2 vols. Chapel Hill: University of North Carolina Press, 1936.

Daniels, Josephus. "The Progress of Southern Education." *Annals of the American Academy of Political and Social Science* 22 (July–December, 1903): 310–19.

Daniels, Pete. *Standing at the Crossroads: Southern Life in the Twentieth Century.* New York: Hill & Wang, 1986.

Dawley, Alan. *Struggles for Justice: Social Responsibility and the Liberal State.* Cambridge, Mass.: Belknap Press of Harvard University Press, 1991.

Dean, Pamela. "Learning to Be New Women: Campus Culture at the North Carolina Normal and Industrial College." *North Carolina Historical Review* 68 (July 1991): 286–306.

Discussions of Our School Problems. Atlanta: Clement Printing Company for the Committee, 1904.

Dittmer, John. *Black Georgia in the Progressive Era, 1900–1920.* Chicago: University of Illinois Press, 1977.

Doyle, Don. *New Men, New Cities, New South: Atlanta, Nashville, Charleston, Mobile, 1860–1910.* Chapel Hill: University of North Carolina Press, 1990.

Du Bois, W. E. B. *The Souls of Black Folk.* New York: Vintage Books, 1990 [originally published in 1903].

Dyer, Thomas G. "Higher Education in the South since the Civil War: Historiographical Issues and Trends." In *The Web of Southern Social Relations: Women, Family, and Education,* ed. Walter J. Fraser and R. Frank Saunders. Athens: University of Georgia Press, 1985, 127–45.

———. *The University of Georgia: A Bicentennial History, 1785–1985.* Athens: University of Georgia Press, 1985.

Eaton, Clement. "Edwin Alderman: Liberal of the New South." *North Carolina Historical Review* 23 (April 1946): 206–21.

Finkenbine, Roy E. "'Our Little Circle': Benevolent Reformers, the Slater Fund, and the Argument for Black Industrial Education, 1882–1908." *Hayes Historical Journal* 6 (1986): 6–22.

Fite, Gilbert. *Cotton Fields No More: Southern Agriculture, 1865–1980.* Lexington: University Press of Kentucky, 1984.

Foner, Eric. *A Short History of Reconstruction, 1863–1877.* New York: Harper & Row, 1990 [abridged].

Fredrickson, George M. *The Black Image in the White Mind: The Debate on Afro-American Character and Destiny, 1817–1914.* Middletown, Conn.: Wesleyan University Press, 1971.

Gaston, Paul M. *The New South Creed: A Study in Southern Mythmaking.* Baton Rouge: Louisiana State University Press, 1970.

Geiger, Roger L. *To Advance Knowledge: The Growth of American Research Universities, 1900–1940.* New York: Oxford University Press, 1986.

General Education Board. *The General Education Board: An Account of Its Activities, 1902–1914.* New York: General Education Board, 1915.

Genovese, Eugene D. *The Southern Tradition: The Achievement and Limitations of an American Conservatism.* Cambridge, Mass.: Harvard University Press, 1994.

Gillette, William. *Retreat from Reconstruction, 1869–1879.* Baton Rouge: Louisiana State University Press, 1979.

Glotzer, Richard Stephen. *Higher Education in the American South 1660–1984: Class and Race in Institutional Development.* Ph.D. diss., University of Wisconsin at Madison, 1984.

Goodenow, Ronald, and Arthur O. White. *Education and the Rise of the New South.* Boston: G.K. Hall, 1981.

Grantham, Dewey. "The Contours of Southern Progressivism." *American Historical Review* 86 (October 1981): 1035–59.

———. *Southern Progressivism: The Reconciliation of Progress and Tradition.* Knoxville: University of Tennessee Press, 1983.

Grob, Gerald. "Reconstruction: An American Morality Play." In *American History: Retrospect and Prospect,* ed. George Athan Billians and Gerald N. Grob. New York: Free Press, 1971, 250–93.

Gutman, Herbert. "Work, Culture, and Society in Industrializing America, 1815–1919." *American Historical Review* 78 (June 1973): 531–87.

Haber, Samuel. *The Quest for Authority and Honor in the American Professions, 1750–1900.* Chicago: University of Chicago Press, 1991.

Hahn, Steven. *The Roots of Southern Populism: Yeoman Farmers and the Transformation of the Georgia Upcountry, 1850–1890.* New York: Oxford University Press, 1983.

Harlan, Louis. *Separate and Unequal: Public School Campaigns and Racism in the Southern Seaboard States, 1901–1915.* Chapel Hill: University of North Carolina Press, 1958.

Harp, Gillis J. *Positivist Republic: August Comte and the Reconstruction of American Liberalism, 1865–1920.* University Park: Pennsylvania State University Press, 1995.

Hawkins, Hugh. *Banding Together: The Rise of National Associations in American Higher Education, 1887–1950.* Baltimore: Johns Hopkins University Press, 1992.

Higham, John. "The Matrix of Specialization." In *The Organization of Knowledge in Modern America, 1860–1920,* ed. Alexandra Oleson and John Voss. Baltimore: Johns Hopkins University Press, 1979, 3–18.

Hill, Walter Barnard. "Nationalism Not Opposed to Truest Sectionalism." *Atlanta Constitution* (April 9, 1905), Hill Papers, UGA.

———. "Negro Education in the South." *Annals of the American Academy of Political and Social Science* 22 (July–December 1903): 320–29.

———. "Relation of the Universities and Colleges to the Public Schools." *Southern Educational Association Journal of Proceedings and Addresses of the Eleventh Annual Meeting Held at Columbia, South Carolina, December 26–29, 1901.* Knoxville, Tenn.: The Association, 1902, 271–74.

———. "Southern Education a National Responsibility." *Southern Workman* (February 1904), in box 7, Hill Papers, UGA.

———. "What Is the University?" *Bulletin* 3 (July 1902): 2–11.

Hollis, Daniel W. "Samuel Chiles Mitchell, Social Reformer in Blease's South Carolina." *South Carolina Historical Magazine* (January 1969): 20–37.

———. *University of South Carolina: College to University,* Vol. 2. Columbia: University of South Carolina Press, 1956.

Hunt, Michael. *Ideology and U.S. Foreign Policy.* New Haven, Conn.: Yale University Press, 1987.

Karina, Stephen J. *The University of Georgia College of Agriculture: An Administrative History, 1785–1985.* Athens: University of Georgia Press, 1985.

Keller, Morton. *Affairs of State: Public Life in Late Nineteenth Century America.* Cambridge, Mass.: Belknap Press of Harvard University Press, 1977.

Kennedy, David M. "Overview: The Progressive Era." *Historian* 37 (May 1975): 453–68.

Kilgo, John. "Some Phases of Southern Education." *South Atlantic Quarterly* 2 (April 1903): 137–51.

Kirkendall, Richard S. "The Agricultural Colleges: Between Tradition and Modernization." *Agricultural History* 60 (Spring 1986): 3–21.

Kirkland, James H. "The Teacher and the State." *Annals of the American Academy of Political and Social Science* 22 (July–December 1903): 249–56.

Knight, Edgar W. "Education in the South." *Outlook and Independent* 154 (1930): 47–49, 78–79.

Leloudis, James L. *Schooling the New South: Pedagogy, Self, and Society in North Carolina, 1880–1920.* Chapel Hill: University of North Carolina Press, 1996.

Leslie, W. Bruce. *Gentlemen and Scholars: College and Community in the "Age of the University" 1865–1917.* University Park: Pennsylvania State University Press, 1992.

Lewis, David Levering. *W. E. B. Du Bois: Biography of a Race, 1868–1919.* New York: Holt, 1993.

Link, William. *A Hard Country and a Lonely Place: Schooling, Society, and Reform in Rural Virginia, 1870–1920.* Chapel Hill: University of North Carolina Press, 1986.

———. *The Paradox of Southern Progressivism 1880–1930.* Chapel Hill: University of North Carolina Press, 1992.

———. "The Social Context of Southern Progressivism 1880–1930." In *The Wilson Era: Essays in Honor of Arthur S. Link,* ed. John Milton Cooper and Charles E. Neu. Arlington Heights, Ill.: Harlan Davidson, 1991, 55–82.

Malone, Dumas. *Edwin Alderman: A Biography.* New York: Doubleday, 1940.

Marcus, Alan I. *Agricultural Science and the Quest for Legitimacy: Farmers, Agricultural Colleges, and Experiment Stations, 1870–1890.* Ames: Iowa State University Press, 1985.

Mathis, Gerald Ray. *Pilgrimage to Madison: Correspondence Concerning the Georgia Party's Inspection of the University of Wisconsin, November 22–23, 1904.* Athens: University of Georgia Press, 1970.

———. *Walter Barnard Hill: Chancellor, the University of Georgia, 1899–1905.* Ph.D. diss., University of Georgia, 1967.

———. "Walter B. Hill, a New Chancellor for the University of Georgia." *Georgia Historical Quarterly* 57 (Spring 1973): 76–84.

———. "Walter B. Hill and the Savage Ideal." *Georgia Historical Quarterly* 60 (Spring 1976): 23–34.

Mathis, Mary Kathryn. "Hill, Walter Barnard," Vertical File, Hargrett Rare Book and Manuscript Library/University of Georgia Libraries.

McBryde, John M., Jr. "Womanly Education for Woman." *Sewanee Review* 15 (October 1907): 467–84.

McCandless, Amy Thompson. "Progressivism and the Higher Education of Southern Women." *North Carolina Historical Review* 70 (July 1993): 302–25.

McDonald, Christina R. "To Educate neither Belles nor Bluestockings": Women and Higher Education in the South during the Progressive Era." *Studies in American Culture* 20 (1997): 59–70.

McIver, Charles D. "Current Problems in North Carolina." *Annals of the American Academy of Political and Social Science* 22 (July–December 1903): 293–303.

Meier, August. *Negro Thought in America, 1880–1915: Racial Ideologies in the Age of Booker T. Washington.* Ann Arbor: University of Michigan Press, 1966.

Merriam, Lucius. *Higher Education in Tennessee.* Washington, D.C.: Bureau of Education, Circular No. 5, 1893.

Miller, Kelly. "The Function of the Negro College." *Dial* 32 (April 1902): 267–70.

Mims, Edwin. "The University in the South." *Annals of the American Academy of Political and Social Science* 22 (July–December 1903): 261–65.

Mitchell, Samuel. "An Aftermath of Appomattox: A Memoir of the Life of Samuel Chiles Mitchell," Unpublished memoir, South Caroliniana Library, University of South Carolina, 1954.

———. "The American Spirit in Education." *South Atlantic Quarterly* 8 (July 1909): 255–59.

———. "Do Our Colleges Pay?" *South Atlantic Quarterly* 39 (July 1910): 213–21.

———. "Education for Constructive National Leadership." *Religious Herald* (March 23, 1911): 4–5, Mitchell Papers, LOC.

———. "The Ideal of the State University." *Bulletin of the University of South Carolina* 34 (July 1913): 3–11.

———. "Jubilee Address." *Alumnus* 5 (April 1910): 112–13.

———. "The Nationalization of Southern Sentiment." *South Atlantic Quarterly* 7 (April 1908): 108–13.

———. "Phases in the Educational Movement of the Day." *Sewanee Review* 16 (1908): 18–25.

———. "Practical Tendencies in Education." *Richmond College Bulletin* (n.d.): 3–6, Mitchell Papers, LOC.

———. "Proposed Solutions of the Negro Problem." *Southern Workman* (n.d.): 545–50, Mitchell Papers, LOC.

———. "The Task of the College in the South." *South Atlantic Quarterly* 6 (July 1907): 259–62.

Mitchell, Theodore. "From Black to White: The Transformation of Educational Reform in the New South, 1890–1910." *Educational Theory* 39 (Fall 1989): 337–51.

Moger, Allan W. *Virginia: Bourbonism to Byrd, 1870–1925.* Charlottesville: University Press of Virginia, 1968.

Montgomery, James R. "The Summer School of the South." *Tennessee Historical Quarterly* 22 (December 1963): 361–81.

———. *The Volunteer State Forges Its University: The University of Tennessee, 1887–1919.* In *University of Tennessee Record* 69 (November 1966): 18–89.

Montgomery, James R., Stanley J. Folmsbee, and Lee Seifert Greene. *To Foster Knowledge: A History of the University of Tennessee, 1794–1970.* Knoxville: University of Tennessee Press, 1984.

Moore, Lauri Ann. *Reforming Southern Education: Charles William Dabney and the University of Tennessee.* Master's thesis, University of North Carolina at Charlotte, 1992.

Moton, Robert R. "Hampton's Gift to the Negro." *Southern Workman* 48 (June 1919): 297–98.

Munford, Mary Cooke Branch. "Woman's Part in the Educational Progress of the South." In *History of the Social Life,* ed. Samuel Chiles Mitchell, Vol. 10 of *The South in the Building of the Nation,* ed. Julian Alvin Carroll Chandler et al. Richmond, Va.: Southern Historical Publication Society, 1909.

Murphy, Edgar Gardner. *Problems of the Present South: A Discussion of Certain of the Educational, Industrial and Political Issues in the Southern States.* New York: Longmans, 1910.

Neufeldt, Harvey, and Clinton Allison. "Education and the Rise of the New South: An Historiographical Essay." In *Education and the Rise of the New South,* ed. Ronal K. Goodenow and Arthur O. White. Boston: G.K. Hall, 1981, 250–93.

Novick, Peter. *That Noble Dream: The "Objectivity Question" and the American Historical Profession.* Cambridge, U.K.: Cambridge University Press, 1988.

Ogden, Robert. "The Conference for Education in the South." *Annals of the American Academy of Political and Social Science* 22 (July–December 1903): 271–79.

O'Steen, Neal. "The University of Tennessee: Evolution of a Campus." *Tennessee Historical Quarterly* 39 (Fall 1980): 257–81.

Ownby, Ted. *Subduing Satan: Religion, Recreation, and Manhood in the Rural South, 1865–1920.* Chapel Hill: University of North Carolina Press, 1990.

Page, Walter Hines. "The University of Virginia and Its President." *World's Work* 8 (September 1904): 5224–25.

Parker, Franklin. "George Peabody's Influence on Southern Educational Philanthropy." *Tennessee Historical Quarterly* 20 (March 1961): 65–74.

Peeps, J. M. Stephen. "Northern Philanthropy and the Emergence of Black Higher Education: Do-Gooders, Compromisers, or Co-Conspirators?" *Journal of Negro Education* 50 (Summer 1981): 251–69.

Presley, John Carroll. *Samuel Chiles Mitchell: A Biography of a Southern Educator.* Ph.D. diss., University of Virginia, 1992.

Quantz, Richard. "Edwin Alderman and the Founding of the University of Virginia School of Education," unpublished paper. Charlottesville: University of Virginia School of Education, April 1979.

Reed, Thomas Walter. "The University of Georgia." *Southern Association Quarterly* (November 1946): 607–24.

Rodgers, Daniel T. "In Search of Progressivism." *Reviews in American History* 10 (December 1982): 113–32.

Ross, Dorothy. *The Origins of American Social Science.* New York: Cambridge University Press, 1991.

Rudolph, Frederick. *The American College and University.* New York: Vintage, 1962.

Shepherd, H. E. "Higher Education in the South." *Sewanee Review* 1 (November 1892): 283–89.

Singal, Daniel Joseph. *The War Within: From Victorian to Modernist Thought in the South, 1919–1945.* Chapel Hill: University of North Carolina Press, 1982.

Skiffington, Florence. "The Broader Education for Women." *University of Tennessee Record* 6 (1901): 358–61.

Smith, Ronald A. *Sports and Freedom: The Rise of Big-Time College Athletics.* New York: Oxford University Press, 1988.

Snider, William D. *Light on the Hill: A History of the University of North Carolina at Chapel Hill.* Chapel Hill: University of North Carolina Press, 1992.

Stephenson, William Holmes. *Southern History in the Making: Pioneer Historians of the South.* Baton Rouge: Louisiana State University Press, 1964.

Stetar, Joseph M. "In Search of Direction: Southern Higher Education after the Civil War." *History of Education Quarterly* 25 (Fall 1985): 341–67.

Stewart, Joseph S. "The Accredited High School." *Bulletin* 5 (January 1905): 1–3.

Tindall, George Brown. *The Emergence of the New South, 1913–1945.* Baton Rouge: Louisiana State University Press, 1967.

———. *The Ethnic Southerners.* Baton Rouge: Louisiana State University Press, 1976.

Torrence, Ridgely. *The Story of John Hope.* New York: Macmillan, 1948.

Trachtenberg, Alan. *The Incorporation of America: Culture and Society in the Gilded Age.* New York: Hill & Wang, 1982.

True, Alfred C. *A History of Agricultural Experimentation and Research in the United States, 1607–1925.* Washington, D.C.: Government Printing Office, 1937.

Turner, James. *Without God, without Creed: The Origins of Unbelief in America.* Baltimore: Johns Hopkins University Press, 1985.

Urban, Wayne J. "History of Education: A Southern Exposure." *History of Education Quarterly* 21 (Summer 1981): 131–43.

Veysey, Laurence. *The Emergence of the American University.* Chicago: University of Chicago Press, 1965.

Wagoner, Jennings L. "Higher Education and Transitions in Southern Culture: An Exploratory Apologia." *Journal of Thought* 18 (Fall 1983): 104–18.

Wagstaff, Henry McGilbert. *Impression of Men and Movements at the University of North Carolina.* Chapel Hill: University of North Carolina Press, 1950.

Wallenstein, Peter. *From Slave South to New South: Public Policy in Nineteenth Century Georgia.* Chapel Hill: University of North Carolina Press, 1987.

Ware, Louis. *George Foster Peabody: Banker, Philanthropist, Publicist.* Athens: University of Georgia Press, 1951.

Washington, Booker T. "Chapters from my Experience: Observations on Negro Colleges." *World's Work* 21 (April 1911): 14232–34.

———. "A University Education for Negroes." *Independent* 68 (March 1910): 613–18.

Wiebe, Robert. *The Search for Order 1877–1920.* New York: Hill & Wang, 1967.

Wiener, Jonathan. "Class Structure and Economic Development in the American South, 1865–1955." *American Historical Review* 84 (October 1979): 970–92.

Williamson, Joel. *The Crucible of Race: Black-White Relations in the American South since Emancipation.* New York: Oxford University Press, 1984.

Woodman, Harold D. "Economic Reconstruction and the Rise of the New South, 1865–1900." In *Interpreting Southern History: Historiographical Essays in Honor of Sanford W. Higginbotham,* ed. John Boles and Evelyn Thomas. Baton Rouge: Louisiana State University Press, 1987, 254–307.

———. "How New Was the New South?" *Agricultural History* 58 (October 1984): 529–45.

Woodward, C. Vann. *Origins of the New South, 1877–1913.* Baton Rouge: Louisiana State University Press, 1951.

Index

MICHAEL DENNIS is an assistant professor of history at Acadia University, Nova Scotia. He earned a B.A. from the University of St. Jerome's and a Ph.D. from Queen's University.

Typeset in 10.5/13 Minion
with Minion display
Designed by Dennis Roberts
Composed by Jim Proefrock
at the University of Illinois Press
Manufactured by Maple-Vail
Book Manufacturing Group

University of Illinois Press
1325 South Oak Street
Champaign, IL 61820-6903
www.press.uillinois.edu